Stephen Sayre

JOHN R. ALDEN

Stephen Sayre

AMERICAN

REVOLUTIONARY

ADVENTURER

LOUISIANA STATE UNIVERSITY PRESS

BATON ROUGE AND LONDON

Copyright © 1983 by Louisiana State University Press
ALL RIGHTS RESERVED
Manufactured in the United States of America

DESIGNER: Barbara Werden
TYPEFACE: Linotron Garamond #3
TYPESETTER: G&S Typesetters, Inc.
PRINTER: Thomson-Shore, Inc.
BINDER: John H. Dekker & Sons

Illustration on title page courtesy of Princeton University Library.

LIBRARY OF CONGRESS CATALOGING IN PUBLICATION DATA

Alden, John Richard, 1908–
    Stephen Sayre.

    Bibliography: p.
    Includes index.
    1. Sayre, Stephen, 1736–1818. 2. Diplomats—United
States—Biography. I. Title.
E302.6.S33A64   1983   973.3'092'4 [B]   83-771
ISBN 0-8071-1067-1

For Kathleen C. Smith Alden

Contents

Preface

This biography of Stephen Sayre has no predecessors, in part, no doubt, because a large body of his papers has not been found. He was a person of importance in the period of the American Revolution, and his career was spectacular. His story has been put together from bits and pieces of information gathered from many sources on both sides of the Atlantic. Access to manuscripts, newspapers, and rare books was generously given by the staffs of the British Public Record Office, the British Museum, the Lincolnshire County Record Office, the Massachusetts Historical Society, the Yale University Library, the New-York Historical Society, the East Hampton (N.Y.) Public Library, the Southampton (N.Y.) Historical Museum, the Suffolk County (N.Y.) Historical Society, the American Philosophical Society, the Library of Congress, the National Archives of the United States of America, the University of Virginia, and the Archives of the Church of Jesus Christ of Latter-Day Saints. The book could not have been written without the unfailing and cheerful assistance of the staff of the Perkins Library of Duke University, the help of Mr. Emerson Ford, director of the interlibrary loan department, being of special importance. Mr. Ford even opened my locked automobile for me with a coat hanger. I received aid from several other persons, including Mr. Albert Ackermann, Lord Bathurst, Mr. Lester Brown, Dr. Paul Chesnut, the earl of Dartmouth, Professor R. Don Higginbotham, Mrs. Vivian Jackson, Dr. Eldon Jones, Miss Sandra Markham, and Professor Peter Marshall. Of special importance was the kindness of Professor David Griffiths, who supplied me with copies of documents he has collected in the course of his researches into international diplomacy during the Revolutionary era. I am indebted to the Princeton University Library for the painting of Sayre reproduced herein. Kathleen Smith Alden and Madaleen Smith Thébaud supplied unending encouragement.

[ix]

Stephen Sayre

1

The New York Puritan

RECISELY how much Stephen Sayre learned when he was a student at the College of New Jersey cannot be determined. In maturity, by the American standards of his time, he spelled fairly well, and he did not brutally attack English grammar—his studies were not devoted to sociology, professional education, or methods of persuading the unwary to part with their cash. There is evidence that he read a book or two after graduation from Princeton in 1757. He wrote quite extensively. Certainly he was the man of his class who had the most dramatic career. Almost half of his classmates, as was usual at that time, propounded more or less eternal truths from the pulpit, including three who served as chaplains in the War of Independence; one, presumably unfortunate, died in the poorhouse; one became a musical composer; Joseph Reed concentrated his efforts upon law, warfare, and politics, achieving before the end of his short life the highest office, President of the Council, in Pennsylvania.[1] Sayre was soldier, merchant, banker, ship-builder, politician, speculator, propagandist, diplomat, inventor, and occupant of prisons. It has also been suggested or asserted, not always with cause, that he was a most active gallant, a wicked schemer, a liar, a fool, a madman, an embezzler, and a traitor.[2] He was a remarkably attractive man, a gracious and charming revolutionary who moved in high English social circles, who sacrificed hugely for liberty, who deserved better from his fellow countrymen than he received—like many another American who participated in the struggle for American freedom.

1. Regarding the Princeton class of 1757, see Stewart M. Robinson, "Campus Evangelism Two Centuries Ago," *Proceedings of the New Jersey Historical Society*, LXXVIII (1960), 118–24.

2. Lewis Einstein peremptorily dismisses Sayre as "a brainless adventurer" in *Divided Loyalties* (Boston, 1933), 246.

In childhood, he grasped a quill pen and wrote his name on the inside of the back cover of his father's account book, "Stephen." He did it a second time.[3] He was the tenth and youngest child, the third son of John and Hannah Howell Sayre of the village of Southampton on the south shore of Long Island, New York. There was nothing in his heredity or boyhood environment that marked him for fame or ill-fame. His father was an artisan. Had Stephen followed pattern, he would have been a carpenter, a mason, a blacksmith, a tanner, a millwright, a farmer, a sailor, or some combination thereof. His father was a tanner, a descendant of Thomas Sayre, also a tanner, one of the eight "undertakers" who founded Southampton in the late spring of 1640. For Stephen Sayre was of that sturdy Puritan stock that peopled New England and eastern Long Island in the first half of the seventeenth century. The "undertaker" was a Bedfordshire man who landed at Lynn, Massachusetts, in 1638 and moved southward to a lovelier and gentler land. A coat of arms has been provided for him and his, but it is unlikely that he had aristocratic pretensions.

Stephen Sayre was in maturity to refer to himself as a gentleman and was recognized as such by others. His father and mother would hardly have claimed to be patrician, but they were highly respectable residents of Southampton. John Sayre was at least briefly a soldier,[4] but he settled down after marrying Hannah Howell in the spring of 1717. The Howells were as prominent in the early history of Southampton as the Sayres and may have been even more numerous. John Sayre was about twenty-five at the time of his marriage, his wife a trifle younger. Beginning in 1718, they produced Prudence, Abigail, John, Luce, Eunice, Hannah, Sarah, Matthew, Ann, and finally, Stephen, on June 12, 1736. It is to be suspected that Stephen, born when his parents had passed the age of forty, was spoiled by his sisters, particularly because there was a gap of five years between him and Matthew.[5]

Stephen was reared in rural comfort with his siblings. His father tanned hides, made and repaired shoes and saddlery, and prospered.

3. The account book of John Sayre is preserved in the Southampton Historical Museum, Southampton, New York.

4. *An Index of Ancestors and Roll of Members of the Society of Colonial Wars* (New York, 1922), 416.

5. Family data in this paragraph can be checked in George Rogers Howell, *The Early History of Southampton, L.I., New York, with Genealogies* (2nd ed.; Albany, 1887), 375.

John Sayre was able to buy gloves, garters, lace, a fan, a mirror, as well as beds, chairs, and buckets. He purchased not only beef, pork, oats, and potatoes, but coffee, tea, ginger, and "Chalkalit." He paid for carting away "6 load of dung," but he also bought an almanac, a "testament," and a "histre book." He made many purchases of "rhumb." He bought a boy's hat as well as the "histre book." Both may have been for Stephen. The senior Sayre might write in his account book, "Command you may your mind from play," but he would not abstain from *all* the pleasures of life.[6]

John Sayre was also a deacon in the Southampton church, which was of the Presbyterian variety—a circumstance that may help somewhat to explain his son Stephen. The minister of that church for many decades after 1727 was the Reverend Mr. Sylvanus White, a Harvard College man and the husband of one Phoebe Howell White. Conceivably Phoebe was a sister of Hannah Howell Sayre. Certainly there was much intermarriage between Sayres and Howells that would normally stimulate the interest of the clergyman in both families. Late in life, Stephen Sayre asserted that he did not believe in predestination and declared his allegiance to Tom Paine—presumably as a deist rather than as a devout subscriber to the doctrines of John Calvin or John Knox.[7] He could not as a boy have escaped immersion in their tenets. He must have heard many a sermon in the village church, many an adjuration to walk in the narrow path prescribed by the dour saints of the Presbyterian sectaries.

But he was not required to follow that path in near or entire darkness, for the Presbyterians, like their Congregational brethren, valued learning, at least learning that was not impious or vicious. Almost all of the men of Southampton in the later decades of the eighteenth century could write their names. To be sure, if they could indite their names correctly, their spelling, like that of John Sayre, might be personal rather than conventional. There must have been a school of sorts where Stephen learned his letters and where he acquired a desire for a more advanced education.[8] He may have been profoundly influenced by Sylvanus White.

6. John Sayre Account Book.

7. Howell, *Early History of Southampton*, 109, 374; Sayre to William Duane, August 4, 1803, in William Duane Papers, Yale University Library, New Haven, Connecticut.

8. Howell, *Early History of Southampton*, 137–38. All but two of a company of eastern Long Island troops were able to sign a payroll in 1776.

If Stephen did not become and remain sound in soul, he did in body. The Puritan stock from which he sprang was sturdy as might be, and even though he was a tenth child, he inherited a strong physique. It was not injured by an inferior or scanty diet, for Southampton offered the bounty of the adjacent waters of the Atlantic as well as that of the good land along its shores and delicacies from distant places, imported by venturesome merchants and sailors. His strength must have been maintained by activity on land and water, for he survived perils and hardships that would have destroyed a man of feeble constitution. Moreover, he acquired at maturity, if he did not possess it in childhood, an almost astonishing comeliness. He became tall, lean, dark, and handsome. It is to be suspected that he was not only spoiled by adoring sisters, but that he came to derive excessive pleasure from his reflection in the mirror.

Decision regarding the means by which Stephen would secure his living was, in view of the circumstances of his family, long delayed. Almost inevitably his brothers inherited his father's land. Little is known about John, who was alive as late as 1811. Matthew was assigned the inheritance of the Sayre homestead. Except for service as a soldier in the War of Independence, Matthew lived quietly in Southampton, married a Mehitable Herrick, fathered seven children, and died at his native place not long before his eighty-eighth birthday. Normally, Stephen would have become an artisan or farmer, perhaps acquiring land by marriage. He might have migrated to New Jersey in search of better land and greater opportunity—two younger brothers of his father, Thomas and Jonathan, had settled there.[9] Perhaps he did go to that colony to seek his fortune. In any event, he lacked permanent occupation at the age of twenty.

On September 23, 1756, Stephen Sayre became a student in the College of New Jersey at Princeton, an institution devoted to the polishing of young Presbyterian males.[10] One may guess that Sylvanus White was his sponsor. Did Stephen contemplate a career in the pulpit? Nearly

9. Frederic Gregory Mather, *The Refugees of 1776 from Long Island to Connecticut* (Albany, 1913), 557; wills of John Sayre, Sr., and Matthew Sayre in East Hampton Free Public Library, East Hampton, New York; Ackerley Record Books, XII, 10, in Suffolk County Historical Society, Riverhead, New York; Howell, *Early History of Southampton*, 375.

10. James McLachlan, *Princetonians, 1748–1768* (Princeton, 1976), 2041.

half of the Princeton men of his time became clergymen. He was much older than most of his fellow students, of whom there were about sixty, residing in the new and attractive Nassau Hall. Graduation at the age of seventeen was not uncommon. However, Stephen had already acquired a stock of information in theology and philosophy, and now he added to it. There was a religious revival at the college in the spring of 1757. Almost all of the students were "saved"—at least nearly all of those who had not yet been converted. The Reverend Gilbert Tennent went to Princeton to see for himself "an extraordinary appearance of the divine power and presence there." His brother, the Reverend William Tennent, also visited Nassau Hall, where he saw "a memorable display of God's power and grace in the conviction of sinners." Various circumstances stimulated the students to look Heavenward, including the death of the president of the college, the Reverend Mr. Aaron Burr. The odds are that Stephen was converted or re-converted to Calvinism.

He was rapidly changed into a college graduate, for "Stephanus Sayre" was granted the title of Bachelor of Arts in October, 1757. More than half of his class occupied the pulpit or taught school, or both. Seven men, including Sayre, went into business. A historian of the class, mentioning that one man who died in the poorhouse, declares, "So far as we know, business, music, the law, medicine, and the ministry gained, in every case but one, a man of sound religious faith and a commensurate life," and that Sayre had "the most spectacular career." [11] Sayre may have retained for a time a sound religious faith; his life, however, was not commensurate with Calvinistic morality.

11. For the revival and the class of 1757, see again Robinson, "Campus Evangelism Two Centuries Ago," 118–24.

2

The Colonial
Climber

T MAY well be that Sayre, like many graduates in the liberal arts, did not quite know what to do with himself when he left Nassau Hall. If he continued very long to be gravely concerned about the eternal welfare of his body and soul, evidence of that fact is lacking; and preaching, except in politics, was not one of his various fortes. In the eighteenth century, there was no Princeton Club in New York City to serve as a base for a career in bond-selling, publishing, or banking. Did he return home to Southampton for a time, like many another bachelor of arts uncertain what to do with himself? By 1759 he had embarked upon a military career, which, however, he soon abandoned for one with brighter prospects.

In the early spring of that year, Sayre was a captain of militia in his native county. The French and Indian War—the great imperial contest between Britain and France known in Europe as the Seven Years' War, which was begun by the aggressive George Washington in the upper Ohio Valley in 1754—had continued during five campaigns and was still in bloody progress. The tide of battle had begun to turn against the French in 1758. Colonials had joined with redcoats in the struggle against the forces of the detested Bourbons defending Canada with the help of Indian allies, but the militia performed only limited duty, which was perhaps more social than soldierly. Captain Sayre undertook to enlist a company of Suffolk County men as provincial troops to serve with the British regulars during the approaching campaign. Empowered to offer bounty money to entice men to take part in attacks against Canada, he collected a company. Most of the recruits were young, but all of them were not superb physical specimens from the sturdy Puritan stock of Howells, Terrys, Wellses, Halseys, and Tuthills of Suffolk. Among the enlistees were farmers, laborers, seamen, Indians, and blacks. Sayre recruited energetically in the Shinnecock tribe, then rather numerous in the vicinity of Southampton. One of the new soldiers was "an ugly black Indian," another "a homely Indian." A third man had "an Indian face full of pimples." A fourth was "a very black mustee." Elias Halsey and Jonathan Baker, who agreed to serve under Sayre as lieutenants, were doubtless white. Sayre was formally commissioned on April 29, and he and his men proceeded up the Hudson River in May. They moved westward from Albany as part of a New York regiment, with redcoats, in June to attack a strong French garrison at Niagara.[1]

Captain Sayre participated in actions that led to the capture of Niagara and the defeat of a French relieving force which appeared from the west. After the end of the campaign, he was offered a commission as major in the New York provincials, but the capture of Québec in September by James Wolfe indicated that the war would not long continue in North America. In any event, there was no bright future for a man in a New York regiment that would surely be disbanded when hostilities ceased, and Sayre refused the appointment. Had he hoped to earn a commission in the British army by a display of valor and to embark upon a military career? It was difficult at any time to obtain such a commission without money and powerful influence. Moreover, he probably foresaw that the British forces would also soon be reduced. He prudently chose to return to civilian life in New York City.[2]

Presumably Sayre returned to Princeton in 1760, for he was awarded the degree of Master of Arts by his alma mater in that year. He made friends, among them Francis Lewis, a wealthy merchant, and Isaac Sears, a not-so-rich businessman—both soon to be passionate defenders of

1. *Second Annual Report of the State Historian of the State of New York* (Albany, 1897), 950−51; *Third Annual Report of the State Historian of the State of New York* (Albany, 1898), 515, 523, 525. Clifford K. Shipton's sketch of Sayre in *Sibley's Harvard Graduates* (Boston, 1968), XIV, 204, confuses militia with provincial troops and has Sayre leaving service immediately after stealing the bounty money. New York *Mercury*, May 14, June 11, 1759. The name of Sayre rather often appears as Sayer and occasionally as Sayers and Sears. It is Sears in the newspaper cited.

2. James Sullivan *et al.* (eds.), *The Papers of Sir William Johnson* (Albany, 1921−45), III, 90; Vicente Dávila (ed.), *Archivo del General Miranda* (Caracas, 1929−50), VI, 212; William Nelson and A. Van Doren Honeyman (eds.), *Documents Relating to the Colonial History of the State of New Jersey* (Paterson, N.J., 1917), 1st Ser., XXIX, 5−6.

American rights against Britain. He attracted the attention and won the respect of Governor Richard Penn of Pennsylvania, who was alarmed lest Yankees seize and occupy a part of the Quaker colony. More important, he entered the employ of William Alexander, a New York merchant who claimed to be the earl of Stirling. He acquired experience in business under the direction of Stirling, who sent him to Connecticut late in the spring of 1762 to secure information regarding plans of the Susquehannah Company, composed of citizens of that colony, to plant new settlements in the Wyoming Valley without the approval or consent of the Penn family. He went from Connecticut to London and appeared before the British Board of Trade—which collected information about the colonies and could recommend action to high officers of state—in August in defense of the rights of his employers. He was not timid, was indeed overbold—he could be and often was calmly indiscreet. He dared refer to "false insinuations" on the part of General Sir William Johnson, formerly his commander at Niagara, superintendent for the crown of the Six Nations and their allies, and one of the most influential men in North America.[3] Sayre was soon established as a merchant in Tokenhouse Yard in the City of London, near the Bank of England. He had begun a rapid rise in business and politics.

Let it not be thought that Sayre had been exclusively devoted to getting on in the world, with occasional attention to arrangements for a satisfactory locale beyond the grave. He was also enthusiastically enjoying himself. In 1766 he declared confidentially, "I am afraid to say a word of the luxurious paths of pleasure which I have for so many years rolled along."[4] It is certain that the persons he met upon those paths were not exclusively males, that Sayre pleased many ladies. But, like most educated men of the Western world of the eighteenth century who knew their society, he sought to avoid marriage without arrangements whereby he obtained property and a bride whose attributes did not make it impossible to enjoy the use of her money. He also had a penchant for politicking.

In London he soon became a habitué of the house of Dennys De Berdt,

3. Julian P. Boyd (ed.), *The Susquehannah Company Papers* (Wilkes-Barre, 1930–71), II, 152.

4. Sayre to Reed, September 3, 1766, in Joseph Reed Papers, New-York Historical Society, New York.

an aging merchant, a native of Ypres in Belgium, who lived in Artillery Row, not far westward from the Houses of Parliament.[5] De Berdt was a devout Protestant and a man of excellent reputation. He had a petite and very attractive unmarried daughter named Esther, known as Hetta and Hettie among the De Berdts and their intimates, and a son, Dennis, who was still a boy. Sayre did not immediately court the daughter, perhaps because he was anticipated by Joseph Reed, who appeared in London late in 1763.[6]

Sayre soon had another alliance in view. Somehow he met and won the liking of Charlotte, a daughter of Sir Henry Nelthorpe, a baronet, of Barton and Scawby in Lincolnshire. Charlotte Nelthorpe, born on January 29, 1743, was young, charming, and propertied (her father had died only three years after her birth), but unfortunately for Sayre, she apparently could not dispose of her wealth without the consent of her mother. Charlotte was socially active in Lincolnshire and also at Harrogate, the watering place.[7] Sayre was seriously interested in her, despite the fact that she was not free to endow him with her property, but her magnetic attractions were not sufficient to prevent him from paying attention to another woman when he was separated from Charlotte by the Atlantic.

According to Sayre, he very quickly acquired a measure of political importance in London. He undoubtedly did become familiar with British policy regarding the American colonies, and he denounced it. The triumph of Britain in the Seven Years' War over the Bourbon monarchies of France and Spain expanded the British possessions over the eastern third of North America. By the Treaty of Paris of 1763, the Spanish were

5. The street still exists. It runs from Victoria toward the Thames. John Milton once lived in Artillery Row.

6. John F. Roche, *Joseph Reed: A Moderate in the American Revolution* (New York, 1957), 15.

7. A. R. Maddison, *Lincolnshire Pedigrees* (London, 1902–1904), II, 705. In his correspondence Sayre refers only to a Charlotte, omitting her surname. However, he sent at least one letter to her through a Mr. Neate, who was a business advisor of Lady Nelthorpe. Moreover, as related below, Sayre tried to secure the investment of money belonging to a daughter of Lady Nelthorpe in a plantation on St. Croix by securing the approval of Mr. Neate and through him of Lady Nelthorpe. Sayre to Joseph Reed, December 5, 1764, February 20, 1765, both in Reed Papers. See also Albert Mathews (ed.), "Letters of Dennys De Berdt, 1757–1770," *Publications of the Colonial Society of Massachusetts*, XIII (1911), 317.

expelled from the Floridas, the French from Canada and from all of Louisiana east of the Mississippi except for the town of New Orleans. Becoming excessively proud of territorial grandeur and wealth and simultaneously concerned about taxes and the costs of their enlarged empire, British politicians in ministries led by John Stuart, earl of Bute, and George Grenville changed policy. They undertook to maintain a substantial body of redcoats in North America, to make the Americans contribute toward defraying imperial expenses by parliamentary taxation, to add hurtful rules to the Acts of Trade and Navigation that restrained American commerce, to limit American westward expansion, and in general to assert British authority. "The ministry are determined to make you pay for the peace which you like so well," Sayre wrote to Isaac Sears. He predicted that "you will soon have a parcel of Marmadonian[8] ravens who will feed upon, and rip your very vitals." A stamp tax was coming, and there would be an effort to reduce a profitable trade between North America and the West Indies. The prophet indulged in very strong language in describing the new policy, and he would continue to use pungent adverbs, adjectives, nouns, and verbs to describe British blows—real, mythical, and potential—to America. Sayre was already embarked upon a political course that would lead him to extremities. He was simultaneously seeking to win friends for himself and to influence people, including enemies of America. He had made the acquaintance of Wills Hill, the earl of Hillsborough, who was at that time president of the Board of Trade. Sayre claimed that he had acquired easy access to Hillsborough and that he had managed to instill a less hostile attitude in government toward the commerce of the Americans with the West Indies.

Another feature of Stephen Sayre was his remarkable mobility. As his solicitude for trade in the Caribbean indicates, he was developing a personal stake in that area. In 1764 he went to St. Croix as agent for Dennys De Berdt, who had interests there as well as business connections on the North American mainland.[9] Sayre intended to proceed to New York before the end of that year but apparently remained on the island until 1765. He saw an opportunity to marry a wealthy woman there. Had his ardor for Charlotte Nelthorpe cooled? He wrote to Joseph Reed

8. Myrmidonian, evidently.
9. Dávila (ed.), *Archivo del General Miranda*, VI, 212.

in London, "My dearest friend,"—Reed was a channel by which he exchanged letters with Charlotte—"I expect you will exert all your abilities to keep up whatever little warmth of affection yet exists between us, and I fear I stand in most need of your services; she is excluded from many temptations from her very situation. I am exposed to all by mine. I am the first object of her choice; she is the last of mine, her inclination like the needle centers entirely in the stone, mine like common gravitation is expanded and diminish'd by every surrounding object." He mingled immature philosophy with youthful conceit. "I hope," he wrote, "never to commit an error that can forfeit her friendship or yours." But he also reported that his attention had turned toward an Englishwoman on the island whose husband was at death's door. She was "almost too charming to be passed by." She was young, beautiful, sensible, agreeable, had no children, and would have £10,000 at her disposal as a widow. He was pledged in some fashion to Charlotte: "As I am in the strictest sense bound to keep my firm covenant I reject every thought of any other long engagements and am content; otherways every thing should give way to make me roam whenever the weeds grow tiresome and decency permits." He continued, "I am resolved to try her resolution and tempt her with every artifice. I am master of nothing but the eye of the husband which has forever been watchfull has prevented me forming some judgment long before this, how much reason I may have to hope for success." Was he joking? Apparently the continuance of the attachment between him and Charlotte, including marriage, was dependent upon his financial success. Conceivably Charlotte could not secure consent for marriage to a less-than-rich colonial. Sayre indicated that he was fond of Reed as well as of Charlotte. He signed a letter to Reed "once more my precious friend farewell," and another, "God bless you my sweetest friend, once more I must bid you most affectionately farewell." [10]

Early in 1765 Sayre was still hoping to acquire a plantation on St. Croix by purchase and by marriage. One Augustus Boyd of London, owner of an estate upon the island worth £30,000–40,000, was reported to be dead or dying. There was reason to believe that his estate

10. For Sayre's adventures during the years 1764–1765, see *Magazine of American History*, X (1883), 508–509; Sayre to Joseph Reed, December 5, 1764, February 20, 1765, both in Reed Papers.

could be bought for £25,000 or even less. Sayre had accumulated four or five thousand pounds that could be used toward purchase of the property, and he hoped to persuade Lady Nelthorpe to permit Charlotte to invest enough of her money to buy it. He estimated that with care the plantation could produce after two or three years an income of two thousand pounds per annum, enough so that he could marry Charlotte and live handsomely in England. If the Boyd estate were not for sale, he would search for another. "Can't bear the thought of living in America or starving in England," he wrote. He was confident that his "dear Charlotte" would like the arrangement and would marry him. It would be necessary for him to visit the plantation only occasionally after it had been made as efficient as possible. His devotion to liberty did not extend to blacks, for he obviously intended to produce sugarcane by the labor of slaves directed during his absences by an overseer—he wished to be one of the many absentee proprietors who lived like gentlemen in England upon the toil of black slaves. Sayre hoped that Joseph Reed would also settle comfortably in England. He wrote to Reed, "I here swear you shall be a large partaker with me in my better fortune." [11] But the "better fortune" did not appear, and the money of Charlotte Nelthorpe was apparently withheld from him.

Sayre promised eternal friendship to Reed, who seems to have responded in kind. Reed also had problems. He had fallen in love with Esther De Berdt, described by Sayre as "that amiable little goddess of your heart." Reed wished to marry Hetta, but her father for a time refused his consent, declining to explain why he opposed the match. Since Reed was beginning to prosper in business in New Jersey and Pennsylvania, he would not leave it to start life anew in England without good prospects. It was more probable that he would take his bride to distant America—reason enough for a prudent English father to forbid the union. But Sayre wrote, "I really am astonish'd to hear the old man so averse to such a connection as I think he might justly be proud of, and, thank his God for so happy an event, where in the circle of all his acquaintance would he find a single man (supposing him in love with his daughter) that is half so likely to please her and at the same time be agreeable to the parent. His actions in this affair ill agree with his common lectures on the uselessness of money. . . . You have one mate-

11. Sayre to Joseph Reed, February 20, 1765, in Reed Papers.

rial comfort that the old codger must soon pop off and leave his fortune on this side the ferry." It would be splendid, Sayre thought, if Reed could marry Hetta and establish himself in England.[12] It turned out that Reed received little help from Sayre, and Dennys De Berdt did not patronize Charon at the River Styx until 1770. Reed, toiling away at business and then at law in America, was separated from his Esther by the Atlantic for five years.

Sayre returned to England in 1765, by way of New York. He doubtless visited Southampton. Before the end of the year he was again in London. If he had acquired West Indian property—he did afterward own some—he spent no time developing it. His Charlotte had not deserted him, nor had he abandoned thought of marrying her. He assured Reed that "the soft and delicate sentiments that apparently possess the whole soul of my Charlotte cannot but inspire the object of her affections; who you know is equal'd by few in this kind of tenderness." The lover did not promptly marry his English sweetheart—was she only one of several? Instead he plunged deeper into business and politicking.

THE WINTER of 1765–1766 was a critical one for Britain and America. The Americans, profoundly disturbed by the restrictions and burdens arranged for them by the Bute and Grenville ministries, had defied the mother country. Almost all of them condemned the Stamp Act as an unconstitutional and iniquitous infringement upon the freedoms they enjoyed as British citizens, and they saw to it that very few stamps were sold in the old thirteen colonies. Muscular colonists destroyed the property of British officials and their few American sympathizers; rioters manhandled persons who dared to suggest that obedience should be rendered to the will of king and Parliament. To enlighten men of London regarding the nature and extent of their authority, many Americans ceased to buy British goods and deferred payment of debts to British merchants. Trade between the mother country and the colonies dwindled alarmingly.

It was known in London before the end of 1765 that the Stamp Act had been nullified in America. There were those in and out of Parliament who were disposed to resort to armed force to compel the colonists to do and pay the duties required by a government that rightly wielded at least

12. *Ibid.*

as much power over contumacious colonists as it did over the superior denizens of Britain. Of such was George Grenville, and many lords and landed gentlemen rallied behind him. However, a new prime minister, the marquis of Rockingham, with allies including other nobles and gentlemen and a brilliant orator, Edmund Burke, was inclined to compromise—to repeal the detested Stamp Act and to assert the unlimited right of Parliament to tax the colonists by a Declaratory Act. The most beloved and trusted English politician, William Pitt, who had led Britain to triumph in the recent war, agreed with the Americans—or thought he did—and demanded rescission of the obnoxious duties. Pitt had only a few followers in Parliament but could exert enormous influence upon the British public. Merchants engaged in trade with America were suffering—colonists were bringing pressure by declining to order goods and were neglecting to pay their debts—and they also called for repeal. Among those who put their names on petitions for repeal was Stephen Sayre. Another signer was Dennys De Berdt, who acted both as a merchant and as a newly appointed agent for the House of Representatives of Massachusetts.[13] Rockingham was less than a gifted leader, but young George III, also a person of modest abilities, supported his chief minister. The Stamp Act was reluctantly repealed in March, 1766, and a Declaratory Act, asserting the right of Parliament to legislate for America "in all cases whatsoever," was enthusiastically voted.

Contributing only in small degree to the erasure of the stamp duties, Sayre was doubtless much concerned for the preservation of American rights. Was there no way to preserve them, to avoid another crisis, to prevent another damaging interruption to business? He prepared a plan to bridge the gap between Britain and America and sent it to William Legge, earl of Dartmouth, who was president of the Board of Trade in the early months of 1766. That nobleman was a devout Christian and a friend of Dennys De Berdt, who undoubtedly brought Sayre and his scheme to the attention of the official. Dartmouth had voted to cancel the stamp duties and was a man of good will, so it was logical to seek his help.

Sayre proposed the creation of an American Board of Trade to meet at New York and to correspond with the British one. Each of the colonies

---

13. Jack M. Sosin, *Agents and Merchants: British Colonial Policy and the Origins of the American Revolution, 1763–1775* (Lincoln, Neb., 1965), 78–79.

should choose one member. The American board would settle vexing boundary disputes among the colonies, such as the Connecticut-Pennsylvania quarrel that had earlier occupied his attention and threatened bloodshed. Its members would also regulate trade between the colonists and the Indians—a traffic in which the Red Men were cheated, enticed into alcoholism, and abused to such an extent that they took up musket and hatchet against their pale-skinned brothers and sisters. Especially important, the board would consider and arrange for American donations toward carrying the burden of imperial defense and would from time to time send recommendations regarding policy to the British board and also to Parliament.[14]

Like other schemes advanced by Americans for new imperial machinery in the colonies that might stifle, or at least soften, disputes, Sayre's proposal did not stimulate action in London. Dartmouth left office before he could act upon the plan, but had he had time, he would hardly have bestirred himself. He was not a great man and lacked sufficient understanding, imagination, and energy to envision and to ward off a dark future. Which is not to assume that the addition to the imperial constitution proposed by Sayre would have been enthusiastically welcomed by the colonists, many of whom desired neither to donate cash for the support of the British army in North America nor to create a colonial union—except, perhaps, as an engine to use against English tyranny.

Sayre was also involved in a successful attempt to secure from Parliament a special favor for American merchants trading in the West Indies. He actively joined William Kelly, a rich New York merchant, and other men of business in a campaign to secure the naming of the island of Dominica, recently acquired from France, as a free port. They gained the support of the brilliant English politician Charles Townshend, and Parliament gave the desired status to Dominica for a period of seven years, thus opening a channel for clandestine trade with the Spanish empire. Probably Sayre hoped for a rather direct economic gain from the measure. He was enjoying his increasing importance in public affairs, and he cultivated the acquaintance of Townshend, acquired through Kelly.[15] It

14. *Royal Historical Manuscripts Commission, Fourteenth Report* (London, 1895), Appendix, Part X, 52. The plan is not dated, but circumstantial evidence definitely points to presentation early in 1766.

15. Sayre to Joseph Reed, June 19, 1766, in Reed Papers; Lawrence H. Gipson, *The*

was likely that Townshend would become before long the leader of the British cabinet.

Indeed, in the spring of 1766, Sayre believed that he was on the high road to prosperity and position. The appointment of Dennys De Berdt as agent for the Massachusetts House of Representatives, making him a spokesman for one of the most populous and prosperous colonies in America—he similarly represented Delaware after 1766—did not arise from intimate knowledge in Boston of his personality and affairs. He was unquestionably a man of integrity, but he had entered upon the eighth decade of life. Affected by the stone, he could not walk much. He did not have easy access to the most potent British politicians, and his business was shaky. His American customers owed him large sums—£50,000, according to De Berdt [16]—and were tardy in their payments. He had a partner, Wright Burkitt, who seems to have been inactive, and his finances were in almost desperate condition. He was worried about the future of his children as well as about money and politics—his son Dennis was still under age. He was undoubtedly ignorant of Sayre's description of him as "an old codger" and also of the young man's eager pursuit of pleasure. De Berdt decided that Sayre would be a valuable junior partner, a guide for young Dennis after his death, and a reliable friend for Hetta. "I trust," declared the elderly merchant, "he is a man after my own heart who will take my son by the hand and animate him to fill up my place in the church and the world when I shall be no more." [17] One must doubt that Sayre was still devout, or that he was peculiarly fitted to lead the younger De Berdt into the paths of orthodox Christianity. In any event, the father sent Sayre back to America to solicit new business and especially to secure cash needed to satisfy the creditors of De Berdt and Burkitt.

Sayre enthusiastically accepted the partnership and set off across the

---

Triumphant Empire, 1763–1766 (New York, 1956), 247–54, Vol. IX of *The British Empire Before the American Revolution*, 15 vols.; Allan Christelow, "Contraband Trade Between Jamaica and the Spanish, and the Free Port Act of 1766," *Hispanic American Historical Review*, XXII (1942), 309–343.

16. William B. Reed, *The Life of Esther De Berdt, Afterwards Esther Reed of Pennsylvania* (Philadelphia, 1853), 63–79.

17. Mathews (ed.), "Letters of Dennys De Berdt," 319–20. There is much information about De Berdt and his affairs in this collection.

Atlantic, leaving Charlotte to wait a second time for his return. He hoped not only to raise money for the firm but to cement an alliance with Townshend and to secure with his support a British land grant at Niagara—Sayre had doubtless described the magnificence of the Niagara region for the benefit of that politician as well as other fogbound Londoners. Townshend, the De Berdts, and Sayre were all expected to profit from speculation in the area of the falls, which was still in the Indian country. Sayre planned that De Berdt would push the scheme with his good friend Dartmouth; Joseph Reed was also to participate in the enterprise. With sufficient influence in London, a little money, a little luck, and time, the speculators might acquire handsome estates, if not for themselves, then for their heirs. Sayre had still another bit of business—to do what he could to foster the romance of Reed and Esther De Berdt by helping Reed to attain early prosperity.

The dream of easily gained and valuable properties in the distant American interior soon collapsed and with it an agreement whereby Sayre was to supply information about America to Townshend. Sayre optimistically hoped that British officers of state and members of Parliament had learned about American grievances and that they would exhibit greater wisdom in the future in the making of policy regarding the colonies, and he saw Townshend as a leader who might promote Concord. However, in an age when British politicians were unusually remarkable for shifting party allegiances and deviations in policy, Charles Townshend was becoming notorious for inconstancy and trickery. He turned against the young American. In the summer of that year he informed De Berdt that he regretted that the aging merchant was connected with such an impertinent young fellow. De Berdt wrote to Sayre that Townshend was "a meer weather cock." The agent was not aware that Townshend was also a crook.

Sayre did not know for some months that he had lost Townshend's good will and assistance. The American enjoyed an easy voyage across the Atlantic and landed safely in Boston late in the spring of 1766. From that place, which he thought sufficiently attractive, he wrote semi-humorously to Reed, still in America and still enamored of Esther De Berdt, whose father had tentatively consented to their engagement, that "I know you don't want inclination to serve your father in law, but perhaps you can't conceive how difficult it is just at this time to support credit as it ought to be, and most of the money due to the old partnership is in Philadelphia where they are beyond example remiss in payment." He urged Reed to persuade merchants of that city to open their purses. Then, seeking orders for goods from men who could offer cash, Sayre went to Newburyport and Portsmouth, Rhode Island, to see fishermen and whalers. If he did not make much money in Boston, he won new friends, including at least one influential person at Harvard College. Upon payment of the customary fee, Sayre was awarded the degree of Master of Arts at Harvard, as if he were a member of the class of 1757 of that institution rather than Princeton—testimony to the appearance, manners, and charm of a man who had spent only one year at Nassau Hall. He also established a cordial relationship with Richard Cary, a wealthy and influential Bostonian and henceforth a stout champion of Dennys De Berdt. Sayre found Elizabeth, Cary's daughter, most attractive, but he did not fail to write to his Charlotte in far-off England.[18]

The man of large affairs, after many weeks of toil and pleasure in New England, planned to visit his family in Southampton en route to New York City.[19] It may be assumed that he very pleasantly crossed Long Island Sound by ferry from New London, Connecticut, to a harbor on eastern Long Island, thence to Southampton. One may also suspect that the appearance of a polished and mature man of the world in that secluded village aroused much gossip. Was he really the son of Deacon Sayre who had gathered clams and crabs in Shinnecock Bay, who had caught weakfish and bluefish in Peconic Bay, who had led the company of local men and boys off to fight the French and their Indian allies seven years earlier? Indeed, was Sayre perhaps becoming too smooth, too elegant, too sophisticated for many of his fellow Americans? Was he putting on the airs of an English gentleman? Admitted that he was soft-spoken and good-humored—he remained so to the end of his life—had he not come to think of himself as superior to plain folk?

Proceeding to New York City, he spoke slightingly there, as he had in Boston, of the Reverend Mr. Nathaniel Whitaker. Eleazer Wheelock,

18. Reed, *Life of Esther De Berdt*, 73, 89–90, 92, 96–97; Sayre to Joseph Reed, June 19 and September 3, 1766, both in Reed Papers; Mathews (ed.), "Letters of Dennys De Berdt," 317, 318; Shipton, *Sibley's Harvard Graduates*, XIV, 205. Dr. Shipton includes a sketch of Sayre in the class of 1757 that is enjoyable but occasionally errs in detail.

19. Sayre to Joseph Reed, September 3, 1766, in Reed Papers.

the founder of a school for Indian boys in Connecticut that was eventually to blossom into Dartmouth College and University for favored
white youths, had employed Whitaker as a money-raiser in England for
his great work. That clergyman had persuaded English contributors to
donate generously, but he had not found the De Berdts to be his sort. He
reported that De Berdt was "a good man, but old & quite under the
influence of his wife & two flirting children." De Berdt, according to
Whitaker, was not to be trusted. Sayre would have it that Whitaker was
"unpolished," that he gave "great disgust" to people of good taste, and
that he was a poor performer in the pulpit, inferior to the Reverend Mr.
Sampson Occom, an Indian brought into the clergy by Wheelock.[20]
Sayre may have correctly assessed the merits of the offended clergyman as
an expounder of Christianity—it is likely that he had heard both men
preach, since Occom was active on southern Long Island when Sayre was
young. But was it for him to speak as if he were himself a superior person
who could assess English manners and niceties of behavior with the
authority of an initiate?

Traveling on through New Jersey to Philadelphia and southward as
far as Virginia, Sayre offended as well as pleased. In Virginia, reported
Dr. William Shippen afterward, Sayre sought commissions to sell tobacco and "did not behave well." Aristocratic planters of the Old Do-
minion, accustomed to receive credit and sink further and further into
debt, would hardly wish to engage in business with a sufficiently elegant
representative of a firm that could not buy with cash or advance it against
prospective sales of tobacco in Britain. Many New Yorkers and Jersey-
men in public life soon made it clear that they did not wish to be
represented in London by an American who seemed too attractive to be
trusted. But the condition of De Berdt, Burkitt, and Sayre did improve
somewhat, in consequence in part, one may believe, of the efforts of the
junior partner.[21]

It is likely that Sayre suffered at least one blow in 1767. In March his
father died in Southampton at the age of seventy-five. The death of John
Sayre was to be expected, although his breed commonly lived into their

20. Leon Burr (ed.), *An Indian Preacher in England* (Hanover, N.H., 1933), 82, 90,
113, 199–200, 203, 208, 215, 216, 255–56, 269.

21. *Southern Literary Messenger*, XXVIII (1859), 184; Reed, *Life of Esther De Berdt*,
131.

eighties. Making provision for his widow, he bequeathed his land and cattle to his older sons, John and Matthew. Stephen was only a residual legatee, along with his surviving sisters. There is no evidence that he was displeased by the division of property, since he had doubtless received special favor in the form of education. In any event, a tie with South-ampton was gone.[22]

SAYRE may have been in Southampton at the time of his father's death. He was in Philadelphia in June, 1767. Either there or in Trenton, where Joseph Reed was established, Sayre condoled with his friend, who had encountered defeat. An effort to secure an appointment for him as an assistant agent to De Berdt for the Massachusetts House of Representatives—which might have opened the way for him to succeed De Berdt as the spokesman for that body—had failed. Nor was there much hope that the lawmakers in Boston would later select Reed to act for them.[23] Reed was making progress in Philadelphia; he could not afford to abandon his career in America to begin life anew in London, not even for his Esther.

   Some time before the close of his American jaunt in search of better business, Sayre heard news of public affairs that must in all likelihood have bad consequences for him and for Reed, probably for all America. Delighted by the revocation of the stamp levies, the Americans had sensibly chosen to ignore the Declaratory Act. Nevertheless, men of business in America continued to grumble, not without cause. Sayre had found discontent among the merchants of Boston, New York, and Phila-delphia regarding both the British laws channeling their trade and the behavior of British officeholders entrusted with the task of enforcing the will of Crown and Parliament. The rules hurt. They hurt even more because they were executed by men who needlessly injured the interests and feelings of Americans. Sayre had written about the situation to the earl of Dartmouth in December, 1766. Learning of added blows aimed at the colonists by Charles Townshend, he wrote again to Dartmouth to re-port protests against "Parliamentary proceedings" instigated by Town-

22. Theodore Melvin Banta, *Sayre Family: Lineage of Thomas Sayre, A Founder of Southampton* (New York, 1901), 53; Will of John Sayre, Sr. Hannah Sayre inherited a black slave named Tom. Stephen Rogers and Silas Cook are mentioned as men who married sisters of Stephen.

23. Reed, *Life of Esther De Berdt*, 108–109, 113, 125.

shend.[24] A second Anglo-American crisis was developing by the time Sayre arrived in England by ship from Boston.

There were British gentlemen and lords who resented the extorted repeal of the Stamp Act. Charles Townshend, chancellor of the Exchequer, took control in 1767 of a new ministry that had been formed by William Pitt. Pitt, as the earl of Chatham, became ill and retired in large degree from politics. This situation permitted Townshend to frame policy regarding the Americans, who had not made it clear that parliamentary import duties for revenue were no more acceptable than stamp duties had been. Townshend, fond of colonies but not of colonists, easily secured the passage of an act placing taxes upon tea, paint, lead, and papers imported by Americans. He was also responsible for the establishment of a new Board of Customs Commissioners in Boston. Britain intended in the future not only to collect all levies upon American maritime commerce but to enforce the Navigation Acts in all their rigor, and Townshend publicly dared the colonists to resist. He died in September, 1767, but men of his cast of mind in the Chatham cabinet continued his work. They established several new admiralty courts to make sure that violators of the Navigation Acts would be punished. What was far more serious, in 1768 they ordered concentration of the army in America—hitherto stationed chiefly on frontier duty—along the Atlantic seaboard. It was clear enough that the redcoats were placed so they could be used if necessary to subdue the colonists. Further to cramp the colonists, the ministry established a new boundary line barring westward expansion of the colonies.

The De Berdt family welcomed the long-distance traveling-man. They had eagerly read Sayre's letters and had received "with great joy" the news of his safe arrival in Boston. The father, at least, hoped "it was an answer of prayer" and that Providence would attend Sayre in all his journeying. The firm was not much better off than it was when Sayre left London—its Philadelphia debtors were not remitting cash or the equivalent in sufficient quantity—but he brought word that Reed was healthy and that he remained in Philadelphia against the wishes of his heart— news that pleased Esther more than it did her father.[25]

24. *Royal Historical Manuscripts Commission, Fourteenth Report*, Appendix, Part X, Vol. II, 54–55.

25. Mathews (ed.), "Letters of Dennys De Berdt," 317–18; Reed, *Life of Esther De Berdt*, 114.

Esther reported in a letter of October 22 to Reed about "our good friend Sayre, who arrived about a week ago. He makes us very happy by his company." "Mr. Sayre is exceedingly well," she wrote, "and gives us great encouragement to hope that our previous difficulties will soon be at an end; and I think everything has a better appearance than some time ago. We are vastly happy in our connection with him, and he seems, and I hope is so with us. Indeed, I do not know any other person that could have been so perfectly agreeable." Did she intend to make her distant sweetheart jealous? Friends knew, she said, that she was in love with an American, but they believed that Sayre was the man. Reed was given cause for additional twinges as time went on. A letter from Sayre of December related that "your dear sweet and justly beloved Hetta stands by me and tells me that she will one day or other reward you a thousand fold with so many kisses—and with these happy expectations I salute you and afresh assure you that these things add fuel to friendship & strengthen that friendship which shall last if God pleases to eternity. Thus I say adieu." The same letter and subsequent ones of 1768 and 1769 make it clear that Sayre was doing what he could to help Reed in commerce and politics and to encourage him to come to London. [26]

Sayre could not report that the finances of the house of De Berdt had materially improved. Nor did his relationship with Charlotte lead to marriage. By 1768 she had decided—or perhaps it had been decided for her—that a match with him was unsuitable. [27] In March of that year Sayre wrote to Reed, "The old Duchess, I mentioned before, would have shared her £3000 a year with me with all her heart, and tho' we have taken a friendly parting upon her refusal to advance a good sum for our trade yet she has again sent me a kind invitation to come often to see her. I fancy she has some inclination to fall into my own terms; but I can't easily reconcile myself to the embraces of an old woman." He said that "your dear little Hetta is likewise earnest in her remonstrances against it." He continued, "the connection would greatly gratify my ambition, mortify my enemies, and fix me in an independent station . . . but the price of acquisition is too precious to part with." He could not "well quit

26. Reed, *Life of Esther De Berdt*, 122–23, 125; Sayre to Joseph Reed, December 19, 1767, in Reed Papers.

27. She married, at an unknown date, the Reverend Robert Carter Thelwell. Maddison, *Lincolnshire Pedigrees*, II, 705.

the dear expectation of refined love & mutual enjoyment with some sweet girl who may possess my whole heart—and tho' we are in the utmost distress for money, yet I had rather endure the present pain than subject myself to unhappiness for life."[28] The faint possibility of marrying the aging duchess—how old was that widow of a deceased duke?—still existed three months later, but Sayre hoped to find a younger wife with money. The firm could meet its obligations, but the partners had ceased to seek business and were trying only to collect from their debtors. "As to the old lady I must confess myself rascal enough to play her off in case of absolute necessity, and should have married her rather than see myself with a family who I now must sink or swim with, subjected to the misfortunes of poverty, my own misfortunes are supportable, and I could live happyer in any station, than with a disagreeable companion but I could never have supported the dreadfull sight of Mr. De Berdt's family becoming bankrupt or drove to the necessity of embarking for America." Was Sayre nerving himself for a wretched sacrifice? Was a duchess actually willing, even eager, to marry the American, bringing ridicule upon herself? One cannot deny the possibility of an affirmative answer to the second question, although it is most unlikely that a woman of such exalted rank would condescend to make such a match. In any event, he did not exchange vows with a duchess—and he escaped the contempt which that sort of union would have brought him.

But all was not gloomy for Sayre. He could relate for Reed "a most frolicksome tour" of two days to Windsor that he made with Hetta, a reference that might well disturb the lover beyond the ocean. It was, however, coupled with earnest advice that Reed travel to Boston, where he might renew his efforts to secure an appointment to the agency for the Massachusetts House of Representatives, and also that he come to England to seek his fortune. Reed seems to have suggested that his engagement to Esther be abandoned. In October, Sayre urgently advised him to come to England, where De Berdt and Sayre were striving to get a governmental appointment for him. The firm was in desperate straits—De Berdt had concealed the true extent of its troubles from Esther and from Sayre. If the prospects of Reed and the De Berdts did not improve within a year, they must all go to America rather than remain in En-

28. Sayre to Joseph Reed, March 27, 1768, in Reed Papers.

gland, where a bankruptcy would expose the family to contempt. In March, 1769, Sayre again pleaded with Reed to seek the Massachusetts appointment, which De Berdt and Sayre were recommending to Richard Cary. Reed should get a letter of endorsement from John Dickinson, the wealthy Pennsylvania lawyer who had become the foremost spokesman for American rights against British tyranny, Sayre urged. And Reed must come to London, for if he did not, he must expect the end of his engagement to Esther. She was very unhappy, and Sayre feared that she would go into a decline. At last Reed resolved that he must follow that advice. He solicited the Massachusetts appointment—in vain—and arrived in England to find the De Berdt family in serious financial trouble.[29]

In January, 1770, a company consisting of the De Berdts, father and son, William Lee, and Stephen Sayre announced that it would engage in trade with Virginia, carrying finished goods to the Chesapeake and bringing away tobacco. The company would use a new ship. William Lee, who had come to London in 1766 with his older brother Arthur, was a member of *the* prominent Virginia family, and the two men had become frequent visitors in Artillery Row. The venture was apparently stillborn, however. The older De Berdt died in April, and his mercantile enterprises collapsed with him. It seems that there was not much of value left in the wreckage for the De Berdts. Reed married—at last—his Esther. Winding up the estate, Reed estimated that it might produce a balance if those who owed it money would pay their debts. The older De Berdt had been credulous, and some men in America dealing with him had been dishonest. Reed also sought to separate Burkitt and Sayre from the affairs of the De Berdts—they had become "incumbrances"—and Burkitt was advertised as a bankrupt in 1773.[30]

The newly married couple, with Mrs. De Berdt, left England, and Reed eventually succeeded as a lawyer and merchant in America. He and

29. Sayre to Joseph Reed, July 3, 1768, October 13, 1768, March 10, 1769, all in *ibid.*; Reed, *Life of Esther De Berdt*, 136–39.

30. Worthington C. Ford (ed.), *Letters of William Lee* (Brooklyn, 1897), I, 11; Reed, *Life of Esther De Berdt*, 146–48; *Gentleman's Magazine*, XLIII (1773), 104. In 1769 Sayre wrote that the books of the firm were in arrears and in disarray. Sayre to Joseph Reed, March 10, 1769, in Reed Papers. It may be that American debtors neglected to meet their obligations as a means of expressing anger against the Townshend measures.

his Esther were quite humanly inclined to place blame for the collapse of the De Berdt enterprises upon Sayre. When the younger De Berdt went into business for himself in London, Reed wrote to him: "You have this much in your favor, that the horrible faults committed in conducting the late partnership are all laid at Sayre's door, so that you have no difficulties in that respect." Apparently Reed, even knowing that Sayre was not seriously at fault, did not regret the injustice done to his friend's reputation. The Reeds—at least Mrs. Reed—turned sharply against him. Some three years later, being informed that Sayre had become a banker in London, Esther wrote to her brother about

> our old friend Sayre. Certainly never was anything stranger or more unaccountable. Every person here is as much astonished as we were—a remark which one gentleman made, is, I think, a very just one. "I see," says he, "what ignorance and impudence will do in London"—certainly these two qualities had some hand in his advancement. Pray do send me word how he goes on, and if the bank succeeds: we have heard that it was never opened. I think he will yet fall to the ground unless he has recourse to matrimony, and if he does not make haste, that will not succeed, as his beauty must be pretty well faded. However, I must leave him, wishing very much his heart and life mended with his fortune.

The judgment of others concerning Sayre's relationship with the De Berdts was apparently much kinder. The Lee brothers did not foreswear all acquaintance with him, nor did Dennis De Berdt, who remained in England, married prosperously, was successful as a London merchant in Colman Street, and did not avoid all association with Sayre.[31]

The fall of the house of the elder De Berdt did not entail the ruin of Stephen Sayre. Presumably he was not legally responsible for the obligations incurred by his senior partners before he joined them. His personal fortune may even have grown somewhat during his association with them, even though it hardly added much to his stock of money. The relationship with De Berdt did bring to him new connections, both helpful and injurious. He became increasingly involved in politics after his return from America as a London radical associated with the irrepressible and irresponsible John Wilkes.

31. Reed, *Life of Esther De Berdt*, 161, 186–87. De Berdt supplied a mail address for Sayre and did at least a little business with him.

THE SECOND crisis in relations between Britain and America that developed in consequence of the labors of Charles Townshend grew alarmingly after Sayre's return to England. Townshend died in September, 1767, but his spirit lived on in the British cabinet. In October Dennys De Berdt took Sayre in his coach to call upon William Petty, earl of Shelburne, the secretary of state for the Southern Department, who was supposedly more responsible than his colleagues for colonial affairs and who was well disposed toward America. Shelburne had been unable to stop the arrogant and heedless Townshend, but perhaps, on being informed about rising tempers in America, he would act to soothe them. He assured the two men that he wished America well, but he was unable to alter British policy.[32] Indeed, early in 1768 Shelburne was deprived of immediate authority over the colonies. American business was given to a new secretary of state for the colonies, an office placed in the hands of the earl of Hillsborough, no friend to Englishmen beyond the Atlantic. De Berdt and Sayre found Hillsborough narrowminded, addicted to punctilio, and hostile. Sayre recalled that Hillsborough had once declared he would "rather see every man in 50 in America put to the sword than the Stamp Act repealed." The new secretary refused to accept a petition from the Massachusetts House of Representatives early in 1768 on the petty ground that it was not prepared in proper form.

There were men in America at least as determined to challenge British tyranny as Hillsborough was to compel obedience to British authority. John Dickinson of Pennsylvania supplied them with constitutional ammunition. The Townshend levies, being intended to raise revenue without the consent of those who would pay them, differed in no fundamental way from the stamp duties and similarly violated the constitutional rights of Englishmen. American propagandists thundered at this and other less onerous indignities heaped upon them by the heedless and wicked denizens of Whitehall and Westminster. The new Board of Customs Commissioners established at Boston in the fall of 1767 became a popular target, and its employees were threatened and pushed about by muscular Americans. The commissioners, fearing rioters, called for military defense in March and again in June, and the governor, Francis Bernard, endorsed their pleas for help. The British cabinet responded by

32. Mathews (ed.), "Letters of Dennys De Berdt," 453.

ordering four regiments of redcoats—afterward reduced to two—into the city to protect the worried officials. Soldiers remained in the city from October, 1768, to April, 1770. Inevitably they quarreled with aggressive civilians, and just as inevitably they were described as tools of tyranny who ought not be in a peaceful American port—where remarkably well-behaved sailors and workmen never indulged in strong language or physical encounters. These paragons of colonial gentility, if one is to believe their defenders, would never fail to stand aside while opening a tavern door for a soldier, never ask a redcoat to cease annoying a buxom barmaid without a polite by-your-leave. Tension mounted in Boston—and elsewhere, gradually, in America.

Although he had never crossed the ocean, Dennys De Berdt was an ardent champion of American rights. He and his junior partner acted together in politics as well as in business, and they did what they could to assert those rights and to defend Americans struggling for them. Sayre solicited business for his friend Isaac Sears, who would achieve fame of sorts as a most energetic fighter for American liberty in New York. De Berdt and Sayre petitioned the British government to act in behalf of Alexander McDougall, also a New York radical, who was arrested and imprisoned by Danish authorities on St. Croix when he tried to collect a debt owed him by a citizen of that island.[33]

Sayre toiled at his desk and blossomed into a vigorous polemicist in behalf of America in 1768 with a long pamphlet entitled "The Englishman Deceived." Published in London and reprinted in Salem and New York, the pamphlet was ostensibly intended to open the eyes of Britishers who did not understand the situation in America or American reasons for resisting the Townshend duties and defying the authority of Parliament. It said little that had not been earlier and better said by John Dickinson, and it lacked fire, except for a denunciation of presumably vicious British officials in America. But it did forthrightly deny Britain the right to tax the Americans or to maintain an army among them. It contained a soothing accusation that France was responsible for British tyrannies.

33. Kenneth W. Porter, *The Jacksons and the Lees: Two Generations of Massachusetts Merchants, 1765–1844* (Cambridge, Mass., 1937), I, 184, 192, 193; "The Memorial of Dennis De Berdt and Stephen Sayre on behalf of Alexander McDougall Merchant of New York," 1768, in Egerton MSS. 2697, fol. 9, British Museum, London.

Esther De Berdt reported regarding its author in May, 1768: "He has been very busy in writing his political piece." He sent copies of it to "the most considerable of the nobility and House of Commons, by the desire of his patron, General Ogelthorpe, who has a very high opinion of Sayre's understanding and genius. I am so really his friend that I begin to fear the effect this applause may have on his mind." [34] The pamphlet was published anonymously, but there was no attempt to conceal authorship, and it gave its composer a measure of fame. However, it did not penetrate far into the minds or hearts of many Englishmen who needed enlightenment, in part perhaps because it was the product of a man of business who was not a master of English prose and who primarily stressed economic gains that would come from a liberal colonial policy. Sayre's arguments might appeal to British merchants, but they could not exert as much influence upon the lords and gentlemen whose wealth was in the form of land.

Sayre not only condemned British policy in print but also bearded Lord Hillsborough in person. Acting in behalf of Dennys De Berdt, he presented a petition from Massachusetts to the colonial secretary in June. Although lacking much ability, Hillsborough, the owner of an extensive estate in Ireland, placed a more-than-sufficient value upon himself and was disposed to deal peremptorily with contumacious colonials. The petition had little chance of success. Sayre was carefully polite in the conference, but he flatly asserted that the worst one might say about the people of Massachusetts was that they were "deluded with false ideas of preserving their freedom." [35] Accordingly, Sayre stated, they were not to be condemned, since their only possible fault was minor—an excessive devotion to an ideal to which all British subjects enthusiastically subscribed. The colonial secretary could not have been pleased by such a forthright challenge.

A most important political activity of De Berdt and Sayre—especially Sayre, as it turned out—was their attack upon Massachusetts governor Francis Bernard, who had successfully urged the sending of British troops to Boston. The House of Representatives of Massachusetts and its agents would not concede that the troops were needed to main-

34. Reed, *Life of Esther De Berdt*, 129.
35. Sayre to Hillsborough, June 2, 1768, in Main Papers, November 28, 1768, Number 59, House of Lords Record Office, London.

tain order in the province. They believed that the governor misrepresented the situation in Boston and in the colony—indeed, it became an article of faith with them and other Americans in London that Bernard and his successor, Thomas Hutchinson, instigated harsh British measures by sending deceitful and malicious reports to London of disobedience, rioting, and the sinister machinations of Massachusetts politicians. It must be said in behalf of Bernard that there was some limited defiance of British law, mob action against minor British officials, and persistent uproar in Massachusetts because of the bustle of James Otis, Samuel Adams, and other champions of freedom who refused to be satisfied.

Early in 1769 Parliament, goaded by the duke of Bedford, always hostile to America, responded to reports from Massachusetts by requesting the ministry to obtain information regarding acts of treason there and to bring the perpetrators, if any, to Britain for trial. Sending back to Boston copies of letters to the ministry from Bernard, De Berdt and Sayre supplied ammunition to Samuel Adams and other members of the House of Representatives for an attack upon the governor. The opportunity was not neglected. The House petitioned for the removal of Bernard, and the task of presenting and supporting the petition fell upon the agent and his partner. There was never the slightest chance that the Privy Council, which heard the petition, would return an affirmative answer when it was finally considered in February, 1770. By that time, Bernard, whose wife was a cousin of Viscount Barrington, secretary of war (who had the ears of the ministry and even of the king), had been rewarded for his services with a baronetcy, pensions to maintain himself and his family in a style suitable to his new title, and a leave of absence that ended in his resignation from his troublesome office. Presented by De Berdt, Sayre, and Arthur Lee, the petition was summarily rejected on March 14.[36] Sayre later resumed the campaign against Bernard.

Nine days before the exoneration of Bernard, the second Anglo-American crisis reached both climax and anticlimax. Tumult in Boston

---

36. Bernhard Knollenberg, *Growth of the American Revolution, 1766–1775* (New York, 1975), 67. The dissertation of Louis W. Potts, "Arthur Lee: American Revolutionary" (Ph.D. dissertation, Duke University, 1970), has been useful with respect to this affair. Many details concerning the activities of De Berdt and Sayre are to be found in Mathews (ed.), "Letters of Dennys De Berdt," 368–410.

did not end with the arrival of the redcoats in the city. On the contrary, the presence of the troops supplied new issues for all Americans and new targets for the more muscular men and boys of Boston, no longer remarkable for straitlaced Puritan morality. Altercations between soldiers and civilians became chronic; all the care and prudence of British officers could not assure maintenance of the peace. In February came the first slaying of the Revolution—the killing of Christopher Snyder, a youthful member of a mob who was shot by Ebenezer Richardson, a customs informer defending himself against unwanted attentions by taunting and threatening tormentors. On March 5 came the famous "Massacre" in which five older and uncivil civilians were slain by a squad of redcoats. On that same day, however, Frederick, Lord North, chancellor of the Exchequer in succession to Charles Townshend and prime minister after January, 1770, introduced in Parliament a bill repealing all of the Townshend duties except that upon tea. It was approved by Parliament as a not-utterly-unacceptable compromise. In Massachusetts, no one had been arrested for treason or brought to trial as an enemy of the British state, and the colonists gradually relaxed their boycott of British goods. As for the tax, the Americans were able to buy teas from Dutch smugglers at prices below those set by the British.

And how did Stephen Sayre emerge from that crisis? He acquired notice among the British politicians who dominated Parliament and cabinet with the king after 1767 as a turbulent and aggressive colonial who might deserve a bit of attention in the event that new troubles arose beyond the Atlantic. Sayre had become remarkably forthright in asserting American rights, but had he in consequence gained many powerful friends on the far side of the ocean? Not at all. In the fall of 1769 his old friend, Isaac Sears, leader of energetic Liberty Boys in New York, urged the assembly of that colony to elect Sayre as a joint agent in London with the man who then held the office, Robert Charles, who was in failing health. When Charles died, as he soon did, the appointment would doubtless lead to his replacement by Sayre. The agency was valuable, not merely for its salary but for the influence it gave its holder. But a motion to favor Sayre was lost by a vote of 16 to 6, for there were New Yorkers who disliked him for putting on English airs and regarded him as a "young giddy foolish coxcomb." The office passed to Edmund Burke, a more prudent man whose devotion to America was less than passionate. Sayre was also, with his friend Arthur Lee, brought forward for the agency vacated by the death of Dennys De Berdt. Lee recommended Sayre and vainly tried to persuade John Dickinson to intervene for him. Joseph Reed, however, saw to it that Sayre did not receive the blessing of the De Berdt family and came forth for Lee. Benjamin Franklin was chosen; he would doubtless have received the post in any event. Ironically, Franklin had been on less than friendly terms with the Artillery Row people, especially after Dennys De Berdt, struggling as best he might for the colonists, had assailed Franklin for lack of vigor in opposing the Stamp Act, and there remained a bit of bad blood between Artillery Row and Franklin's quarters on Craven Street. Sayre's efforts on behalf of Massachusetts were not rewarded. Failing to inherit the De Berdt agency, he received from it a legacy of hostility on the part of Franklin.[37]

But surely Sayre retained some friends from his Princeton days? In March, 1768, the rapid graduate of the class of 1757 met in London the Reverend John Witherspoon, the Scottish clergyman who was soon to become president of the College of New Jersey. The two men conversed about its condition, and Witherspoon reported to alumnus Benjamin Rush, then a student of medicine at the University of Edinburgh, that Sayre seemed to be "as warm a friend to the college as yourself. However, I had the mortification to learn from him that at present there are [only] about 50 students at the college." Nevertheless, Witherspoon accepted the presidency and commissioned Sayre, Rush, and Dr. Thomas Rushton to procure scientific apparatus for Princeton. Sayre also agreed to

37. Edward P. Lilly, *The Colonial Agents of New York and New Jersey* (Washington, 1936), 132; David M. Griffiths, "American Commercial Diplomacy in Russia, 1780–1783," *William and Mary Quarterly*, 3rd Ser., XXVIII (1970), 233–34; Richard Henry Lee, *The Life of Arthur Lee* (Boston, 1829), II, 303; William B. Reed, *Life and Correspondence of Joseph Reed* (Philadelphia, 1847), I, 43; Reed, *Life of Esther De Berdt*, 161–62. John Dickinson begged off Lee's request that he help Sayre on the ground that he was not sufficiently familiar with Massachusetts leaders. Regarding the operations of the American agents in England and especially the relations between Franklin on the one hand and the De Berdts, Lee, and Sayre on the other, see Michael G. Kammen, *A Rope of Sand: The Colonial Agents, British Politics, and the American Revolution* (Ithaca, 1968), particularly pp. 129–30, 148–51.

assist in securing gifts of money and books.[38] It does not appear that anything came from his efforts, if he made any. Nor has evidence been found that he had strengthened his old school ties or that either Witherspoon or Rush afterward befriended him.

Sayre continued to have contacts in Massachusetts, including Samuel Adams, and he did not cease to assert himself in London. He developed new associations there, with, among others, John Wilkes and Mrs. Sophia Baddeley.

38. Lyman H. Butterfield, *John Witherspoon Comes to America* (Princeton, 1953), 72, 81–82; John Maclean, *History of the College of New Jersey* (Philadelphia, 1877), I, 296.

3
The English Arriviste

HE COLLAPSE of the house of De Berdt was a severe blow to Sayre, even though he escaped bankruptcy. Whatever economic occupation he had during the following three years remains unknown, but it may be assumed that he was not entirely idle. He reappears, surprisingly, as a banker in London. Among the new connections established by the American were a number of men and women in high places, including the earl of Chatham. Sayre became especially intimate with John Wilkes, the notorious Radical, and he acquired in consequence office as sheriff of London. Another association into which he entered, a liaison with Mrs. Sophia Baddeley, was even less appropriate for a banker. Nor did his political activities in behalf of America, as time would reveal, conduce to success in an English countinghouse.

Whatever else may be said about Sayre, he was venturesome. Banking is an occupation that normally rewards the cool and cautious adherent to the status quo rather than a bold and passionate enemy of the political powers-that-be. By 1773 Sayre was managing a bank in Oxford Street—then a rapidly growing part of London—as the senior partner of Bartholomew Coote Purdon, a likable Anglo-Irishman of the same age as Sayre.[1]

Purdon was apparently even less fitted by temperament or experience for banking than was Sayre, but he did have property in Ireland. He was of distinguished Protestant ancestry, and he had relatives and friends of high social standing who, it is likely, brought business to the bank.

---

1. Esther De Berdt could hardly believe that her former friend had become a banker. Frederic Reynolds, *The Life and Times of Frederic Reynolds, Written by Himself* (London, 1826), I, 368–69, 372–73.

Purdon was a descendant of Cootes who held the earldoms of Bellomont and Mountrath, and he was also the grandnephew of the first earl of Carbery. His father was Robert Coote, one of the numerous offspring of Chidley Coote, D.D., of County Limerick, brother of General Sir Eyre Coote, who served brilliantly in India during the Seven Years' War and the War of American Independence and who was one of the principal architects of the British empire in India. Robert married Anne, the daughter of Bartholomew Purdon of Ballyclough in County Cork, in February, 1730. The Cootes were prolific—Robert and Anne had at least six children. Sayre's partner was a second son. He was nine years of age when his grandfather died in 1745. He took the family name of his mother and grandfather and became known as Bartholomew Coote Purdon.

In April, 1762, Purdon married Mary, daughter of Henry Wrixon of Glinhill in County Cork. He and his wife were living comfortably, even luxuriously, in London when he linked his fortunes with those of Sayre. The Purdons were fond of music, and they entertained liberally. They maintained a "splendid establishment," which was "visited by personages of the highest rank," including the famous Georgiana, duchess of Devonshire. They befriended the young Richard Brinsley Sheridans before Sheridan achieved fame as a playwright. The charming Mrs. Sheridan had a lovely voice and sang in their home, sometimes with the Purdon girls. The Purdons introduced the Sheridans to the duchess. The Purdon daughters appear with Mrs. Sheridan, appropriately posing as St. Cecilia, in a painting by Sir Joshua Reynolds, who also frequented the Purdon house. Afterward, Sayre recalled that Purdon possessed an estate that gave him an income of £1,500 per annum. It may be that he and his wife lived beyond their means; it is certain that they were an attractive couple. Presumably both Sayre and Purdon invested cash in the bank. Rather surprisingly, it did not quickly fail.[2]

If the new partnership did not enjoy large profits—at that time one could still see oxen in Oxford Street—Sayre enjoyed sufficient income to

2. For the background and early history of Purdon, see the entries regarding the Cootes of Bellomont and Mountrath in John Lodge, *The Peerage of Ireland*, ed. Mervyn Archdall (London, 1789), II, especially pp. 69–71; also A. de Vlieger, *Historical and Genealogical Record of the Coote Family* (Lausanne, 1900), 69, 106, 138, 155 (Purdon's parents were apparently cousins). Reynolds, *Life and Times of Frederic Reynolds*, I, 372—

indulge in the social activities of an English bachelor as well as those of the Anglo-American political world. As a member of the Society of Supporters of the Bill of Rights, which Arthur Lee could not afford to join (although he did attend meetings of the society), Sayre associated with Sir Francis Blake Delaval, Lord Mountmorris, John Sawbridge, and John Horne Tooke—a pugnacious Radical second only to Wilkes in notoriety—together with Wilkes, John Reynolds, and sundry other notables. He continued to entertain visiting Americans, such as Henry Marchant of Rhode Island. He was upon friendly terms with Mrs. Catherine Macaulay, the celebrated historian and avowed republican, and later with the beautiful Mary Robinson, who would achieve a bad reputation as the mistress of the Prince of Wales and of Colonel Banastre Tarleton, who would keep better company and earn better repute as a novelist.[3]

Many Englishmen, especially courtiers, came to feel that Sayre kept bad company. To them, Wilkes was corrupt and unprincipled, and his American friends, including Sayre and the Lee brothers—with whom Sayre remained on good terms after the death of Dennys De Berdt—were mischievous. Of the three Americans, Sayre enjoyed the greatest intimacy with Wilkes, that extraordinary Englishman. He possessed a measure of the elegance and good manners for which Wilkes was distinguished, and he also shared with Wilkes a taste for luxurious living. But he did not possess the wit, cynicism, or family money that enabled the oblique-eyed Wilkes to pursue his riotous way as a champion of personal liberty, especially of freedom of the press. Putting forth censure of the royal family and of Scottish followers of George III, Wilkes and his publishers had been arbitrarily imprisoned; there is even reason to believe that the government arranged to add forged blasphemy to his

---

73; Thomas Moore, *Memoirs of the Rt. Hon. Richard Brinsley Sheridan* (New York, 1853), I, 99–100; W. Fraser Rae, *Sheridan* (London, 1896), I, 279; Dávila (ed.), *Archivo del General Miranda*, VI, 212. The painting is reproduced in Fitzgerald Molloy, *Sir Joshua and His Circle* (London, 1906), II, opposite p. 562. Reynolds also painted, in 1774, Charles Coote, earl of Bellomont (Ellis K. Waterhouse, *Reynolds* [London, 1941], 156).

3. Lee, *Life of Arthur Lee*, I, 22; Reynolds, *Life and Times of Frederic Reynolds*, I, 9; Franklin B. Dexter (ed.), *The Literary Diary of Ezra Stiles* (New York, 1901), I, 83, 251, 293, 318, 320; Mary Robinson, *Memoirs of the Late Mrs. Robinson, Written by Herself* (London, 1801), I, 104.

writings in order to discredit him.[4] He had successfully sued a secretary
of state, Lord Halifax, for damages on the score of false arrest, obtaining
an award of £4,000. Wilkes was a hero to many Londoners—he was even
able to charm the redoubtable Dr. Samuel Johnson, whose principles
and behavior in no way resembled his own. The Radical was more
interested in asserting himself than in fundamental reform, and he
championed America primarily because his English enemies were also
hostile to the colonists. Americans supplied him with money to carry on
his struggle against British authorities; he used it to pay some of his large
debts.

Sayre was associating with Wilkes as early as 1769. In August of that
year, while he was sojourning at Bath and recovering from a recent
illness, Sayre wrote to Wilkes, facetiously informing him that Earl
Jersey "died here last night, and now lies very cold, on the warm side of
the parade." Reporting that he had not neglected "the great cause of
freedom" in visits to Bristol and Wiltshire, Sayre expressed pleasure that
"many of the corporation" of Bath were "impressed with a proper sense of
the dangers we are exposed to." He voiced hope that "perhaps we may in
the event save this distracted and oppress'd people; for there appears a
noble spirit of freedom still existing among us." He did not confine his
hyperbole to politics. He was, "while life lasts," Wilkes's "cordial and
unalterable friend."[5]

Sayre and the Lees assumed that the cause of American liberty was the
same as those of English liberty and Wilkes. They recommended Americans for membership in the Society of Supporters of the Bill of Rights,
for they did not realize that the primary purpose of that society, so far as
Wilkes was concerned, was to raise money to pay his debts. In 1773,
upon the recommendation of Samuel Adams, his cousin John was unan-
imously elected to membership. Sending the news to John Adams, Sayre
declared, "It affords me great pleasure to find so very respectable a

4. That the British government resorted to such an unworthy attempt to discredit
Wilkes seems to be established in Charles C. Trench, *Portrait of a Patriot: A Biography of
John Wilkes* (Edinburgh, 1962), 144–46. Sayre believed that the government was guilty
of it (Sayre to Joseph Reed, March 29, 1768, in Reed Papers). Wilkes was capable
of blasphemy.

5. Sayre to Wilkes, August 29, 1769, in Additional MSS. 30870, folio 185, British
Museum, London.

gentleman of America, disposed to unite with the friends of liberty in England for our mutual safety and defence."[6] John Adams, never a roisterer or one to admire persons addicted to gaiety, might well have doubted that he had so very much in common with Wilkes.

Sayre and the Lees, becoming socially involved with the foremost English Radical, also became friends of his friends. One of them was John Reynolds, a solicitor who was to play a large and not uniformly pleasant role in the career of Stephen Sayre. Born in 1728, a year earlier than Wilkes, Reynolds was the son of a substantial landowner in Wiltshire. One may infer that Sayre visited the Reynoldses when he was in that county in 1769. John Reynolds was gay, handsome, hospitable, extravagant, bold, and devoted to Wilkes. Indifferent to business, he served nevertheless as lawyer for both Wilkes and the earl of Chatham. Marrying an heiress, he had acquired an income of as much as £5,000 per annum; he lived liberally in a large house in Lime Street in London and owned a villa at Southbarrow near the suburb of Bromley. Reynolds would have been at home as a character in a Henry Fielding novel or as a fox-hunter of superior social class in the stories of Robert Surtees. He loved a laugh, and there were those who thought him ignorant and vulgar. He, his wife, and his sister-in-law were fond of entertaining Wilkes. Reynolds was not excessively moralistic. He went to jail in 1768 for corrupt practices in parliamentary elections, and he was compelled for his sins against and in behalf of candidates to beg pardon from the House of Commons. Nor was he easily intimidated. Some months later, supporting Wilkes in a London election, Reynolds was struck in the mouth by Charles Dingley, an opponent of Wilkes, and lost some teeth. He responded by knocking Dingley down. Bold and carefree, Reynolds was a stout and reliable friend and a fearless and resolute enemy. When Wilkes became mayor of London in 1770, he saw to it that Reynolds as under-sheriff became the channel by which citizens could best approach the mayor. Reynolds also served as a lawyer for Sayre and the Sayre-Purdon bank.[7]

6. Charles Francis Adams (ed.), *The Works of John Adams* (Boston, 1850–56), II, 325.

7. There are many data regarding Reynolds in the autobiography of his son, *The Life and Times of Frederic Reynolds*. See also Horace Bleackley, *Life of John Wilkes* (London, 1917), 272–74; W. S. Lewis *et al.* (eds.), *Horace Walpole's Correspondence with Sir Horace*

Wilkes was very popular in the City and in Westminster, and voters in Middlesex County—that is, London—elected him again and again to the House of Commons. The House, however, just as repeatedly denied him a seat on the ground that he was unfit for that body because he had been found guilty of criminal libel. Many a citizen of the capital insisted that the House of Commons, not exclusively an abode of high-minded men, must accept the results of polling in London. In consequence, the voters, organized in liveries, technically including men on the basis of occupation, rallied behind Wilkes as a hero. The king and the royal court were challenged at the very center of their power, in Westminster, and Wilkes and his allies gave proof of their sway by electing two Americans as sheriffs of London and Middlesex County in 1773.

The first of the colonials to seek the office of sheriff was Sayre, on June 23. He was put forward as a "frame-work-knitter," although he was interested only in fabricating rope with which to tie enemies of the Wilkesites and the Americans. He testified afterward that he was inducted into office "upon public principles, and as a partizan with a set of men who were of a decided character." His associates were indeed of a special stamp. Arthur Lee eloquently and successfully urged the election of Sayre amidst tumult. "We have just now carried Mr. Sayre sheriff for London," he reported, "& in great triumph, solely on public ground, and the interest of the bill of rights. No men can be more determined in the cause of liberty than the livery of London." Elected with Sayre as sheriff was William Plomer, officially a bricklayer. When the two men addressed voters at a meeting at the Guildhall, Plomer said little. Sayre proclaimed, "I will strain every nerve in combating our common foe; I will labour assiduously to stop the progress of despotism; at least I will, by a vigorous exertion of those powers with which you have entrusted me, prevent its making any inroads into this great, this opulent, this free and independent city." [8]

In September, after Plomer had resigned, William Lee was chosen as Sayre's colleague. In mild surprise about the two elections, Benjamin Franklin wrote: "(Could you think it?) both Americans viz. Mr. Sayre,

---

Mann (New Haven, 1960), VI, 584; Trench, *Portrait of a Patriot*, 243–44; George Rudé, *Wilkes and Liberty: A Society Study of 1763 to 1774* (Oxford, 1962), 62.

8. Ford (ed.), *Letters of William Lee*, I, 15; *Southern Literary Messenger*, XXVIII (1859), 184; Lee, *Life of Arthur Lee*, I, 224; London *Chronicle*, June 24–26, 1773.

the New Yorker and Mr. W." They took office on September 29. Issuing instructions to their assistants, they urged obedience to law and mercy for the weak and innocent, promised to watch executions of criminals as a part of their duties, and urged that citizens be spectators in order to strengthen their moral principles. The two men might be plain and virtuous Americans, but they did not serve without ceremony. Sayre came forth in a coach with attendants in silver, white, and black; Lee appeared in a carriage with servants adorned in white, silver, and green, "with the cuffs and collars elegantly trimmed." They pledged themselves to keep order in elections, then commonly riotous. Two days later, they went with Wilkes and other celebrants in the city barge upon the Thames to the Court of Exchequer, where they were "sworn in & performed the ceremony of 'counting the horse-shoes and hobnails according to ancient custom.'"[9]

As it happened, Sayre held office in London for only one year. A successful politician might advance from sheriff to alderman and thence to lord mayor, but Sayre was defeated in a contest for alderman in November by one Robert Peckham, a wheelwright, whose name has not been preserved as that of an ally of Wilkes.[10] William Lee did become an alderman in 1775. Sayre was a conspicuous officeholder for only one year, but he moved into higher political circles. It is not recorded that the new sheriffs enjoyed the sights and sounds of the frequent hangings of criminals they were required to witness—although such pleasures were sought by English persons of high as well as low degree.

The two Americans were convivial with Wilkes and Reynolds. Sayre dined with them on June 29, 1773, at the London Tavern, on July 2 on Tower Hill, on July 3 at the London Tavern in a party including the Lees, and on September 14 on Tower Hill in a party including one of the Lees. On January 25, 1774, they dined at the home of Mr. Crosby in Essex Street with Wilkes and his daughter, Mr. and Mrs. Reynolds, a Miss West, and Sir Watkin and Lady Lewes. A month later Sayre took dinner with Wilkes and others at a chophouse in Duke's Court. In April Wilkes dined twice at Sayre's house in Berners Street. The sheriffs ate with their English friend at the Latham Brickyard in Camberwell on

9. Albert H. Smyth (ed.), *The Life and Writings of Benjamin Franklin* (New York, 1905–1907), IV, 97; London *Chronicle*, September 28–30, 1773.

10. Alfred B. Beaven, *The Aldermen of London* (London, 1908), I, 112, II, xxxviii.

July 15, at the Mansion House a week later, at the George & Vulture in the City in mid-September.

At the end of their term of office, they had the duty and pleasure of instructing Wilkes that he had once more been elected to the House of Commons. So they challenged that body, in behalf of the voters of London, to deny Wilkes his seat. Wilkes received a "presentation dinner" at the Joiners Hall on November 3. Weary of struggle with him and the City, the House at last accepted Wilkes without comment. Before they left office, the sheriffs, as friends of humanity, gave "a hot dinner for the poor inmates in the Compters and Ludgate prison." They also supplied "an entertainment for the sergeants and yeomen" of the County of Middlesex.[11]

OTHER activities of the senior sheriff were more exposed to censure, for he sprang once more to the defense of his native land as a third and ominous crisis began to develop between Britain and America. Growing variations between the British citizens kept apart by the seas were preserving and creating antagonisms that threatened the continuance of the imperial community. There was cleavage between the inhabitants of the British islands and the venturers into North America at the very beginning of the colonies. The settlers of New England were overwhelmingly Puritan, while those who remained in England were largely Anglican. Very few nobles voyaged westward from Plymouth or Bristol to seek their fortunes in the New World, nor was the English gentry decimated by the departure of a large fraction of its members for the far shores of the Atlantic. Both the nobility and the gentry continued to flourish in eighteenth-century Britain, whereas those who came from Britain—and from the European continent—to the possessions of the Stuart and Hanoverian rulers beyond the ocean were in the main from the middle and lower echelons of society. Such contrarieties, and others, did not materially diminish. Josiah Quincy, Jr., of Massachusetts, in 1775, after a tour of southern England, declared that "the commonalty in this country are no more like the commonalty in America than if they were two utterly distinct and unconnected peoples."[12]

11. William Purdie Treloar, *Wilkes and the City* (London, 1917), 280–84; Ford (ed.), *Letters of William Lee*, I, 16, 19.

12. Josiah Quincy, *Memoir of the Life of Josiah Quincy, Junior, 1774–1775* (Boston, 1874), 259.

Isolated from Europe and increasingly conscious of their common enemies, the colonists tended to become one people different from all others—Americans. Securing by means of elected assemblies substantial authority over their domestic affairs, they had pruned away the power of British governors, councilors, judges, and customs men. At the end of the Seven Years' War in 1763, they were relieved of a Bourbon menace when the French flag vanished from Canada and eastern Louisiana and Spain was compelled to cede the Floridas to Britain. Now largely free from danger of foreign attack, the colonists had become sufficiently numerous and wealthy to challenge even the authority of Parliament. They had also emerged victorious from two Anglo-American crises: they had secured the repeal of the detested Stamp Act in 1766, and they had obtained withdrawal of several British duties upon their imports four years later. Thus they felt that they had rather effectively asserted their view that they were exempt from parliamentary taxation for revenue. But their triumphs were incomplete. The crisis that loomed awesomely after 1773 began primarily when the prime minister, Lord North, secured parliamentary consent to a scheme that permitted the East India Company of Britain to sell tea very cheaply in America—so cheaply that the colonists would be enticed to buy it and to pay an import duty surviving from the second crisis. By this decision, Lord North revived the issue of taxation for revenue and thereby triggered the clash that led to the Boston Tea Party and similar frolics in several American ports.

In January, 1774, exasperated officers of the crown began to strike back. Benjamin Franklin had obtained "private" letters sent by Thomas Hutchinson and other royal officials in Massachusetts which condemned Samuel Adams and his like and urged that British authority in the province be buttressed. Sending the letters to Boston, Franklin, as agent for Massachusetts, was instructed to ask for the removal of Hutchinson from the governorship. Presenting a petition for that purpose to the Privy Council, Franklin was pilloried before that body as a thief, a spy, and a sinister conspirator seeking American independence. American resistance also induced crown and Parliament in the spring of 1774 to punish Massachusetts in general and Boston in particular. The colonists outside Massachusetts were to learn by example that they could not continue to flout imperial authority. A Port Bill closed the harbor of Boston to commerce until such time that payment was made for the teas destroyed there, and some weeks later Parliament passed a series of

Coercive Acts to remodel the government of Massachusetts toward making it less American and more British.

It was doubtless fortunate for Sayre that he did not secure the agency for Massachusetts at the death of Dennys De Berdt. To Samuel Adams and many other vigorous citizens of Massachusetts, Hutchinson, like Bernard, was a treacherous traducer who blackened the virtuous behavior of honest colonists in letters that were carefully read in London and stimulated British resentment. Hence came eagerness in the House of Representatives to inspect such missives and pressure upon the agent to secure them so that the wicked machinations of the writers could be exposed. Sayre had tried to obtain copies of official reports sent by the governors to the Colonial Office but had been turned away.[13] He had learned of the existence of the "private" letters from Hutchinson and his sympathizers, but it was reserved for Franklin to obtain them and to pay a penalty for relaying them to Massachusetts. Had he had the opportunity, Sayre would hardly have behaved otherwise than did Franklin. He shared the feelings of Samuel Adams and Franklin regarding Bernard and Hutchinson, but he escaped embroilment on that account until 1775.

Nevertheless, Sayre continued to be involved in the affairs of Massachusetts. He remained in touch with Samuel Adams, who was not fond of Franklin. Immediately after receiving news of the death of Dennys De Berdt, Adams had resolved to support Sayre for the Massachusetts agency because, as he informed Sayre, he valued "your honest zeal for the rights of America" and "your ability to defend them." Then, being told that Sayre wanted the post to go to Arthur Lee, Adams had pushed for Lee. Adams would not have peace between Britain and America. He continued to insist, after Captain Thomas Preston had been found innocent by a jury of committing murder in the Boston "Massacre," that Preston was guilty. When an arrangement was made in London to place Hutchinson in royal pay, so as to make the governor less subject to the influence of the Massachusetts legislature, Adams asked Sayre, "Is this not perfect despotism?" Sayre undoubtedly answered that query in the affirmative, if not in print. He must have been flattered by the attention he received from Adams.[14]

13. Richard Frothingham, *The Life and Times of Joseph Warren* (Boston, 1865), 160.
14. Harry A. Cushing (ed.), *The Writings of Samuel Adams* (New York, 1904–

Did Sayre resent his rejection for the Massachusetts agency? Apparently not, although he did desire the appointment. If he continued to be cool toward Franklin, he did not turn jealously against Arthur Lee because Adams had thrown his support to Lee. He sent to Adams propaganda pieces written by Lee under the pseudonym *Junius Americanus*, which passionately and windily defended the colonists against the capricious tyranny of British ministers. Sayre also arranged for a correspondence between Adams and Lee, thus encouraging the creation of an alliance between Adams, Lee, and the numerous Lee brothers of Virginia, which also came to include John Adams, a second cousin of Samuel. That alliance was to play a large part in the American Revolution. It would also ultimately injure Sayre.[15]

Sayre managed to remain on good terms with the Lees until the War of Independence was well under way—a testimony to his own graciousness. William Lee, Arthur's older brother, was a colorless man, although not quarrelsome. Arthur, however, was addicted to feuding. Having qualified to practice medicine, he preferred to mix bitter potions for English politicians hostile to America. He was a prolific and verbose writer, and eventually he became a lawyer. He was by American definition and in his own opinion a gentleman. Ascribing the loftiest motives to himself, he was remarkably disposed to question those of other men. There was a serious defect in his psyche that time would glaringly reveal. For some years, however, the Lee brothers remained stout allies of Sayre, and all three men looked upon themselves in London as American gentlemen united in a great cause.[16]

Too much can be made regarding ill feeling between Franklin and Sayre, even respecting hostility between the Philadelphian and the Lees.

1908), II, 67−68. For the development of the relationship between Samuel Adams and Sayre, see *ibid*, II, 56−61, 66, 134−35.

15. Lee, *Life of Arthur Lee*, I, 249. It was suspected in 1773 that Sayre was the author or coauthor with Arthur Lee of the *Junius Americanus* essays. Nelson and Van Doren (eds.), *Documents Relating to the Colonial History of the State of New Jersey*, 1st Ser., XXIX, 5−6. The suspicion was unwarranted.

16. The Lees saw to it that Sayre became a member in 1774 of the Mississippi Company, formed by Virginia speculators, including Washington, to secure a grant of land north of the Ohio River. Clarence W. Alvord and Clarence E. Carter (eds.), *The Critical Period, 1763−1765* (Springfield, 1915), 23, Vol. X of *Collections of the Illinois State Historical Library*. The venture failed.

Sayre and Arthur Lee rallied to Franklin's support in the affair of the Hutchinson letters. Moreover, Sayre and the Lees did what they could in the early months of 1774, with Franklin and other champions of American rights, to moderate British policy. In January, Franklin was assailed not only by government before the Privy Council but by William Whately because of his behavior in the affair of the Hutchinson letters. Whately had acquired possession of the letters from the estate of his brother, Thomas, the recipient, and began a suit in chancery against Franklin, accusing him in effect of theft of the papers. Sayre and Arthur Lee actively assisted Franklin and Franklin's lawyer, John Dunning, in the preparation of a defense. As it happened, the charge against Franklin was abandoned by Whately because the American was out of England and out of reach before the case could be heard.[17]

The Americans were less fortunate in their efforts to induce the government to deal judiciously with Massachusetts. At a meeting in the Thatched House Tavern presided over by Sheriffs Lee and Sayre, twenty-nine men, including Franklin and Arthur Lee, signed a protest against the Boston Port Bill. Sent to the House of Lords, it was ignored. Nor was heed given to a petition against the Coercive Acts prepared by Arthur Lee and brought forward by the sheriffs. Sayre tried to present it, but he was turned away.[18] The government was determined to proceed against the obstreperous colonists, who, it was assumed, would yield to a display of imperial power.

But neither Boston nor Massachusetts meekly accepted chastisement, and colonists from New Hampshire to Georgia rallied to support them. In May, General Thomas Gage, commander-in-chief of the British army in North America, appeared in Boston as governor of Massachusetts. It was his task to execute the Port Bill and the Coercive Acts. Gathering troops in the city, he rigidly enforced the Port Bill. One of the Coercive Acts required the formation of a new royally appointed council, but when Gage undertook to establish it, Massachusetts, except for Boston—which was helpless under military control—rose in revolt. In August, royal authority outside the city collapsed. In September, Gage fortified the narrow peninsula which then connected Boston with

17. Worthington C. Ford, "Franklin's Accounts Against Massachusetts," *Proceedings of the Massachusetts Historical Society*, LVI (1922), 107–116.

18. Kammen, *A Rope of Sand*, 291–92; Sosin, *Agents and Merchants*, 179, 182.

the mainland. Stripping garrisons elsewhere in North America, Gage brought more and more troops into the city, and a naval squadron collected in adjacent waters to assist him. In the meantime, the Americans quite generally responded by aligning themselves with Gage's adversaries. They sent food to nourish Bostonians who lost employment in consequence of the closing of their port; and twelve of the thirteen colonies—all except Georgia—commissioned delegates to the First Continental Congress, which met at Philadelphia in early autumn to speak for all America.

There was good reason to expect that worse was to come. Sayre had become friendly, perhaps through the medium of John Reynolds, with Lord and Lady Chatham as early as June. During the summer he sent information about events in America to Chatham, along with a gift of venison obtained from a royal preserve and a hint that the great Englishman, who had more or less retired from politics because of ill health, should exert himself for the benefit of both countries. Chatham, always ready to face realities, did indeed recognize that the situation was becoming desperate. In mid-August he expressed worry that "the streets of Boston have already run with blood" and that a general American rebellion loomed. Two weeks later he wrote to Sayre, "I fear the bond of union between us and America will be cut for ever. Devoted England will then have seen her best days." [19]

ALL OF Stephen Sayre's time was not engrossed by public business that summer, nor were all of his connections upon the level of the Chathams. Were one to accept as social gospel *The Memoirs of Mrs. Sophia Baddeley*— that scandal-filled chronicle of the life of a most beauteous actress— Sayre was then enmeshed in personal as well as public troubles. Moreover, he appears as a thoroughgoing rake in that juicy history, which relates that he became a lover of Mrs. Baddeley in 1773, her keeper, and the father by her in 1775 of a son she named Stephen Sayre. He is also depicted in those recollections as short of money, ungenerous, and unfeeling, except for seeking pleasure. The *Memoirs* in addition assert that he deceived and despoiled another, but innocent, woman. Its author, or authors, knew Sayre, and their testimony cannot lightly be set aside.

19. William S. Taylor and John H. Pringle (eds.), *Correspondence of William Pitt, Earl of Chatham* (London, 1840), IV, 349, 359, 360–61.

Sophia Baddeley, born in 1745, was a daughter of Valentine Snow, a trumpeter at the court of George II. She learned to sing from her father. She eloped with Robert Baddeley, a distinguished actor, at the age of eighteen or nineteen, went on the stage, and soon achieved fame. Possessing a delicate loveliness, she sang light and frivolous songs superbly. She soon parted from Baddeley and went from lover to lover. George III and his Queen Charlotte were so entranced by one of her performances in London that the king requested that she sit for her portrait by his favorite artist, Zoffany. The "divine Baddeley" was, unfortunately for her, frivolous, vain, empty-headed, and wildly extravagant. Pursued by a fraction of the House of Lords, she came to prefer what seemed to be the ease of a mistress to the grease of the actress. She produced at least two children after 1777. Worn by dissipation, she turned to the solace of opium. She was supported by kind fellow actors during the last years of her life and died in Edinburgh in 1786.[20]

The *Memoirs* declare that Sayre obtained money that enabled him to become a banker by fleecing and ruining a Mrs. Pearson of Berners Street, with whom he lived as husband and wife until he deserted her for Mrs. Baddeley. There is no good reason to doubt that Sayre had an affair with a Mrs. Pearson or that she accused him of dissipating her property, although he denied that he had mistreated her. It is certain that he engaged in a liaison with the actress. According to the *Memoirs*, Sayre arranged to make her acquaintance by a device that pleased the empty-headed Baddeley. A fortune-teller whom he employed informed Baddeley that she would meet a tall, thin, rather handsome gentleman in St. James's Park. He would be wearing around his neck a gold chain, the badge of office of a sheriff of London. She went to the rendezvous and soon became Sayre's mistress. He provided an establishment for her in Cleveland Row and later at other addresses. The couple frequently entertained friends, including John Wilkes, in Cleveland Row. Sayre broiled steaks for them, and they burned George III with strong language. Sayre

20. There are many testimonies to the beauty of her face and figure. For examples, see Edward C. Everard, *Memoirs of an Unfortunate Son of Thespis* (Edinburgh, 1818), 58, and John Galt, *The Lives of the Players* (Boston, 1831), II, 217–27. Racy incidents clustered about the actress. One is related in Harold Simpson and Mrs. Charles Brown, *A Century of Famous Actresses, 1750–1850* (London, n.d.), 281–82. There are sketches of both Baddeleys in the *Dictionary of National Biography*.

was "a red-hot patriot." Eventually, according to the *Memoirs*, the actress became pregnant and gave birth to a son in 1775 with the assistance of the famous physician, Dr. William Hunter. It is reported that she named the boy Stephen Sayre and that the father continued to support mother and child for some time. Then they drifted apart, without excessive agony for the lovely Sophia, who is said to have had at least one other lover while she was intimately associated with Sayre.[21]

There is cause to doubt the entire validity of the *Memoirs*. They were ostensibly written by Mrs. Elizabeth Steele, a close friend of Mrs. Baddeley, who claimed to be the benefactress of the actress, although she was actually a dependent who encouraged the amours of the beautiful Sophia. Mrs. Steele was obviously hostile to Sayre. The *Memoirs* relate that Mrs. Baddeley adopted a son of her cook and tried to get assistance from the duchess of Devonshire by the intercession of Mrs. Richard Brinsley Sheridan for the education of a five-year-old "son" in 1782.[22] But there is no evidence other than the statements in the *Memoirs* that Sophia had a child by Sayre.

The *Memoirs* were clearly intended to create a sensation. Mrs. Steele was assisted in writing the biography by one Alexander Bicknell, a minor professional writer who may have had his own reasons for attacking Sayre.[23] It is to be suspected that he supplied at least one unquestionably malicious passage savoring of forgery. Supposedly taken from a letter written by Sayre in 1771 to a political friend, the passage ran: "We are likely to have some serious matters, of the political kind 'ere long. Wilkes has brought the Commons into a damnable dilemma, by attacking his two old friends, the K— and Lord Halifax. I hope there still

21. Elizabeth Steele, *The Memoirs of Mrs. Sophia Baddeley, Late of Drury Lane Theatre* (Dublin, 1787), III, 192–93, 147–48, 172–73, 177–78, 210.

22. For the appeal through Mrs. Sheridan to the duchess and for a good account of Mrs. Baddeley, see Philip H. Highfill, Jr., Kalman A. Burnim, and Edward A. Langhans (eds.), *A Biographical Dictionary of Actors, Actresses, Musicians, Dancers, Managers & Other Stage Personnel in London, 1660–1800* (Carbondale, Ill., 1973–), I, 202–208.

23. John Fyvie, *Comedy Queens of the Georgian Era* (London, 1906), 232–34. There is a sketch of Bicknell in the *Dictionary of National Biography*. He also wrote a biography of Alfred the Great, *A History of England and the British Empire*, and *Instances of the Mutability of Fortune*. Sensational exposés of prominent persons were commonly published in England in the latter part of the eighteenth century, notoriously in the *Town and Country Magazine*.

remains some spirit of Englishmen among us, which will soon blast the
men who are striving to ruin this great kingdom. That you and I may
live to share the spoils of those rascals, and be rewarded with what we
really merit, is my ardent wish." Vehement as Sayre might have been, he
would hardly have written about dividing the "spoils of those rascals." It
is likely that Bicknell inserted a bogus passage in a Sayre letter. Further
doubt concerning the trustworthiness of the *Memoirs* arises from a general denial of their authenticity by Sayre.[24]

But, again, the *Memoirs* cannot be set aside as utterly false. The
author or authors did know Sayre, and there is a substratum of truth in
the sensational opus. That Mrs. Baddeley bore him a son seems unlikely.
Still, because the account of the birth of Stephen Sayre, Jr., is so circumstantial, it may be that the son did indeed make an appearance, but that,
like so many babies of the eighteenth century, he lived only briefly.[25]

The *Memoirs* throw some light upon a formal and much more dignified union into which Sayre entered, for he married into a very prominent
English family at the age of thirty-eight. The *Memoirs* would have it that
he took to wife, before the birth of Stephen Sayre, Jr., an "old lady for
her money," that he "absolutely hated her and should have shrunk from

24. Steele, *Memoirs of Mrs. Sophia Baddeley*, III, 179–80. I also find it difficult to
believe that on one occasion Sayre wrote to his "dearest love" Sophia that "this is the first
moment I could get to inform you, that I can't come out of doors this day; my eyes are
exceedingly inflamed. I am obliged to keep them covered with parsley and cream; can
scarcely look long and nuff to write this" (*ibid.*, III, 248). Sayre's denial is in Sayre to
James Madison, March 10, 1802, in James Madison Papers, Library of Congress,
Washington, D.C. Sayre also said that Elizabeth Steele would have been hanged for
forgery had she not died soon after the publication of the *Memoirs*, and that Bicknell,
"that most infamous of all ministerial hirelings," had falsely accused the brilliant comedian Samuel Foote of sodomy. The accusation was made, and Bicknell may indeed have
had a share in creating the canard. Lucyle Werkmeister, "Notes for a Revised Life of
William Jackson," *Notes and Queries*, CCVI (1961), 44; Simon Trefman, *Sam. Foote,
Comedian, 1710–1777* (New York, 1971), 248–60. Condemnation of the *Memoirs* by
Sayre does not preclude partial authenticity; he did not specifically denounce every part of
it as false. He told Madison that he had never done anything dishonorable—for a
gentleman bachelor in that time and place to conduct an affair with Mrs. Baddeley would
not have been thought dishonorable.

25. Steele, *Memoirs of Mrs. Sophia Baddeley*, III, 177–78, 210. There is a discrepancy
in these references concerning the birth of Stephen Sayre, Jr. One account places the date
in the spring of 1775; the other indicates that it occurred in the following autumn.

the alliance, but that her fortune would save him from ruin." Evidence of weight that Sayre was in truly desperate need of money is otherwise lacking. He may have used financial stringency as an excuse for putting an end to his liaison with Sophia Baddeley, since long afterward he said that his bank "succeeded beyond my most sanguine expectations."[26]

It is certain, however, that Sayre married an older woman. According to the *Memoirs*, he first met his wife when she came with a niece to Sayre & Purdon upon a bit of business. Such may well have been the fact. She was Miss Elizabeth Noel, and she was the guardian of the niece, Lady Frances Sherard, daughter of the earl of Harborough. The wedding took place on February 18, 1775. Notices of it appeared in several newspapers and magazines, including one that "covered" Bath, in part, no doubt, because Sayre thus became connected with one of the oldest and proudest families of England. The London *Chronicle* reported that "on Saturday was married Stephen Sayre, Esq; banker in Oxford-Street, and late one of the sheriffs of this city, to Miss Noel, one of the daughters and co-heiresses of the Hon. W. Noel, Esq; deceased, late one of the Justices of his Majesty's Court of Common Pleas and Chief Justice of Chester."[27]

Like Charlotte Nelthorpe, Elizabeth Noel was a Lincolnshire woman. She was apparently born at Stamford in 1727. The Noels were far above the Nelthorpes in social standing. That Judge Noel had been an important person was evident. In an age when individuals of rank and influence in England commonly held political sinecures, he was the only man who was permitted to hold two judicial appointments while per-

---

26. Sayre to Henry Knox, October 3, 1788, in Henry Knox Papers, Massachusetts Historical Society, Boston. Sayre owed some money to Ralph Izard at the time of the marriage (Lee, *Life of Arthur Lee*, II, 76). Izard, a fellow American who lived in Berners Street after 1771, was afterward a depositor in Sayre & Purdon. Sayre and Izard were friends for several years, and it is quite possible that Sayre had borrowed money from his neighbor before becoming a banker and had neglected to repay it.

27. The niece married army officer George Catchmaid Morgan, apparently a close associate of Sayre, in April, 1776. Morgan, despite his middle name, may not have been a fortune hunter. He ultimately became a general in the British army. Steele, *Memoirs of Mrs. Sophia Baddeley*, III, 210–11; John H. Chapman (ed.), *The Register Book of Marriages Belonging to the Parish of St. George, Hanover Square* (London, 1886), I, 262. Reports of the marriage are included in London *Chronicle*, February 18–21, 1775; Felix Farley's Bristol *Journal*, February 25, 1775; *Gentleman's Magazine*, XLV (1775), 102; *Town and Country Magazine*, VII (1775), 111.

forming the duties of only one.[28] Sayre had become an "Esquire" and had finally contracted the alliance with a lady of family and fortune that he had so long desired.

Certainly Elizabeth Noel possessed at least a small fortune. "I married a woman of one of the first families in England—she had money & landed property," Sayre afterward asserted. She inherited £6,000, together with a one-third interest in lands located in Leicestershire and Lincolnshire, from her father, Judge William Noel, and she may also have received a legacy through her mother. Mrs. Sayre came from the Noels of Kirkby Mallory in Leicestershire, a family that established itself in England at the Norman Conquest, and she was a descendant of *the* Wentworths. Her father was a younger son of Sir John Noel, Baronet, and Mary Clobery, the daughter of Sir John Clobery, Knight, of Devonshire. The mother of Mrs. Sayre was Elizabeth, daughter of Sir Thomas Trollope, fourth Baronet of Casewick in Lincolnshire.[29]

Judge Noel was apparently not remarkable for genius. Horace Walpole is reported to have said that he was "a pompous man of little solidity." He conferred the title of "Honourable" upon himself. When Hogarth portrayed two judges asleep in his unflattering engraving of "The Bench," it was claimed that Noel was one of the somnolent dignitaries. He was satirized as a person always seeking higher office:

> As next in pretence up starts Mr. N—l;
> "Me, your lordship, quo' he, "does certainly
> know well.

28. Copies of the parish register of All Saints, Stamford, preserved in the headquarters of the Church of Jesus Christ of Latter-Day Saints in Salt Lake City and in the Lincolnshire Record Office, report the christening of Elizabeth, daughter of William and Susanna Noel, in 1727. The month and day given in the entry cannot be deciphered with certainty, but the event may have taken place on August 27. Mrs. Sayre's mother was named Elizabeth; the mother of Mrs. Noel and her eldest daughter were named Susanna (or Susan). John Nichols, *The History and Antiquities of Leicestershire* (London, 1795–1811), IV, Part II, 767. It would appear that Mrs. Noel was confused in the record with her mother or daughter. Perhaps she was named Elizabeth Susan. I am indebted to Mr. Lester Brown for an analysis of the parish register. Evidence of Judge Noel's appointments is found in London *Times*, January 9, 1787.

29. Dávila (ed.), *Archivo del General Miranda*, VI, 212; Will of William Noel, in Wills, Public Record Office, London (Professor Peter Marshall kindly arranged to procure a copy of it for me); Nichols, *History and Antiquities of Leicestershire*, III, Part L, 253.

> If a gentleman born, and descendant of high blood,
> And knowledge of law, which I think pretty good:
> If oft being mention'd in all the newspapers,
> At ev'ry promotion, as one of the gapers,
> Can entitle a man to the place in dispute,
> I presume that, with justice, I can't be left out." [30]

Such attacks did not prevent Judge Noel from holding a seat in the House of Commons for thirty-five years, nor from providing for his progeny. Dying in 1762, he bequeathed to his offspring, and ultimately to Sayre, important social and political connections.

Elizabeth was the youngest of the judge's four daughters. Her mother and all of her sisters died before her marriage, but two of the sisters supplied valuable ties for her and her husband. The oldest daughter, Susan Maria, married Thomas Hill, whose son Noel became Lord Berwick of Attingham in 1784. Another sibling, Anne, remained single. Frances, the third daughter, married Bennet Sherard, earl of Harborough. Descendants of the Noels of Kirkby Mallory became famous in the nineteenth century, among them Lady Annabella Milbanke, the wife of Lord Byron, the poet. Lady Byron inherited Kirkby Mallory and lived there in her later years. Through her mother, Mrs. Sayre was also related to the novelist Anthony Trollope, who was the son of her first cousin. But even in the heyday of Stephen Sayre, the Noels and the Trollopes were related or associated with several potent families, including the Wentworths, Rockinghams, Sherards, Portlands, and Verneys. Those connections enabled Sayre to play a special role in the last stages of the third Anglo-American crisis, even before his marriage. [31]

To know who Elizabeth Noel was, to be sure, does not supply full information about her. She remains without much description. Was she, as she was spitefully described, merely an "old lady" whom Sayre married for her possessions? He had earlier resisted the temptation to acquire money and status by such a union. Moreover, he was warned against July

30. Edward Foss, *The Judges of England* (London, 1864), VIII, 351.

31. This genealogy of Elizabeth Sayre has been compiled from Nichols, *History and Antiquities of Leicestershire*, IV, Pt. II, 767, 770, 772; the sketches of Judge William Noel and Frances Trollope in the *Dictionary of National Biography*; and materials under the titles Berwick, Portland, Harborough, Melbourne, and Wentworth in *The Complete Peerage*. None of those works mentions the marriage of Elizabeth Noel to Sayre.

and November nuptials by the experience of John Wilkes, who was twenty-two when he espoused a lady of thirty-two. Wilkes separated from his wife after she bore a daughter. "In my non-age," recalled Wilkes, "to please an indulgent father, I married a woman half as old again as myself; of a large fortune—my own being also that of a gentleman. It was a sacrifice to Plutus, not to Venus. . . . I stumbled at the very threshold of the temple of Hymen."[32] The difference of ages of ten years is not impressive. But did Sayre also stumble upon entering matrimony? He was nine or ten years younger than his wife. One may speculate that an elegant, pleasant, and remarkably good-looking man—even a colonial without an impressive pedigree—was most attractive to a woman without other prospect of marriage, one far beyond the flush of youth, which did not ordinarily last long in her time. It is not likely that Sayre detested her at the period of their marriage, although he may have told Sophia Baddeley that such was the case in order to emphasize his reluctance to put an end to their liaison. There is no doubt that Elizabeth's money attracted him. The union was one of convenience, probably one not entirely pleasing to his wife's relatives, who could not prevent it and so accepted it with the thought that Elizabeth might have eloped with a footman, an actor, or a wild fortune-hunting Irishman. Sayre was, not surprisingly, sexually unfaithful to his marriage vows. It will be remembered that in his English milieu of that time it was rather expected that the male partner in such a couple would engage in extramarital adventures.

32. The life of actress Harriot Mellon supplies two extraordinary examples of July–December marriages of convenience and money. At the age of thirty-seven, she married the enormously wealthy banker Thomas Coutts, when he was seventy-nine. After his death, when she was forty-nine, she espoused a duke of St. Albans, who was twenty-six.

4
Gentleman Between Two Worlds

 OWEVER great were Sayre's involvements with his bank, Sophia Baddeley, and his marriage, they did not occupy all of his energies. The third Anglo-American crisis continued to deepen, and Sayre continued to engage in politicking. He campaigned for a seat in the House of Commons as a champion of American rights, and he strove to create an English coalition to defend them. After the shooting began at Lexington and Concord, he remained in England.

Enough was known in London before the end of August, 1774, about the troubles in America to create serious concern for George III and his cabinet.[1] On the twenty-fourth of that month, the earl of Dartmouth, secretary of state for the colonies, signed orders instructing General Gage to arrest leaders of the refractory colonists of Massachusetts and even to send them to England for trial, if the governor could do so without goading the malcontents into increased violence. It was impossible for Gage even to try to execute the orders without a convulsion, and the meager forces he had in Boston for many months dictated inaction. The king and his cabinet also decided to call a parliamentary election. Law required that one be held not later than 1775, and they wished to avoid contest at the polls when Britain was engaged in a decisive struggle with the Americans. The existing Parliament was dissolved on September 30, and the polls were opened.

How did the monarch look upon America? In one statement he

1. For the last stages of the third Anglo-American crisis and the curious story of the transmission of orders to Gage to begin the shooting, see my "Decision for War, 1775," in John Browning and Richard Morton (eds.), 1776 (Toronto, 1976), 11–51. Herein I offer citations for some quotations and new points.

[53]

declared that "the die is now cast, the colonies must either submit or triumph." He did not wish to come to "severer measures"; however, he believed that "there must always be one tax to keep up the right" and that the duty upon teas must accordingly be maintained.[2] Was George III as determined as those words indicate? He had accepted a decision by the cabinet in 1766 to rescind the Stamp Act, and he had agreed to preserve the duty upon tea only as a symbol at the close of the second Anglo-American crisis. Still, he must have had doubts occasionally regarding the right course to pursue. Although courageous and devoted to duty, George was also scatterbrained and obstinate. Coming to the throne at a time when it was customary for politicians in power to buy the votes of Lords and Commons with titles, positions, pensions, and contracts, he had become the chief dispenser of pelf—a political boss as well as a monarch possessing the profound prestige of a hereditary ruler in eighteenth-century Europe. It remained possible that the cabinet would compensate for the monarch's deficiencies and that he would once more accept a compromise acceptable to the Americans, for he was disposed, when his conscience permitted, to listen to his confidential advisers.

The active members of the cabinet were not utterly committed to repression. They were, except for Lord North, all peers—men who were superior by birth to ordinary British mortals and even more definitely to mere colonials. They had no personal acquaintance with America, and the colonies were as strange to them as they were to the king, who was insular enough in outlook. However, North was averse to quarreling, and his stepbrother, Lord Dartmouth, sincerely desired to avoid a clash of arms. When in the mood, Dartmouth could assess the power of Parliament in the most extreme language. In the preceding summer, he had declared, with respect to the duty on teas, that "the supreme legislature of the whole British empire has laid a duty (no matter for the present whether it has or has not the right so to do, it is sufficient that we conceive it has)."[3] At other times Dartmouth was disposed to try to

2. John W. Fortescue (ed.), *The Correspondence of King George the Third* (London, 1928), III, 131.

3. Dartmouth to Joseph Reed, July 11, 1774, in Reed, *Life and Correspondence of Joseph Reed*, I, 73.

conciliate the Americans. Much depended upon him because of his position and his relationship to North. Other members of the cabinet, who must have had their doubts regarding the wisdom of extreme measures, were more or less committed to them. There was a chance that the colonial secretary would assert himself and insist upon an accommodation with America, but it was doubtful that he would seek to impose his views upon his colleagues, for he was modest as well as peace-loving. A more substantial hope for an Anglo-American compromise rested in those worried British politicians who stood in opposition to the cabinet, if not to the king, among them the earl of Chatham, Lord Rockingham, and John Wilkes.

Even as the royal call for elections began to circulate at the beginning of October, Dartmouth received alarming news from General Gage. The commander in chief declared that New England could not be reduced to obedience without the arrest of the Yankee leaders and the employment of large bodies of troops. The general then believed that other Americans would not rally effectively to help the New Englanders, but he realized that the Yankees were in a mood to fight and would fight very well. He would need substantial reinforcements and a year or two to subdue them. The answer to that ominous appeal for massive help indicated a military weakness that warned against resort to the British army. The beleaguered general was advised not to expect powerful assistance before the spring of 1775. The most that could quickly be done to help him was to send a contingent of six hundred marines to Boston with additions to the naval squadron in its harbor.

That October, Thomas Hutchinson, an intelligent man who had come to London upon a leave of absence that proved to be permanent and who was in rather close touch with high officials, wrote, "I really believe there has never been a set of men more disposed to favor the colonies in every point which can consist with their remaining one state with the kingdom, than the present ministry." Hutchinson also declared, "I know it to be the wish of the King and his ministers to gratify the colonies as far as can be done without an entire separation from the kingdom." However, when he suggested to Lord Dartmouth that hostile measures against Massachusetts should be accompanied by repeal of the duties upon tea, the colonial secretary replied that cancellation of the taxes was impossible. It would induce the Americans to believe that Britain was less than determined to defend its rightful authority.[4]

Benjamin Franklin saw the situation in a very different light. Resenting abuse that he had suffered in the preceding January from the tongue of Solicitor General Alexander Wedderburn at the hearing upon the petition to remove Hutchinson, Franklin had ever since avoided the company of ministers. He had earlier dreamed of a noble and enduring British empire in which the Americans would be recognized as the equals of the English. Like Stephen Sayre, Franklin enjoyed life in England, but he had become increasingly American. He, with other Americans in the imperial capital, believed that Britain must and could be forced to recognize American rights. He estimated that the resistance of Massachusetts might, with colonial boycotting of British goods, lead to the downfall of the North ministry and the formation of a new one more friendly to America, but he feared that such a happy result would be impossible if hostilities broke out in Massachusetts. In that event, Franklin knew that he could expect arrest and incarceration in Newgate Prison or the Tower of London. Nevertheless, he chose to run the risk of imprisonment and remain in England to do what he could for America.[5]

What was the attitude of Stephen Sayre? He had less reason for being attached to America than Franklin, and he had not been abused by the British government. Unlike Franklin, Sayre had no property in the Thirteen Colonies, nor did he have firm and powerful friends in America. He was even less eager to return home than was the Philadelphian, who had preferred to remain in England for eleven years rather than go back to Pennsylvania. Sayre not only was happier in England than in America, he was in the process of acquiring, at last, substantial property and lofty social connections. Were he cautious in politics and banking, he could look forward with confidence to the pleasures of a comfortable position in English society. He nevertheless continued to stand forth energetically for American rights. Discretion was not part of his character.

The odds in the election of 1774 heavily favored the North ministry.

4. Peter O. Hutchinson (ed.), *The Diary and Letters of His Excellency Thomas Hutchinson* (Boston, 1884–86), I, 262, 265.

5. Smyth (ed.), *Life and Writings of Benjamin Franklin*, VI, 238–39, 243–44, 247, 251, 253, 254.

Because of restricted suffrage, with districting remarkably at variance with population, and with government control of patronage, many supporters of the ministry were assured of success at the polls. Leaders of the Anglican church and Scots could safely be counted as adherents of government, and many country gentlemen were inclined to rally behind the monarch. Still, America had many friends among merchants and manufacturers in the cities, especially in London. There were also noblemen who were hostile to the king and to North because they were denied a share of the good things dispensed by government or because they were sincerely convinced that the king was a tyrant whom it was necessary to curb; there were workmen and sailors who could not vote but who could exert a measure of influence upon public opinion; and there were newspapers that dared to demand justice and lenity for the colonists. It was certain that a substantial minority in the House of Lords would defend the Americans, and it was at least possible that such an impressive showing of sympathy for the colonists would be manifested in the election of the House of Commons that the king and his allies would find it necessary or prudent to pursue a more moderate course.

Sayre was one of those who sought to enter the House of Commons as a champion of American and English liberties. He did not permit his defeat for alderman in London to discourage him. He had become rather intimate with Charles, Lord Mahon, who was engaged to marry a daughter of Lord and Lady Chatham and was also a close friend of the younger William Pitt, their second son. Mahon was only twenty-one years of age, an ardent reformer and a seeker for economic and social advance. When Mahon sought election as one of the two members of the Commons from Westminster, Sayre toiled for him at his headquarters in the Standard, a tavern in Leicester Square. Sayre was optimistic: he hoped not only that Mahon would win, but that Chatham himself would come forward to supply leadership for the enemies of government. He told the earl that the men across the ocean who spoke for America were responsible persons with whom Britain could safely negotiate. It became evident, however, that Mahon could not win in Westminster, and he withdrew from the canvass. Sharing Sayre's optimism, he then agreed to stand with the American for the two seats of the borough of Rochester. They did not actually campaign, however, probably because they discovered that they could not win. Moreover, Chatham, assuring Sayre that the "very kindly and friendly share you have taken at the Standard can never be forgot," did not offer a ringing challenge to the ministry during the election because he was crippled by a "severe attack of the gout."[6]

Undismayed, Sayre then entered the lists with one John Chetwood as a partner at Seaford, a seaport in Sussex, where they stood as allies of John Wilkes rather than of Chatham. They were opposed at Seaford by Viscount Gage, the older brother of the general, and George Medley—a pair who offered allegiance to the king and to North. When the votes were counted on October 8, Gage and Medley were declared the victors. Sayre and Chetwood claimed that Thomas Washer, the returning officer, had illegally refused to let many of their supporters vote and that Sayre and Chetwood actually deserved to win by large majorities. They petitioned the House of Commons for a reversal of the returns and for seats in it. Consideration of their plea was twice deferred. It was opposed, of course, by the ministry and was at length rejected.[7] George III and North had secured a new Parliament almost as pleasing to them as the one that had been dismissed.

But the·king and his allies were still unable to proceed to deal with the American crisis without concern lest Parliament rebel against them. The City of London had elected John Wilkes, a sufficiently forthright defender of the Americans, and two of his followers, although other parts of metropolitan London, including Westminster, chose adherents of the ministry. Scores of followers of Lord Rockingham and Chatham were returned outside London, but all the enemies of the North regime together could muster no more than one-third of the House of Commons or of the House of Lords. But what if public opinion and many uncommitted country gentlemen in the Commons, who had reason to believe that a convulsion in America would lead to heavier taxation, turned against the ministry?

The British enemies of the king and Lord North did not accept the result of the election as decisive so far as America was concerned. The

6. See Taylor and Pringle (eds.), *Correspondence of William Pitt*, IV, 366–67, and a letter from Mahon to Sayre of October 4 in Stephen Sayre, *A Short Narrative* (N.p., n.d.; photocopy in Duke University Library).

7. Ian R. Christie, *Myth and Reality in Late Eighteenth-Century British Politics and Other Papers* (Berkeley, 1970), 54–55; *The Journals of the House of Commons from 1774 . . . to . . . 1777* (London, 1803), 30–31.

marquis of Rockingham and the earl of Chatham would have continued to assail the powers-that-were in any event, since Rockingham and the principal followers of both men lusted for office. Chatham was not sufficiently healthy to take a place in the cabinet, but he was determined to assert himself at times when his physical condition permitted. John Wilkes also attacked the ministry, not for preferment, which he could not hope to attain, but for the pleasure gained by embarrassing his enemies. The three men did not cease to contend that the monarch had become, or was becoming, a menace to English as well as American liberty, and that the American policy of the king and his allies was both wrongheaded and dangerous. Rockingham, still young, rich in goods but not in talent, had as Prime Minister pushed through the repeal of the Stamp Act. The Rockinghams, who had earlier waffled a bit upon the issue of parliamentary taxation of the Americans for revenue, now were firmly disposed to contend that Britain had the power to impose it but should not exercise the authority. The marquis had no affection for Americans. Chatham, on the other hand, did not dislike them, although he had been more inconsistent constitutionally than Rockingham. He had given his approval to the Townshend duties, then to their repeal, but he was eager to satisfy the colonists. The marquis and the earl were not stout allies, although neither man was fond of Radical John Wilkes. A body of peers and commoners gave allegiance to Rockingham. Chatham had few politicians behind him, but he was admired and revered by the general public because, as William Pitt, he had brilliantly led Britain to military triumph in the Seven Years' War.

Stephen Sayre shared the belief of other Americans in London that the formation of a common front might still make it possible to force the creation of a more friendly policy toward the colonies. The boycott of British goods arranged by the Continental Congress might persuade, even compel, the British business community to ask for accommodation with America.[8] If merchants and all those opposed to armed contest in America rallied in a Chatham-Rockingham-Wilkes coalition, it might succeed in bringing down the North ministry.

The day before Christmas, Chatham wrote to Sayre that he was

8. For examples of the sentiment of Americans in London, see Quincy, *Memoir of the Life of Josiah Quincy, Junior,* 194, 223, 224; Anne Izard Deas (ed.), *Correspondence of Mr. Ralph Izard, of South Carolina, from the Year 1774 to 1804* (New York, 1844), 35–37.

pleased by the behavior of the Congress, that "America under all her oppressions and provocations holds forth to us the *most fair* and *just opening* for restoring harmony and affectionate intercourse, as heretofore."[9] Sayre was thus encouraged to act. He had become friendly with Ralph Verney, the second Earl Verney, a connection of Elizabeth Noel and a devoted follower of Rockingham. Sayre sought to take advantage of his links with all the factions hostile to the king and North, in particular to bring an end to the estrangement between Chatham and Rockingham. Apparently with Verney's help, he opened the way for a social call by Rockingham upon Chatham on January 7, 1775, and a conference between them at the marquis' London house on the following day. Sayre and Verney were present when the earl made his appearance there. Leaving the two noblemen to converse, Sayre and Verney departed, with Sayre hoping that "*the affairs of Great Britain and America were in a fair way of being put into a course of healing and salutary measures.*"

Sayre had reason to be proud of his labors, but the two peers were unable to resolve their differences in opinion in order to deal with a crisis that both perceived to be alarming. Had they agreed upon a plan of action, Wilkes would have rallied support in London. As it was, Chatham and Rockingham went their separate ways. Reporting the affair to his ally Edmund Burke, Rockingham peevishly expressed concern lest Chatham and Sayre spread an account of the meetings that would not be favorable to the marquis. Afterward, Chatham would not even give early information to Rockingham regarding a plan for conciliation that Chatham developed with the help of Benjamin Franklin. The earl was so haughty that he offended other Americans, and hope to form an effective common front against the North ministry faded.[10]

There is reason to believe that the king and Lord North would not have secured easy majorities in Parliament had they been faced by the effective coalition that Sayre tried to form, especially if members conceived that an American war would be costly and quite possibly unsuc-

9. Sayre, *A Short Narrative*.

10. Thomas W. Copeland *et al*. (eds.), *The Correspondence of Edmund Burke* (Chicago, 1958–78), III, 92; George Thomas, Earl of Albemarle (ed.), *Memoirs of the Marquis of Rockingham and His Contemporaries* (London, 1852), II, 260–67; A. Francis Steuart (ed.), *Last Journals of Horace Walpole* (London, 1910), I, 422.

cessful. There was somewhat greater likelihood that the king and the ministry, faced by an angry opposition and revolt by country gentlemen, would give heed to their own friends who counseled moderation. Dartmouth continued to have misgivings, and a lesser adviser of the king, Viscount Barrington, the minister of war, would go no further than propose a naval blockade to coerce the colonists. Two royal governors in England on leave of absence from their posts in America also urged the wisdom of seeking an accommodation.

The advice of the two governors ought to have been carefully considered. One of them was William Tryon, a true-blue Englishman who was a soldier by profession. He had served as governor of North Carolina and was currently the chief executive of New York. Tryon had used military force to suppress the rebellion of the Regulators in North Carolina and had executed a half-dozen of their leaders. He was established in London in the fall of 1774. Another governor in England, Lord William Campbell, also deserved a respectful hearing. He was a younger son of the fourth earl of Argyll, a scion of a powerful Scottish family. He had been a naval officer, had acted as governor of Nova Scotia after 1766, and had become governor of South Carolina. Both Tryon and Campbell could speak from personal acquaintance with the colonists, and no one could doubt their loyalty.

Sojourning at Bath after Christmas, Tryon wrote a warning letter on January 19, 1775, to Dartmouth in which he declared that the Americans would not accept parliamentary taxation for revenue in any form whatever; that it would be unwise for Britain to adopt half-measures, extending the sword in one hand and the olive branch in the other; and that Britain must give way or exert extreme force. Since the army and the navy could not be quickly and materially expanded, the implication was clear that Britain should undertake to conciliate the colonists. Afterward Tryon recalled that he had freely talked at court against such taxation, that Dartmouth declared agreement with him on more than one occasion, and that the colonial secretary changed his mind after each occasion at the insistence of Lord North. Tryon also later asserted that he had orally urged North to arrange for repeal of the duties upon tea and that Campbell had joined him to make the plea.[11]

11. Hutchinson (ed.), *Diary and Letters of Thomas Hutchinson*, I, 345, 347, 348, 349; *Royal Historical Manuscripts Commission, Fourteenth Report*, Appendix, Part X, 260; Wil-

Other Englishmen also brought pressure upon Dartmouth and North in favor of the Americans. Granville Sharp, a leader of the British abolition movement, begged Dartmouth in a letter of January 19 not to join in punitive measures. Dr. John Fothergill, a Quaker who was Dartmouth's physician, fellow Quaker David Barclay, Lord Hyde, and Admiral Richard Howe initiated negotiations between Dartmouth and Benjamin Franklin during the winter. There was another—and extraordinary—appeal for an accommodation from Brownlow North, the bishop of Worcester, who was a half brother of the prime minister. On Monday, January 30, the anniversary of the execution of King Charles I, the bishop delivered a commemorative sermon before the House of Lords in Westminster Abbey. On that solemn occasion, he used as his text a passage from Philippians, "Let all men know your moderation." Obviously the bishop was cautioning, however mildly or indirectly, against the obstinacy that had brought Charles to the execution block, suggesting that the behavior of that monarch was a bad example for the present king and Parliament with respect to America. The warning was the more poignant in that Charles was virtually a saint to most Anglicans, including bishops who sat in the audience and who were members of the House of Lords.[12]

But the king and the ministry set aside the pleas of their friends as well as those of their political enemies. Indeed, some of the advice from their friends came too late to affect the course of events. Government deceived the country gentlemen, who might have turned against the ministry had they been convinced that a costly and quite possibly unsuccessful war must follow an attempt to reduce the colonists to obedience

---

liam H. Sabine (ed.), *Historical Memoirs from 16 March 1763 to 9 July 1776 of William Smith* (New York, 1956), 236–38. Colonel John Dalling, Lieutenant Governor of Jamaica, was recommending a liberal approach to the colonists in private conversation in London in the fall of 1774. Hutchinson (ed.), *Diary and Letters of Thomas Hutchinson*, I, 272. It was an article of faith among many Americans, especially those of Massachusetts, that the royal governors misrepresented them and urged punitive measures, but even Thomas Hutchinson was able to say that he had no part in framing British policy that winter. Hutchinson to Lord Hardwicke, June 14, 1775, October 12, 1775, both in British Museum, Add. MSS. 35,427.

12. *Royal Historical Manuscripts Commission, Fourteenth Report*, Appendix, Part X, 260–61; Hutchinson (ed.), *Diary and Letters of Thomas Hutchinson*, I, 365; Philippians 2:5 (King James version).

by use of the army. When Parliament opened after the customary long Christmas holiday, it was known in London that the Massachusetts House of Representatives was behaving like a revolutionary body and that the Congress in Philadelphia had demanded repeal of all the still-existing repressive measures taken by Britain after 1763.

Moreover, it was apparent that the ministry was moving toward a decision to employ the army in New England. Presenting "gutted" papers from General Gage—documents edited in such fashion that the military situation in America was made to appear less than alarming—North and Dartmouth succeeded in reducing the fears of the country gentlemen, who then rallied in support of government.[13] Lord Chatham immediately moved that the troops be withdrawn from Boston to prevent bloodshed before an accommodation could be arranged, and he now emphatically denounced taxation of the Americans for revenue as unconstitutional. Rockingham also called for military evacuation of the city. He continued to insist that Britain had the right to levy such taxation but should not use it. Chatham's motion was defeated by a vote in the Lords by 68 to 18.

Chatham persisted. On February 1 he introduced a Provisional Act to serve as a vehicle toward bringing the Anglo-American crisis to an end. The act gave proof of his statesmanship. It stipulated that the army must not be employed against the Americans, but that Britain must retain its authority in general over the colonists and the power to regulate their commerce in particular. Moreover, the act provided that the mother country should renounce the power to tax the Americans for revenue, and that the Continental Congress should be recognized as a legal body and asked to arrange for a permanent revenue. Lord Dartmouth declared that the scheme put forward by Chatham at least deserved serious discussion, but he did not insist upon it. Had he challenged his colleagues, there was still a chance—a slender one—that Britain would draw back. Meanwhile, anticipating the approval of Parliament, the cabinet had resolved to order General Gage to put his troops in motion. Dartmouth

13. See statements regarding the country gentlemen by Edward Gibbon, Thomas Townshend, and the duke of Grafton in Hutchinson (ed.), *Diary and Letters of Thomas Hutchinson*, I, 472; William Cobbett (ed.), *Parliamentary History of England* (London, 1813), XVIII, 450; William R. Anson (ed.), *Autobiography and Political Correspondence of Augustus Henry Third Duke of Grafton* (London, 1898), 238.

had signed the instructions to Gage on the twenty-seventh of January, and they were already aboard ship. As it happened, however, the vessel, H.M.S. *Falcon*, was unable to proceed across the Atlantic because of storms and was back in the harbor at Portsmouth after the middle of February.

Other cabinet members scoffed at the Chatham scheme, its creator, and all those who clamored for conciliation. The Lords, by a vote of 62 to 31, promptly rejected the proposal. Moreover, as the aggressive majority in the cabinet had expected, both houses of Parliament rallied to its support. On February 6 the Commons sanctioned an Address to the Throne which said that "a rebellion actually exists" in Massachusetts and that petitions for redress from separate colonies would be considered in lenient spirit, but that there must be no concession "of any part of the sovereign authority" of Britain. The Lords endorsed the address the next day.

Choosing to employ the army in Massachusetts, the king and his cabinet proposed in addition to offer to the Americans in general the famous Conciliatory Resolution as a settlement of the dispute over taxation. The resolution asserted that Parliament would not levy for revenue in any colony that supplied its fair share toward the cost of imperial defense. They did not perceive that such an offer, to have a chance of success, must at least precede the use of force. King and cabinet decided to take advantage of the *Falcon*'s return to port, and North hastily introduced the resolution on February 20. Then, however, having received a report from Gage which said that the Massachusetts Patriots were momentarily less passionate, they permitted the orders to use the army to proceed to Boston before securing passage of the resolution. The resolution was not considered in America until after the Battle of Lexington and Concord, and by then it was too little and too late.

Persons in England unfamiliar with America, excessively aware of British power, and disposed to be optimistic might be relatively unconcerned about the crisis in empire during many following weeks. "In three months," wrote Horace Walpole, doubtless reflecting opinion in the aristocracy, "we shall hear whether it will be war or peace. The nation will stare a little if it is the former. It is little expected, and less thought of." The profound concern felt by better-informed men of good will in England was well expressed by Henry Cruger, an American merchant who sat in the House of Commons. Cruger wrote on May 3 that "our minds are so big with the *mighty* expectation of approaching events, we can talk of nothing else; our faculties seem benumbed alternatively by hope and fear." It was only too obvious that a clash of arms in Massachusetts could hardly be avoided. William Lee wrote from the imperial capital on March 4, "In short, a civil war is inevitable." Josiah Quincy, Jr., who had crossed the ocean to speak for Massachusetts and had conferred with many men, including Sayre, reached the same conclusion and sailed that day from Portsmouth for Salem. A victim of tuberculosis, Quincy did not live long enough to report orally to his associates in Massachusetts about British men and measures. He died on board his ship before it reached land, on April 26.[14]

Benjamin Franklin lingered in London. Not without reason, he became increasingly concerned lest he be arrested. Before Quincy departed, the earl of Hillsborough, referring to him and to Franklin, declared, "There are now men walking in the streets of London who ought to be in Newgate or Tyburn." On March 13, Solicitor General Wedderburn, informed that Franklin was about to depart for home, declared that he "ought to be stopped." That evening, Thomas Hutchinson, writing to Lord North regarding the motions of Quincy and Franklin, referred to "mischief I apprehended they designed." Six days later, Lord Suffolk, a cabinet member, said that "if he had the sole direction," he would prevent Franklin from leaving England. Had Franklin been in London after the arrival of news of hostilities in New England, he would almost surely have been arrested and charged with treason. However, he took passage for Philadelphia on March 19, and while his vessel was still on the ocean, shooting began in Massachusetts.[15]

Perhaps Stephen Sayre and the Lee brothers, being considered less dangerous than Franklin, were not as yet thought of in government offices as persons who should be incarcerated, and they did not take ship

14. W. S. Lewis *et al.* (eds.), *Horace Walpole's Correspondence with Sir Horace Mann* (New Haven, 1967), VIII, 85; Henry C. Van Schaack, *The Life of Peter Van Schaack* (New York, 1842), 36; Deas (ed.), *Correspondence of Mr. Ralph Izard*, 48; Quincy, *Memoir of the Life of Josiah Quincy, Junior*, 228; London *Chronicle*, March 4–7, 1775.

15. William B. Donne (ed.), *Correspondence of King George the Third with Lord North from 1768 to 1783* (London, 1867), I, 219; Hutchinson (ed.), *Diary and Correspondence of Thomas Hutchinson*, I, 405, 414.

for New York or Yorktown. Sayre had greater reason than the Lees to remain in England, since he had acquired an English wife and a stake in English property in the midst of the crisis, and he was on the verge of attaining the lofty economic and social goals he had set for himself. Even as British troops made final preparations to move out of Boston on that famous march that led to gunfire at Lexington and Concord on April 14, Americans attended a ball given by Mayor John Wilkes at the Mansion House. It was an elegant affair. Among those present were Mr. and Mrs. Sayre, Dr. Arthur Lee, William Lee, Lady Mary Sherard, Edmund Burke, the duke of Richmond, Lord Mahon, the earl of Effingham, Lord George Gordon, sheriffs and aldermen, and James Boswell, who worshipped Dr. Samuel Johnson but did not share his hostility toward America.[16] The son of a Long Island tanner had risen far in the world.

The pain and the heartbreak of war would come soon enough. On May 16 Dr. Joseph Warren, one of the most attractive of the leaders of the Patriots in Massachusetts, wrote to London to say that he wished to correspond with Sayre, whom he had met in Boston, and with the Lee brothers.[17] It was known in London before the end of May that hostilities had begun. Warren was killed in the Battle of Bunker Hill on June 17.

Sayre would also pay heavily for his championship of America. He might have abandoned his banking business, might have chosen to use his own money and that of his wife to establish himself as a country gentleman. Such was the goal of many a man of commerce in his time. However, he was too sanguine, too ambitious to be satisfied with the relatively quiet life. He did not abandon banking, nor did he prudently cease to toil for American liberty. He would suffer in consequence.

16. Treloar, *Wilkes and the City*, 147–49; London *Chronicle*, April 18–20, 1775.
17. Lee, *Life of Arthur Lee*, II, 270–71.

5

The Resident of the Tower

HERE NEVER was good cause for hope that the House of Commons would overturn the election results at Seaford. Sayre undoubtedly petitioned for a reversal only to plague the king, Lord North, and their allies, just as Wilkes had used the refusal of the Commons to accept him as the member from Middlesex as proof that the powers-that-were wickedly and unconstitutionally ignored the wishes of good and true Englishmen who deserved better from the monarch and his manipulating friends. If Sayre entertained even the thinnest hope of a successful appeal, it vanished when news reached London of the outbreak of war. As always, armed clash enhanced anger, on both sides of the Atlantic. A wave of patriotic emotion in England washed away part of the support that had been given to the colonists, and Wilkes lost popularity in London. Was it not disloyal to oppose government, to encourage those who shed English blood and might be striving for independence from the mother country? The king and the ministry began to put warships into commission and to raise fresh troops, even commencing attempts to hire the services of soldiers from Holland, the German states, and Russia. In the autumn of 1775, Lord North and his colleagues were able to muster handsome majorities in both houses of Parliament, securing approval for their measures by votes of three-to-one. And Stephen Sayre was given accommodations, not in the halls of Westminster, but down the Thames in the gray and gloomy Tower in which so many men and women had encountered sorrow and death.

There were men in government, doubtless including Lord North, who were not eager to move decisively against its enemies in England until proof came that the colonists had indeed taken up arms against the mother country, with solid evidence that the rebels had been stimulated

[67]

by their insidious and treacherous allies in Britain. Soon after word reached London of the fighting, the Radical John Horne Tooke undertook to collect gifts for American women and children murdered, as he asserted, by the redcoats on April 19. Action against him was delayed until 1776.

Word of the Battle of Bunker Hill may have goaded officers of state to move against an outspoken American. So long an advocate for America, Sayre was an obvious target for reprisal. A letter from London of September 30, published in America, asserts that the earl of Sandwich, the First Lord of the Admiralty, was plotting to ruin Sayre and William Lee, that Sandwich was "villain enough to make use of every means, however base, to accomplish his wicked purpose." According to the letter, Lord Chief Justice Mansfield, a pillar of government, was assisting Sandwich, and he was denounced as the equivalent of the infamous Judge Jeffreys.[1] We may swiftly set aside the charge against Mansfield, who was too dignified to engage in such conniving. Should Sandwich also be declared obviously above suspicion of conspiring against Sayre and Lee? It may seem improbable that the powerful nobleman should stoop to strike surreptitiously against those gadflies, but Sandwich was not a saint.

It was exasperating, of course, that Americans who sympathized with their fellows across the Western Ocean, who had stimulated them to resist their lawful rulers, and who continued to encourage them, should remain in the British Isles, even within short distances of the palace of St. James and the halls of Westminster. Moreover, Sayre boldly and publicly assailed Parliament and the adherents of the king. There was a meeting of the freeholders of Middlesex County on September 25, presided over by Sheriff William Plomer. Sayre was the principal orator, a "diffident yet able, spirited yet candid, advocate for the Americans." He put forth several arguments in their behalf that were not new: it was idle to apply to Parliament for relief; the royal ministers viciously encouraged "culprits and informers of every kind" in America to misrepresent the colonists and so to supply excuses for punishing them. Then Sayre offered a new accusation against his old enemy, Bernard, who was, of course, one of the wicked tattletales. Sayre said that "there were American papers now recorded in office, charging SIR FRANCIS BER-

1. Essex *Journal*, December 13, 1775.

NARD, with purloining the public money . . . he would repeat the charge . . . Sir Francis Bernard was no stranger to his place of residence, and if he chose personally to call upon him, he was ready at any time to honor Sir Francis with a personal explanation."[2] Obviously, if that explanation did not satisfy Bernard, he could seek redress upon the dueling ground.

Enjoying an income sufficient to maintain a baronet in proper style—provided in substantial part by grants from Whitehall—Bernard was living in the country. He was not young, and his wife was unwell; he probably had no lust for intellectual or physical combat. It may be assumed that he did not charge into the banking house to demand justice. Had he actually embezzled Massachusetts money? Again, no evidence to support Sayre's charge has been found. Bernard had been accused of accepting presents for neglecting to act against American smugglers. If true, the supposed crime was a mere peccadillo rather than a serious misdeed in the colonies until Anglo-American antagonism became rancorous. Nor could the acceptance of handsome pensions from Whitehall, even if undeserved and conferred because of family influence, be defined as outright theft even of British money. In any event, the cabinet soon struck at Sayre so heavily that Bernard could well believe that personal reprisal was quite unnecessary.

Afterward, explaining why he was attacked by the government, Sayre said that he had been commissioned by Chatham to try to collect friends of America in Parliament who would form a new ministry, also that "he had formed a plan by which, all the lords and commons, in opposition to government agreed to secede from parliament, and to hold their meetings, at the mansion-house, in the city."[3] Excuse for this emphatic display of dissent would be the government's plan to hire foreign troops to serve against the Americans, which would be denounced as illegal. He claimed that his arrangements were ruined by his arrest on October 23. Were his own importance and deeds enhanced in memory? He did openly assert in his speech of September 25, it should be observed, that it was useless to appeal to Parliament. In any event, he was assailed by a royal officer and locked up as an enemy of the British state.

2. Pennsylvania *Evening Post*, January 2, 1776.
3. Sayre, *A Short Narrative*.

THE WHOLE affair began rather casually. There was in London in the autumn of 1775 a young American named Francis Richardson, a native of Chester, Pennsylvania, who was of Quaker stock. He is said to have been a well-mannered man of "great personal beauty" and to have acquired a passion for military life in consequence of mingling with British army officers stationed in Philadelphia. Richardson went to England, obtained a commission as ensign, and quickly managed to secure a promotion to lieutenant. He became an adjutant in the First Battalion of the First Regiment of the Foot Guards. In the process of beginning a climb up the British military ladder, he was compelled, in accordance with the practice of that time, to pay for his commissions. In that connection he acquired a bad reputation at Deal, where he was a familiar figure. Elizabeth Carter wrote from that place, "R—— is well known in this neighborhood. A gentleman not very far from hence, had treated him very kindly, and lent him money to buy a commission. He repaid the favor by an arrangement with his wife. As an English esquire does not take to this Chesterfield system [4] quite so peaceably as a French marquis, the husband threw him into prison for the money he had lent him." [5]

Sayre knew Richardson only casually—they had met at the De Berdt house some years earlier—but Sayre and William Lee went to the assistance of a fellow colonial who was an outspoken champion of American rights. They used their knowledge of law and their influence as sheriffs to arrange for his release from the Marshalsea prison. [6] Ironically, Richardson was soon to be instrumental in Sayre's arrest and imprisonment on a charge of high treason.

4. Of debauchery recommended to his illegitimate son by Lord Chesterfield.

5. *Letters from Mrs. Elizabeth Carter, to Mrs. Montagu* (London, 1817), II, 338; John F. Watson, *Annals of Philadelphia and Pennsylvania* (Philadelphia, 1850), I, 560.

6. For the connection between Sayre and Richardson and the legal proceedings that followed, the fullest and most reliable account is the shorthand record of *Sayre* v. *Rochford et al.*, in Treasury Solicitor, Series 11, Bundle 542, Public Record Office, London. It is supplemented importantly by Nicholas Nugent, *The Case of Nicholas Nugent, Esq.; Late Lieutenant in the First Regiment of Foot Guards* (London, 1776), and by Francis Richardson's *An Appeal to the Officers of the Guards* (London, 1776). Evidence from sources other than these will be cited concerning various details. Reports of *Sayre* v. *Rochford et al.*, which appear in the London *Chronicle*, June 27, 1776, and T. B. Howell (comp.), *A Complete Collection of State Trials* (London, 1814), XX, 1286–1316, are not completely trustworthy.

Government was also kind to Richardson. Because of his incarceration for debt, he had been required to resign from the Guards. However, after he had made arrangements to satisfy his creditor or creditors, he was permitted to resume his commission. On Friday, October 19, about one o'clock in the afternoon, Richardson approached Captain[7] Nicholas Nugent of his battalion while Nugent was on duty in the tiltyard at Whitehall. A gallant young Irish officer and a man-about-town, Nugent had earlier lent money to Richardson. The loans had been repaid, and there was no ill feeling between the two men. The lieutenant went to the captain as a friend, telling him that he had a matter of the utmost consequence to disclose. The two men went into the guardroom, locked the door, and the American unfolded a remarkable tale. So Nugent asserted afterward, but he was contradicted by Richardson, who stated that they conversed in the tiltyard.

Nor did the two men agree entirely regarding the content of their conversation. Richardson told Nugent that, about noon on the preceding day, he had gone to the Pennsylvania Coffee House in Birchin Lane, where Sayre was writing letters. Sayre had led him upstairs into a private room, revealed an extraordinary plan, and asked for his assistance. According to Richardson, Sayre said that he could rely upon the services of some fine fellows. He proposed that they should be employed to abduct the king as he went to open Parliament upon October 26 and to take him to the Tower. He asked Richardson to assist his men by corrupting the Tower's garrison. John Wilkes, as mayor of London, was to place constables around the Tower to prevent the king's escape, and George III was to be transported to Hanover. The rebels would create a new cabinet and seize control of the nation. The Guards officer averred that Sayre had already distributed £1,500 among the household troops to win their help and offered him ten or fifteen pounds more to gain popularity among the soldiers. According to Nugent, Richardson also asserted that the duke of Devonshire was party to the plot and that he had supplied money to win over some of the Guards. Nugent told Richardson that his story was incredible. But the younger officer declared, "By God," it was true. Then Nugent mentioned that an unnamed City man had, in an earlier conversation with him, expressed sympathy for the Guards,

7. Nugent was a lieutenant. Commonly described as a captain, he must have held that rank by brevet.

whose pay was inadequate, and had suggested that men of the City ought to help them financially. Richardson interpreted that statement to mean that an effort had been made to corrupt Nugent. Asked for advice by Richardson regarding the course he should take, Nugent declined to give it.

The conversation between the two officers was interrupted, and Richardson went to General Francis Craig, their commanding officer, with the story, leaving behind him an increasingly troubled Nugent. The Irish captain realized that his reference to the unnamed City man might be used to bolster Richardson's story. He had incautiously mentioned the man, who he did not believe had any connection with Richardson's supposed conspiracy. Nugent had reason to be concerned.

General Craig listened to the tale of the young American. He expressed disbelief in the conspiracy, but he immediately conducted Richardson to the Whitehall office of Lord Rochford, who as secretary of state for the Southern Department was responsible for internal security. Rochford did not promptly dismiss Richardson's story as unbelievable. Clearly, neither John Wilkes nor the duke of Devonshire, neither of them a determined enemy of the British state or the status quo, could be suspected of taking part in such a plot, but there might be a core of truth in Richardson's tale. Was not the Guy Fawkes conspiracy unthinkable until it proved to be only too real? Besides, the war in America was going very badly. The British had sustained heavy losses in the battles of Lexington-Concord and Bunker Hill, and General Gage with his army was penned against the sea by the Americans under Washington. If it were feasible, it might be worthwhile to strike at the American Patriots in England and their English sympathizers, and Sayre might be a useful target. Rochford arranged for Richardson to tell his story under oath and to put it in the form of an affidavit. He also instructed the informant to guard his tongue, to seek out Sayre, and to try to secure further information from him.

Before the day ended, Nugent became uneasy indeed, and during the evening he saw Richardson again. The adjutant's behavior worried the Irishman. He assured Richardson that the unnamed City man had done no more than express sympathy for officers of the Guards in economic distress and that he surely had no part in a conspiracy against the king. The following morning Nugent went to General Craig to seek his advice. Craig refused to listen to him but insisted that he give information to Rochford. About noon, a soldier came to Nugent to escort him to the War Office. There he found the general, who took him to Rochford's headquarters. The secretary was at Court. Nugent and Craig thereupon agreed to meet at midday on the twenty-first at St. James's Coffee House and to go a second time to Rochford's office.

The secretary and his undersecretary, Sir Stanier Porten—a connection of historian Edward Gibbon—were there when the two officers arrived on that second visit. Nugent then related his version of the conversation with Richardson to Rochford in the presence of Craig. He said that Richardson was honest about money but that he was "apt to rattle away," especially about American affairs. He asserted again that the unnamed City man had no connection with any conspiracy against the monarch and declared that it would be unworthy of him as a gentleman to reveal the City man's identity. Rochford apparently agreed that Nugent was correct upon both points.

But Nugent's troubles had only begun. Horace Walpole tells us that Richardson's accusation was a subject at a meeting of the cabinet, its members being in town for the opening of Parliament. According to Walpole, Lords Mansfield and Thurlow attended that meeting, and Thurlow laughed at the Richardson story. The cabinet, however, allegedly decided to proceed against Sayre but was able to get legal assistance only from the blind magistrate, Sir John Fielding.[8]

Whether or not there was such a meeting is not certain, but Rochford did not let the matter drop. On Monday the twenty-third, Nugent was away from his quarters from eleven o'clock in the morning until ten at night. Craig insistently tried several times to find him there and left a letter ordering him to meet the general on the parade ground at nine the following morning. Receiving the command, Nugent became alarmed and hastened, despite the lateness of the hour, to Craig's house in Cleveland Court. The general was not at home. Unable to see him, Nugent must have slept uneasily. He presented himself to Craig in accordance with the order of his superior officer on the twenty-fourth. The general took the captain a second time to Rochford's office. The secretary made his appearance soon after ten, and Craig retired. Then the secretary led

---

8. Steuart (ed.), *Last Journals of Horace Walpole*, I, 481.

Nugent into a private room, where he was questioned under oath by Rochford and Joseph White, solicitor to the Treasury.

The two officials examined and cross-examined the captain for about four hours. Rochford ceased to talk to him as one gentleman to another. Nugent again refused to identify the mysterious City man. It would be "an act of villany," he said, to do so, thus involving an individual for making a harmless remark in a social hour. Nugent would do no more than agree to sign a deposition containing the statements he had earlier made. Rochford now uttered threats against the captain. He told Nugent that failure to give the required information constituted misprision of treason—a major crime—and if the officer continued to refuse to comply, Rochford would commit him to Newgate Prison. Nor would the secretary permit Nugent to ask a friend for advice. Rochford sent for Craig and departed, leaving the Irishman in Porten's care. He did permit Nugent to have breakfast brought to him from the St. James's Coffee House.

The grilling went on. Craig urged Nugent to talk while the captain consumed·his belated breakfast, but Nugent refused. Returning, Rochford asked whether Nugent had changed his mind. Discovering that Nugent remained obdurate, the secretary became very angry. If the captain maintained his silence, he must expect to be dismissed from the army. Rochford threatened again to send him to Newgate, and Craig suggested that Nugent, as an army officer, should be locked up in the Tower. Rochford indicated that he might take the Irishman before the cabinet for examination. Standing firm, Nugent was then taken to the guardroom at St. James's and kept in custody. He was denied visitors, and he was not permitted to send out letters without examination of their content by unfriendly eyes. Richardson came to visit him there. The American expressed regret, Nugent afterward recalled, because he had involved his fellow officer in a bad scrape. Was Richardson sent to try to secure the information that Nugent had refused to give to Rochford and Craig?

About nine o'clock that night, Craig came for Nugent and conducted him in a hackney coach to Rochford's house in Berkeley Square, where the captain was again put to the test by the minister and the general. Rochford indicated that Nugent might just as well identify the City man, since the government already had his name. The Irishman did not fall into that trap. Rochford then laid a more subtle snare. He proposed to read off the names of City men. Nugent could protect innocent individuals by exculpating them, one by one. But the captain, under great pressure, displayed intelligence as well as courage. As a gentleman, he could not lie. If he answered in the negative regarding several persons, he could not do so when the name of the City man was brought forward. He therefore refused to respond to the reading of any name. Then Rochford forthrightly asked him three times whether Sayre was the man. Nugent kept silent.

At last, abandoning the interrogation, the minister informed the captain that he was free to leave and expressed a hope that Nugent would not make a public issue of the questionings to which he had been subjected. Nugent declined to give such a commitment. Craig then ordered the captain to make the pledge. Refusal would be marked against him by the general—a hint that Nugent's career would suffer if he did not obey. Believing that Craig had no right to issue such a command, Nugent again remained silent. Nugent was then escorted by Craig and Joseph White to St. James's. The general said not a word to Nugent during the journey. At St. James's the captain was given his freedom. His ordeal had ended. He said afterward that the strain he had undergone was such that he fell into a fever and was confined for about two weeks. Recovering, the gallant captain sought redress for the abuse he had undergone.

That Richardson had also tried to secure further information from Nugent is indicated by the fact that he sought out Sayre on Saturday, the twenty-first, for that purpose. Richardson tells us that he had not received the ten or twenty pounds supposedly pledged by Sayre. He met Sayre and John Reynolds that morning in the street, where they were in a coach en route to the Reynolds house. Richardson refused an invitation to enter the coach and walked behind it to the house. There he had another tête-à-tête with Sayre. The banker told Richardson that he did not have the money with him, but that he would supply it to Richardson at the New England Coffee House at one o'clock. Sayre had obviously become suspicious that the lieutenant was not a reliable friend, and he fixed a cold eye upon his fellow American. Had Richardson, he asked, mentioned their conversation to anyone? Only to General Craig, the lieutenant ineptly lied. His reply could not fail to arouse concern in Sayre, who did not appear at the New England Coffee House.

The Sayre ménage on Oxford Street was apparently a comfortable one. The firm of Sayre & Purdon carried on its business below, and Sayre and his wife had their quarters above. They had servants, and they maintained a coach. The routine of the bank and the household was interrupted on Monday, October 23.

If the Richardson tale contained a core of truth, it would be imprudent to permit Sayre to remain at large. Accordingly, Lord Rochford in his capacity as magistrate issued a warrant for Sayre's arrest. It was executed early in the morning. A company of infantry was not sent to seize the conspirator—apparently a desperate resistance was not expected. Two king's messengers accompanied by Joseph Wood, a constable, were admitted into the Sayre house by a maid. Sayre was still in bed, and he and his wife were about to go to Bath for a holiday. The three men informed John Tally, a clerk in the bank, that they wished to consult his employer regarding a forged note of two hundred pounds. A porter went upstairs twice to inform Sayre that his services were desired. At length he appeared, still not dressed for the day. He was then informed that he was under arrest for high treason and that the three men were authorized to search through his papers. He quietly asserted that he was innocent and that he did not object to the ransacking of his papers. His clothes were brought to him, and he shaved. He was not permitted out of sight of his captors, but he was allowed to go to a room where his wife was having breakfast and to inform her of his arrest. He was also able to send an appeal for help to John Reynolds. The three men found a letter from Mrs. Macaulay and a copy of an essay entitled "Barnard's Ghost" addressed to the citizens of London—presumably intended as another attack by Sayre upon Sir Francis Bernard. After somewhat more than an hour, the four men entered the Sayre family coach and proceeded in dignity to Lord Rochford's office, where Sayre was formally charged before Rochford and Sir John Fielding, who had been pressed into service by the crown to make sure that the cabinet member conducted himself according to law and to help protect the king.

Did Sayre lack experience in criminal proceedings? According to one report, he immediately and unwarily responded to questions, asserting that he hardly knew Richardson. A clerk began to write down his declarations. A report by someone friendly to the accused man says "it would be a scandalous omission to conclude this narrative without doing justice to the behavior of Mr. Sayre. As a subject of a free state, his demeanor was manly; as a patriot, it was intrepid; as a gentleman, it was polite. He treated the malice of informers with the utmost contempt, when preferred by the creatures, and countenanced by the authority of government, this he smiled at with utmost disdain." He accused Bernard and Thomas Hutchinson of sending lies to "bloody minded" superiors in London and said that "whatever informers government might encourage, integrity was a shield which would protect men of honor from their shafts." Defended by that shield, he would "enter the appartments of a prison conscious that they would prove a safe asylum for virtue."[9]

In another narrative, Sayre is reported to have responded more precisely to the accusation leveled against him. He admitted that "he had expressed himself very fully concerning the unhappy and destructive contest now depending in America" and had asserted that "there was not spirit enough in this country to bring about a total change of men and measures," but he "utterly denied" use of any words that could be construed to mean that he planned or intended to seize the person of the monarch. Had he done so, Richardson obviously should have pretended to be sympathetic so as to secure further information regarding the conspiracy. At that point, Rochford is alleged to have offered "a very handsome apology" because he was "under a necessity of giving attention to the business."

Sayre may indeed have conducted himself with Roman courage and gentlemanly dignity, but it was doubtless well for him that John Reynolds appeared to protect him. The proceeding was interrupted by the arrival of the vigorous lawyer, and Rochford was informed that Reynolds demanded "immediate admission to his client." As under-sheriff of London, Reynolds had been watching executions of criminals at Tyburn when he was informed by one of Sayre's servants that he was needed and hastened to Whitehall. Fielding tried to bar Reynolds upon the remarkable excuse that he had not been asked by Sayre to come to that particular

9. Pennsylvania *Evening Post*, January 27, 1776.

spot. However, officials wished to avoid irregularities in procedure—they remembered the four thousand pounds that Lord Halifax had been forced to pay to Wilkes. After some wrangling, Reynolds was allowed to participate. He immediately advised Sayre to be silent and to sign no paper prepared by his questioners. Richardson's statement was read a second time for Reynolds' benefit. Sayre smiled, and his lawyer laughed, declaring that "the whole thing was too ridiculous to be seriously attended to." Said Reynolds regarding Richardson, "I know that gentleman too well to give credit to anything he says." The informer, who had also appeared at the hearing, exchanged barbed remarks with Reynolds and asked Rochford and Fielding to silence the lawyer. The doughty Reynolds refused to be cowed and said he would "always pay a proper deference to authority, but whatever he had there said of the informer he would repeat in any place whatever." He made it clear that he was prepared to offer Richardson satisfaction at sword or pistol point.[10] The hearing ended with an offer from Reynolds to provide surety for Sayre's appearance in the event that the offense charged against him proved to be a bailable one. Sayre was then ordered into an adjacent room, and a new warrant against him was prepared. The charge against him was reduced. In consequence, an order addressed to Lord Cornwallis, Constable of the Tower, or to his lieutenant or deputy, by Rochford required the reception of "the body of *Stephen Sayre*, Esq. . . . being charged . . . with treasonable practices," and that he be kept "in close custody."

REPORTS of the arrest of the American banker spread through London and created a sensation. Sayre was indeed kept "in close custody"—a phrase that prevented visits to him by his friends and also denied him the privilege of sealed letters. During the afternoon of the day of his arrest, he requested Charles Rainsford, who actually commanded at the Tower, to permit such visits. No one was given access that day save for his wife, who was doubtless allowed to bring him clothing and toilet articles—this after Lord Rochford issued a special order to Rainsford to let Mrs. Sayre enter the Tower. Nor was the prohibition of other visitors soon relaxed. Lawyer John Ellis, employed by Mrs. Sayre, consulted Edmund Burke, who was politically and financially indebted to Lord

10. *London Magazine*, XLIV (1775), 543–44; London *Chronicle*, June 27–29, 1776.

Verney, and the earl of Effingham, an army officer who had refused to serve against the Americans. The three men went together to the Tower, but were refused admission. John Wilkes also failed to reach his friend, although Wilkes saw Sayre at a window and managed to exchange bows with him. Arthur Lee and John Alleyne were turned away, and also James Adair, chosen by Sayre to represent him—this despite the fact that it was illegal to keep a person accused of treasonous practices (rather than high treason) in such rigid confinement. Solicitor General Wedderburn deprived Sayre of early access to counsel by ruling that a lawyer could visit Sayre only upon his request or that of his wife, acting in his behalf.[11]

But the government could not long ward off legal action by the friends of the American. Reynolds and other lawyers sought the prisoner's release upon a writ of habeas corpus, on the ground that the warrant for his arrest was defective, but they were unable on the twenty-fifth to reach a magistrate qualified to act. The following day Sayre's friends renewed his petition for reversal of the Seaford election returns—uselessly, of course, since reversal would have substituted an enemy of the ministry for one of its supporters. Sayre's friends were unable to obtain the writ until the evening of that day. On the twenty-seventh, in response to the writ, two military officers conducted the prisoner from the Tower to a hearing before Lord Mansfield, who ordered that Sayre be brought before him again the following day. Thus Sayre was kept in custody until the king had opened Parliament and had safely returned to his palace.[12]

In the meantime, all sorts of rumors spread through London and beyond the capital. It was correctly reported that iron bars had been placed over the windows of the Tower apartment occupied by Sayre to prevent the escape of the dangerous American, incorrectly that "upwards of thirty persons" in London were involved in his activities and accused of high treason, and that intercepted letters would be brought forward as evidence against men in the city. Excitement ran high, especially because the beginning of the war had been accompanied by extensive

11. Essex *Journal*, January 19, 1776; Fortescue (ed.), *Correspondence of King George the Third*, III, 274–75.

12. Pennsylvania *Evening Post*, January 11, 1776, and Felix Farley's Bristol *Journal*, October 28 and November 4, 1775, offer interesting details regarding events during the period October 23–27.

gossip regarding correspondence with the rebels and conspiracy in their behalf.[13] It was widely believed that Sayre was charged with "remitting money, and conveying information from parties here to the insurgents in America." One report had it that conspirators associated with him had "gone off" and that others were being sought by the king's messengers. A second report declared that "two popular gentlemen of eminence, who are said to have carried on a correspondence with the Americans, have absconded since Mr. Sayre's commitment to the Tower." Another story related that a warship had brought back to an English port a vessel carrying letters that incriminated Sayre, which had been sent to Rochford's office. A rumor of October 26 asserted that at least part of the accusation against Sayre was based upon letters written by him seized by Governor Guy Carleton of Canada and sent by Carleton to Lord Dartmouth—how they fell into Carleton's hands was not explained. Then, according to the tale, Dartmouth hastened to take a packet of the revealing documents to the king at Kew, and the monarch immediately sent for Alexander Wedderburn, who inspected the letters and recommended that Sayre be arrested. Every step taken against Sayre was recommended by Wedderburn. There was reason to believe that Sayre would be questioned by the Privy Council—that is, by the cabinet, perhaps joined by other dignitaries. According to that yarn, "the principal proof against him does not arise from any thing that passed between him and Mr. Richardson, but depends on several intercepted letters of Mr. Sayre." Another piece of gossip had it that the number of the King's Guards—presumably still loyal to His Majesty—had been doubled to assure his safety when he went to open Parliament, also that each of them had been given thirty rounds of ammunition.[14]

In the midst of the excitement, John Scargill, clerk to a lawyer in the Temple, after drinking with a soldier in Southwark, produced a picture of General Israel Putnam, the American Patriot, suggested that Putnam was a brave man, and asserted that the Americans were not entirely

13. Government was indeed trying to intercept "traitorous correspondence." See *Royal Historical Manuscripts Commission, Fourteenth Report*, Appendix, Part X, 368.

14. Felix Farley's Bristol *Journal*, October 28, 1775; *Annual Register*, XVIII (1775), 53; York *Courant*, October 31, 1775; Essex *Journal*, January 19, 1776; Connecticut *Gazette*, February 2, 1776. Edmund Burke was told on the day of the arrest that two or three more men would be seized. Copeland *et al.* (eds.), *Correspondence of Edmund Burke*, III, 234.

wicked. The soldier, with the assistance of another redcoat, seized Scargill and took him to the Tower. Scargill was soon released from custody, but only after his employer had satisfied a bevy of justices of the peace that the clerk was not disloyal.[15]

At Deal, Mrs. Elizabeth Carter heard "stories of plots and conspiracies" and wrote, "they make me shudder." According to those unreliable chroniclers Elizabeth Steele and Alexander Bicknell, Sophia Baddeley underwent agonies when she received the news of her former lover's incarceration. She feared that she would be commanded to testify against him, that "death would be his portion," and she bravely resolved not to say that he was accustomed to speak most disrespectfully of the royal family.[16]

Many persons were especially alarmed because Sayre was locked up in the Tower rather than in an ordinary prison—actually, he was sent to the Tower as a favor to a person who might be a member of the House of Commons.[17] Worldly wise males familiar with the British world were not worried because of danger to the state. Edward Gibbon, a member of the House of Commons soon to acquire fame by publication of part of his *Decline and Fall of the Roman Empire*, did not believe that George III was menaced by abduction and dethronement. He wrote that Sayre "was a fool, Richardson a busy knave." Cynical Horace Walpole described the affair as "a farce . . . ministers cried out, a plot! . . . The ministers, as grave as they looked, could not keep anybody from laughing—no, though they trebled the guards. I have heard this morning that they have blundered in the warrant, just as they did in Wilkes's . . . and he will be at liberty, instead of being, as he ought to be, in Bedlam."[18]

15. Correspondence between Justice John Sherwood, Rochford, and others concerning Scargill is preserved in State Papers, Domestic, Series 44, Bundle 92, Public Record Office, London. One of the documents bears the interesting statement, "Read by the King."

16. *Letters from Mrs. Elizabeth Carter, to Mrs. Montagu*, II, 338; Steele, *Memoirs of Mrs. Sophia Baddeley*, III, 221–22.

17. This was pointed out in the Bath *Journal*, October 30, 1775, the Connecticut *Gazette*, February 9, 1776, and other English and American newspapers to caution those who might look upon imprisonment in the Tower as specially punitive or indicative of the gravity of the charge against Sayre.

18. J. E. Norton (ed.), *The Letters of Edward Gibbon* (London, 1956), II, 91; Lewis *et al.* (eds.), *Horace Walpole's Correspondence*, VIII, 138. Since Gibbon was intimate with Sir Stanier Porten, his judgment may reflect that of Porten. Walpole reported that an

It does not appear that George III, who was brave enough, more than momentarily feared, in consequence of the revelations of Francis Richardson, that he would be deposed and taken to Hanover. Some incendiary handbills were distributed on the twenty-fifth, but the ministry placed troops on the alert, and Sir John Hawkins, who was responsible for keeping order in the city, let it be known that force was available to control any violence. Nor does it appear that the London public was desperately concerned for the safety of the monarch when he rode in his coach from Buckingham House to the House of Lords on the twenty-sixth. A huge and curious crowd estimated to number more than twenty-five thousand persons, chiefly women, gathered to watch his progress, but the route was not lined by bayonet-carrying troops. Nor was his coach surrounded by protecting police or secret service men—he was accompanied by two footmen. George encountered a few hisses, but he was loudly cheered in St. James's Park, and he performed his ceremonial duties without incident. A crowd of justices of the peace who had gathered in the Guildhall of Westminster under the direction of Sir John Hawkins to act in the event that any insult should be offered the king was given no business.[19]

The bizarre proceedings continued on the morning of October 28 at the house of Lord Mansfield in Bloomsbury Square. A phalanx of lawyers appeared in behalf of the prisoner when he was brought before the chief justice. James Adair, John Alleyne, and Messrs. Dayrell and Lucas were presumably ready to offer vigorous argument to win the release of their client, and Mrs. Sayre, John Wilkes, and other friends of Sayre were present to offer moral support. There was no struggle. Mansfield pointed out that a person accused of treasonable practices was eligible for bail, and the government did not protest against Sayre's liberation. Lord

---

eccentric Major Peter Labelliere of the Guards, "a poor mad enthusiast to liberty," was taken up. Was Labelliere the man Nugent refused to name? Labelliere had given money to members of the Guards, was "a Christian patriot" and a "Citizen of the World." He had no connection with Sayre. In his will, Labelliere directed that he be interred with his head downward, "as the world was turned topsyturvy, it was fit that he should be so buried that he might be right at last." Edith Sitwell, *English Eccentrics* (New York, 1957), 23. One of the followers of John Wilkes wrote to him from Bath, "We have been for a week past in perpetual laughter about the late dreadful plot." John Almon, *The Correspondence of the Late John Wilkes, with His Friends* (London, 1805), IV, 173–74.

19. Felix Farley's Bristol *Journal*, October 28, 1775; Pennsylvania *Evening Post*, January 11, 1776; Hutchinson (ed.), *Diary and Letters of Thomas Hutchinson*, I, 547.

North had put the decision whether or not to try to prevent it in the hands of Joseph White, who said that he had no objection to bail. Mansfield set it at £1,000 and accepted guarantees from Sayre for £500, Purdon for £250, and Reynolds for £250. Sayre then thanked the chief justice, saying that he "hoped his lordship would always act in the like impartial manner according to the constitution." "I hope so too," responded the judge, "let us both act according to the constitution, and we shall avoid all difficulties and dangers." The hearing ended quite amicably. Wilkes shook hands with Mansfield. Freed, the prisoner went triumphantly home to dinner with his wife, Wilkes, Reynolds, and Arthur Lee.[20]

THE AFFAIR was by no means ended. On November 6 Lord Rochford asked Lord Chancellor Edward Thurlow whether sufficient evidence was available to prosecute Sayre successfully. Probably the government had not yet decided whether to bring him to trial on November 14 when a batch of letters from General Gage reached the office of the colonial secretary. Wrote that commander, a scapegoat for the dismal failure of British measures regarding America, "I transmit your Lordship a packet of letters that were picked out from a number of papers scattered about Cushings house. They contain no intelligence of present transactions but shew the nature of the correspondence that the two Lees, Doctor Franklin and others kept up with the leaders of this rebellion."

Among the documents was a letter of September 12, 1770, from Sayre to Thomas Cushing, found in Cushing's house in Boston, in which Sayre wrote, "I am under a necessity for my personal safety of begging that this letter may not be trusted in too many hands for could the Attorney General here get a copy of it he would undoubtedly file a bill against me." Could more evidence be found that might be used against Sayre? The letter was taken from its place in the files of the Colonial Office, and it was doubtless inspected with care. It was the message in which Sayre reported that he had been unable to secure letters of Governor Thomas Hutchinson and other Massachusetts officials that would

20. Bath *Journal*, October 30, 1775; York *Courant*, November 7, 1775; Pennsylvania *Evening Post*, January 27, 1776. Horace Walpole states that Mansfield displayed a "dastardly spirit" by "his profuse civility" to Sayre on this occasion. Steuart (ed.), *Last Journals of Horace Walpole*, I, 488. Enemies of Mansfield commonly accused him of cowardice.

serve to condemn that harried governor. Although it hinted that Sayre
had engaged in illegal activity while trying to get at the reports, the
letter could not be used to bolster the flimsy case against him.[21]

Sayre took the offensive. On Friday, December 15, he appeared with
Arthur Lee at the Old Bailey to urge that his bail be set aside. Except for
the evidence of Richardson, there was no case against him. By this time,
it had become obvious that the government did not intend to proceed
further against Sayre. Lord Justice Burland and Lord Mayor Sawbridge,
who heard the plea, accordingly canceled the bail.[22] Sayre was as free
legally as might be.

Did Sayre actually bribe members of the Guards with intent to
abduct George III? Quite certainly, no. Did he propose kidnapping the
monarch when he conferred with Richardson in that upstairs room of the
Pennsylvania Coffee House? He may have talked about a wild scheme to
overthrow the government as a possible theoretical step toward solving
Anglo-American troubles without the slightest intention of executing
it. He was addicted, as will appear, to the concoction of grandiose plans.
Conceivably he was amusing himself, at least in part, at Richardson's expense.

There is another and not utterly implausible explanation of the affair—that Richardson was used as a tool by men in government to strike
at Sayre in particular and to discredit its enemies in England and America in general. Such was the opinion expressed in a brief essay "On Plots
Against Government," which was published in the popular *London Magazine*.[23] Its author, or authors, reminded the readers of the periodical that
the accusation against Sayre bore a strong resemblance to similar charges
made during the reign of Charles II in that it was wildly improbable.
"Most true it is, that the plots set on foot by ministry have ever been of

21. Two packets of the papers found in the Cushing house were sent to London,
copies of the papers being later forwarded by General William Howe. Clarence E. Carter
(ed.), *The Correspondence of General Thomas Gage* (New Haven, 1931–33), I, 422–23;
Howe to Lord Dartmouth, November 30, 1775 (Private), in Colonial Office, Series 5,
Bundle 92, Public Record Office, London. The sentence quoted is taken from an index
to the second set of documents prepared by Dr. Thomas Moffatt. Neither the original
Sayre letter nor the copy of it is now to be found in the Public Record Office. I am indebted to Miss Angela Houstoun of the P.R.O.'s Search Department for the quotation
from Moffatt's index.

22. *London Magazine*, XLIV (1775), 659.

23. *Ibid.*, XLV (1776), 366–67.

the incredible kind. They have abounded with improbabilities, like that lately of Mr. Richardson's concerning Mr. Sayer."

It is by no means impossible that Sayre was the victim of a conspiracy. So Edmund Burke believed. Government sought, he wrote, "to discourage the spirit of petitioning," to make a display of energy, and "to divert the attention of Parliament from the main point—the conduct of the ministers with regard to America." Richardson was savagely attacked on the western side of the Atlantic, where he was classed as a "recent volunteer" with his namesake, Ebenezer Richardson, the customs informer and slayer of Boston. From London, another critic displeased by the lieutenant's conduct wrote, "What will all America think of her infamous countryman Frank Richardson who for a paltry rise in the army has attempted to swear the life of Mr. Sayre away . . . he does not walk the streets, and in a little time he will be consigned even to despair, and a variety of wretchedness; for though there are not many who have yet attempted the lives of their countrymen by perjury, yet there are scoundrels from every part of America, who ought to be execrated to eternity by all good men." The Lee family's version of the affair was that the North ministry first tried, with Lord Sandwich taking the lead, to entrap Sayre and William Lee into bribing dockworkers needed by the navy to leave their jobs and Britain—a criminal offense—then to make use of Richardson. "The ministerial scheme agst Sayre & others was this. The workmen leaving the docks, demanding higher wages, applying to the American friends to supply them with money to convey them out of the kingdom. It was about to take effect when one more honest than the rest of his fellows, disclosed the whole affair to the alderman"—that is, to William Lee. The Lee interpretation continued, "this failing, their next plan is, to make one Richardson . . . swear away the life of Sayre, & it is apprehended the other also. Is it possible that any one can expect anything good from such abandoned villains? from them & their hellish plots good Lord deliver us." The Lee brothers, especially Arthur, were much inclined to claim the purest virtue for themselves and to discern sinister motives and wicked behavior in their antagonists, but the statement concerning the dockworkers is a logical one and is probably one of fact rather than of imagination.[24]

24. Copeland *et al.* (eds.), *Correspondence of Edmund Burke*, III, 234; statement by "Sincerus" in the Pennsylvania *Evening Post*, February 13, 1776; Connecticut *Gazette*,

Nor can testimony by Sayre himself that he was the victim of a conspiracy be lightly set aside. He made the charge in a letter to President George Washington. "You would doubt the possibility of such pointed persecution of a private man," he wrote.

> Mr. Izard can inform you, that I was not only much more active against the views of the British administration against America, at the commencement of the troubles than Mr Franklin, or any other American in England. I was chairman of that first meeting of the Americans in London, when they made their protest against the proceedings at Boston etc etc—I continued an open & avowed opposition, not only in the City of London, but in Middlesex—where being the Sheriff I frequently concerted their opposition also, by county meetings—this conduct, not only excited the hatred of Adn. but all others, their adherents—I lost many friends to my bank, who would, under neutrality, have done me solid services—at last Government took a despotic & desperate measure, by hiring a scoundrel to make a weak & ridiculous information agt. me.

It would appear that Sayre was giving his honest opinion. His use of the word *weak* suggests, as was indicated above, that his remarks to Richardson at the Birchin Lane coffeehouse were such that they could be misconstrued by an enemy. In another letter to Washington Sayre commented,

> I had no personal foes—indeed, I had some real friends, among the very men, who were compel'd to persecute me—my ruin never was in contemplation, 'till I had united all the parties of our cause, into a formidable phalanx—singular as it may appear, I was the only man, who conducted the springs of opposition, in the year 1775. . . . It was my misfortune, not to know, the extent of the power I had acquired; or not to have consider'd the power of the minister to punish.[25]

The sensational affair did not end when the indictment against Sayre was abandoned. He undertook to secure legal redress upon the ground that his personal rights had been violated.

February 16, 1776; William Bell Clark (ed.), *Naval Documents of the American Revolution* (Washington, D.C., 1964–), III, 1234–35.

25. Sayre to Washington, October 15, 1790, January 3, 1795, both in Department of State, Miscellaneous Letters, 1789–1906 (RG 59), National Archives, Washington, D.C.

6

The Banker in Distress

EITHER Nicholas Nugent nor Sayre was content to put an end to the remarkable episode. The courageous captain refused to accept his arrest, with its accompanying trickery and browbeating, without a public protest, and he struck back as best he might against Lord Rochford and General Craig, though without much success. After Rochford and the North ministry vanished from the seats of power, Nugent was rewarded for his bravery. Sayre also sought redress in the courts. He learned again that the English government was a formidable antagonist for a refractory American in England. The notoriety arising from his struggle with the British state put an end to Sayre's career as a banker in Oxford Street. He became a rebel indeed, and he secured appreciation for his services and sufferings neither in Britain nor in America.

In the closing weeks of 1775 there was gossip in London to the effect that Nugent and Richardson had become personal enemies and that a duel between them impended. The rumor was unfounded. The two men met some weeks after the captain's release, and the American expressed regret that he had thought it necessary to involve Nugent in a scrape.

The Irishman bore Richardson no ill will, but he was determined to strike at Craig and Rochford. As soon as his health permitted, on November 8, Nugent undertook to expose them by asking for a military investigation in which he could defend himself against the general's accusation that he had not conducted himself properly as an officer, and could bring forth evidence that Craig had threatened to discriminate against him because of his refusal to name the unidentified City man. Informed by Nugent that the captain desired such an investigation, the general offered no objection. Nugent then placed his request before Adjutant General Edward Harvey, who referred him to Lord Barrington, the latter possessing the authority as secretary of war to act upon the request. According to the captain, he mentioned a court martial as a possible means of bringing forth the facts but asked the secretary to indicate the best method. Nugent could have compelled his superiors to establish a court of inquiry but was not aware that such was the only way in which he could effectively present his evidence.

Barrington informed the captain that the situation was rather delicate and that he, like American Indian chiefs facing a serious problem, needed time to deliberate. After some delay, Barrington told Nugent that a court martial was in order. However, asserted the secretary, it could only consider charges against Craig, since the general was offering none against Nugent. Barrington undertook to frame the court martial accordingly. The burden of proof was thus placed upon the captain, by "a low attorney-like quirk," asserted Nugent.

He sought the advice of his friend, Edmund Burke,[1] who referred him to lawyers John Dunning and Arthur Lee. Describing Barrington to Burke as "an infamous scoundrel," Nugent tried in vain with the help of influential friends, both military and civil, to compel the secretary to abandon the court martial and to create a court of inquiry. He was informed that the king had approved the court martial. Nugent could not hope to prove that Craig had abused him and had threatened to punish him for his behavior in the hearings before Rochford and White. He therefore declined to press charges, and the court martial was set aside. Barrington's conduct was officially quite proper; it was not, however, that of a gentleman seeking to do justice.

Nor had Craig become one. In the midst of the controversy between Nugent and Barrington, the general arranged the captain's transfer from the First Battalion of the Foot Guards to the Second Battalion. The change would inevitably be construed to mean that the government approved of Richardson and condemned Nugent. The captain protested. Craig then cancelled the order, excusing himself on the ground that Nugent had earlier requested the transfer. Thoroughly disgusted, Nugent resigned from the army.

Nugent did not leave in silence, however. He published a short book, *The Case of Nicholas Nugent*, relating in detail his version of his role in the supposed Sayre conspiracy. The book inevitably reflected unfavorably upon Richardson, who replied in a brief pamphlet, *An Appeal to the*

---

1. Mrs. Burke was born a Nugent but was apparently not related to the captain.

Officers of the Guards, that he had told the truth. Nugent never did reveal to the public that name so eagerly sought by the government. In all likelihood it was that of an innocent man, since no reason appears for Nugent to protect Sayre. In any event, the captain emerged from the imbroglio as a chivalrous gentleman.[2]

Nor was Sayre content to let the matter drop. The legal battles between him and the British state continued, and this time Sayre took the offensive. He too recalled that Wilkes had mulcted the government of four thousand pounds by securing a verdict of illegal arrest against Lord Halifax. A report circulated in December, 1775, that Sayre had instructed his solicitor to begin suit against Rochford, his undersecretaries, and the men who had executed Sayre's seizure, "so that the personal liberty of every Englishman may be again asserted in his person." Sayre did indeed sue Rochford for damages. The cabinet minister was served a summons on February 3, 1776, "to appear before the King's justices at Westminster, in eight days of the purification of the Blessed Mary, to answer Stephen Sayre, of a plea of trespass, assault, and imprisonment." Rochford was declared to be responsible for an illegal invasion of the Sayre home, unlawful search of Sayre's papers, and the illegal imprisonment of Sayre. The banker asked for thirty thousand pounds in damages, including serious injury to his business.[3]

The case was opened in the Court of Common Pleas before Lord Chief Justice De Grey on June 28. A battery of lawyers, Sergeant James Adair, Sergeant John Glynn, a Mr. Davenport, John Alleyne, and Arthur Lee appeared in behalf of Sayre. Rochford was also amply supplied with counsel of six men, led by Attorney General Lord Thurlow and Solicitor General Wedderburn—the government did not desert its own. Sergeant Glynn was the chief spokesman for Sayre, Thurlow the principal advocate for Rochford. Glynn contended, quite accurately, that the banker's reputation had suffered and that he must incur heavy financial losses in consequence. Thurlow responded that the secretary had not acted from malice, that Sayre was a person of no importance to his lordship, and that Rochford had merely done his duty as he saw it. Sayre could not win an

2. The Nugent and Richardson publications are cited above. Regarding the affair of the court martial, see also Nugent to Burke, December 27, [1775], and January 1, 1776, in Edmund Burke Papers, Northamptonshire Record Office, Northampton, England.

3. York *Courant*, December 19, 1775; *Scot's Magazine*, XXXVIII (1776), 107.

award unless "a special jury" flatly rejected the defense offered for Rochford and decisively acted to recompense the American for the injuries he had suffered. Had he been English-born, had he not been known as a champion of American rights, he would doubtless have had a greater chance of success.

Neither Sayre nor Rochford took the stand, but the events and the documents of the preceding October concerning them were canvassed. Richardson repeated his story. It was not to be denied that Rochford could legally act as a magistrate when the safety of the nation seemed to be at stake. The entry of his agents into the Sayre house, though accompanied by trickery, was therefore lawful. Moreover, evidence was produced to demonstrate that Sayre had not objected to examination of his papers. Sergeant Glynn pointed out that Rochford could easily have discovered, by consulting John Wilkes, that Richardson's story was utterly ridiculous. More important, he contended that Rochford had arbitrarily denied the plea of John Reynolds for bail. Thurlow replied effectively that successful conspiracies are often foolish in appearance, and he claimed that Reynolds had not officially requested bail.

The case was opened at ten o'clock in the morning, and it went to the jury at four in the afternoon. After the jury had retired, counsel for Rochford enlarged upon two legal points. Could there be damages for refusal of bail? Had it been formally offered? It was agreed that the two questions must be reserved for future judicial determination. The jury was brought back to the courtroom, instructed regarding that decision, and sent back to its deliberations. The twelve good men and true deliberated for some time before returning with their verdict. They proved to be docile. They found Rochford guilty and voted damages of one thousand pounds to Sayre, but subject to the stipulation made by the court.[4]

The jury had placed decision of the case in the hands of judges, and the way was still open to thwart Sayre. On April 25, 1777, after customary delay, Sergeant William Day, with a colleague, asked the Court of Common Pleas to rule in the affirmative regarding both questions raised by the lawyers for Rochford. Compliance would automatically have convicted the secretary of illegal conduct and would have justified the award to Sayre. Again final action was deferred—the two questions were judged too important to be hastily settled. By that time, Sayre had

4. *London Magazine*, XLV (1776), 389.

become openly an American rebel. The following November, both questions were debated once more, with Sergeant Glynn speaking for Sayre and Sergeant Davy for Rochford. Finally Lord Chief Justice De Grey with three other judges ruled that Rochford, acting to protect the state, had not received an offer of bail from Reynolds in due form—although Reynolds had unquestionably expressed a wish for it. Obviously, if there was no illegal refusal, there could be no damages.[5] Rochford, and the government, had won the last battle of the legal war. Defeated in court by a trifling legal technicality, Sayre did indeed suffer financially. By that time he had also lost an economic struggle, had been in the toils of the law a second time, and had left England.

THE BANKING house of Sayre & Purdon was inevitably injured by the arrest, confinement, and trials of one of its partners. Sayre became notorious. Was it safe to entrust money, to have anything financial to do with a man accused of seeking to execute a revolution, a rebellious and desperate American? To be sure, he had married into a superior English family, but one knew that fairest flowers of the aristocracy had at times been lured into marriage by insidious adventurers. Sayre was too elegant, too gracious to be trusted with pound notes or bills of exchange—the very staff and stuff of the good life enjoyed by proper people. It was reported in October, 1775, that "a patriotic nobleman and his friends" had put "£20,000 in the hands of a certain banker, to prevent any ill effects that may arise from the present proceedings of government against Mr. Sayre," but it is apparent that he did not receive such massive help.[6]

Had the bank, one may well ask, ever been sound? It is clear that neither Sayre nor Purdon possessed the cool caution and sagacity that enabled Thomas Coutts to accumulate an enormous fortune from banking in the eighteenth century, and certainly Purdon had reason to believe that he was injured by the political escapades of his partner. In June, 1776, English newspaper advertisements announced that "the notes issued under the firm of Sayre and Purdon will be paid with interest on the 15th of July next, when the house will be opened by Mr. B. Coote

5. Felix Farley's Bristol *Journal*, May 3 and November 29, 1777; London *Chronicle*, November 25–27, 1777.

6. York *Courant*, October 31, 1775. The nobleman and his friends were probably Rockingham and his allies.

Purdon." But one Gregory Bateman and other men secured a commission for bankruptcy against both men on November 21, and the assets of the bank together with their estates were assigned to James Christie, afterward famous as an auctioneer, and Gregory Bateman.[7]

Purdon vanished; his obligations had doubtless become too heavy to bear. Long afterward, Sayre declared that the government exerted its influence to destroy his bank, and the popular *Gentleman's Magazine* announced to the polite world of England that it was defunct. It was later rumored that Purdon had gone somewhere east of Suez to begin a new life—it may be that the influence of Sir Eyre Coote enabled a relative in distress to find a new means of livelihood. John Reynolds, who held an insurance policy of five thousand pounds upon Purdon's life, probably in recompense for efforts to assist him, was told in 1782 that Purdon had died in the Paddington area of London, then that he had been drowned in the Thames. His body was not found in Paddington, and dragging the river proved to be fruitless. A rumor that Purdon had expired in France also did not lead to a death certificate enabling Reynolds to collect the insurance money. Actually, Purdon seems to have died in October, 1780, somewhere on, in, or near the waters of the Indian Ocean.[8]

Despite the fact that he had withdrawn from the partnership, Sayre had to face the consequences of the collapse of the bank in London. Were one to accept at face value a statement that appeared in the London *Chronicle* early in January of 1777, Sayre came out of the bankruptcy proceedings almost in a blaze of glory. The troubles of a dignified gentleman of the greatest probity, who chose not to lament his misfortune, arose in part from the malice of government, in part from the shortcomings of the absent Purdon:

> Saturday, being the third and last meeting under the commission of bankruptcy against Mess. Sayre and Purdon, late of Oxford-street, bankers,

7. Felix Farley's Bristol *Journal*, June 22, 1776; Bankruptcy, Series 1, Bundle 68, pp. 24, 84–85, Public Record Office, London. In his early years in business in London, Christie dealt primarily in real estate. W[illiam] Roberts, *Memorials of Christie's* (London, 1897), I, 3.

8. Sayre, *A Short Narrative*; *Gentleman's Magazine*, XLVI (1776), 531; de Vlieger, *Historical and Genealogical Record of the Coote Family*, 138; Reynolds, *Life and Times of Frederic Reynolds*, I, 332–33. In 1817 an announcement appeared, "Died at her house in Clifton-mall, Mrs. Coote Purdon, relict of Bartholomew Coote Purdon, esq. of Bally-clough, Ireland." *Gentleman's Magazine*, LXXXVII, Part I (1817), 570.

Mr. Sayre appeared, as he had done at the two former meetings, and then finished his examination to the entire satisfaction of all, the creditors who were present; the senior commissioner declared that he had sat in that capacity five-and-twenty years, and that he never experienced an instance of so clear, candid, and satisfactory a state of accounts as Mr. Sayre had given in; in which the other gentlemen in the commission entirely concurred. Mr. Sayre seemed impelled, as he stated facts, to the necessity of shewing that another person had been too deeply involved in debt, from the very commencement of their co-partnership, to be extricated; it appeared that his necessities had drawn a very large sum out of the house; that his estate had been long subject to heavy annuities, unknown even to his own family. Mr. Sayre scarcely mentioned his unhappy commitment to the Tower; he expressed no bitterness against the authors of that fatal stroke, but delicately left every gentleman present to his own opinion on the matter. In short, it appeared to the most prejudiced persons at the meeting, that every report which had been propagated to his disadvantage was totally groundless.[9]

But newspapers were partisan and even less reliable in the London of that time than their counterparts of the nineteenth century. One could buy a "puff" in them for himself—a flattering report thinly disguised as news—and it is to be suspected that the laudatory paragraph quoted above was prepared by a person or persons associated with the American and disposed to enlarge upon his virtues.[10]

Sayre afterward claimed that his troubles arose in part from an unpaid loan of £10,000 he had made to Purdon. In any event, his financial difficulties were not yet ended. Late in January, sued by Robert Albion Cox and eight other men for more than £1,400, he was brought a second time before Lord Mansfield and was sent to jail for debt, and he was housed in quarters less commodious and less dignified than those he had occupied in the Tower. However, with the help of John Reynolds, a true friend in time of need, he was soon able to satisfy his creditors sufficiently to secure his release. It was announced in the London *Chronicle* at the beginning of February that "the late partner" of Bartholomew Coote Purdon had been "granted a certificate" that would lead to his liberation on February 22—he was actually discharged on February 27.

9. *Gentleman's Magazine*, January 4–7, 1777.
10. Lucyle Werkmeister, *The London Daily Press, 1772–1792* (Lincoln, Neb., 1963), 6–7.

Sayre did not emerge from his second confinement with the respect and unanimous praise of the London press. Two years later, the *Morning Post* of the capital described him as "the notorious Mr. Sayre, by some called Sheriff Sayre, others Tower Sayre, and others Banker Sayre." Other unflattering comments would continue to appear in London and provincial papers.[11]

Nor did the released prisoner come forth from jail without financial strain. No evidence has been found that wealthy relatives of his wife surged forward to his assistance. It may well be that, except for spendthrift Lord Verney, who was himself somewhat embarrassed for money and who was forced more than once to flee to France to escape jail, the Noels and allied families were not disposed to help the colonial who had inserted himself into their midst. John Reynolds generously—and perhaps recklessly—came to the rescue and put up £5,000 in order to secure the release of his friend. Property of Elizabeth Sayre that brought an income of as much as £600 per annum, sufficient for her support in comfort, was at least temporarily saved from the wreckage. Long afterward, Sayre claimed that his losses from the bankruptcy and subsequent legal proceedings, including land in Leicestershire, Essex, and the island of Dominica, amounted to more than £50,000. In that estimate there was, one is inclined to believe, multiplication as well as addition. In any event, Sayre had to begin life almost anew at the age of forty, and his political prospects in England were severely damaged by his financial collapse.[12]

DESPITE all his difficulties, there is no evidence that Sayre went so far as to demand separation of America from Britain until some months had passed after the news of the Declaration of Independence reached En-

11. Charles Isham (ed.), *The Deane Papers* (New York, 1886–90), V, 443–44, Vol. XXIII of *Collections of the New-York Historical Society*; London *Chronicle*, February 1–4, 1777; Prisons, Series 4, Bundle 6, p. 34, Public Record Office, London; Isham (ed.), *Deane Papers*, III, 276, Vol. XXI of *Collections of the New-York Historical Society*.

12. Reynolds, *Life and Times of Frederic Reynolds*, I, 172–73. Ralph Izard wrote to William Duer in October, 1777, "You must long ago have heard of the misfortunes" of Sayre & Purdon. "Their creditors," said Izard, "will, I fear, be considerable sufferers." But Izard also informed Duer that a debt of Duer to Sayre & Purdon of £163 "has been made over to me . . . by Messrs. Christie and Bateman . . . the assignees . . . in satisfaction for my demand upon them" (Deas [ed.], *Correspondence of Mr. Ralph Izard*, 205). Sayre, *A Short Narrative*.

gland. To be sure, it would have been imprudent for him to announce allegiance to the new republic emerging beyond the Atlantic. In the midst of his money troubles, in September, 1776, he approached Lord Effingham and the immensely rich duke of Portland, a political ally of Lord Rockingham, with a scheme to put an end to the war beyond the ocean. He proposed that the British opponents of government take advantage of news of failures of the king's forces in America to protest massively against continuing the war. Lord Mayor Sawbridge of London, an ally of John Wilkes, could assemble its citizens for a dramatic demonstration; a number of peers and respectable commoners should attend as if they were brought together impulsively because of "impending danger"; all present should combine to declare that the nation was averse to the war and to send circulars to all the counties in Britain urging similar denunciations of the conflict.

Portland conveyed the scheme to Rockingham, who declined to take part in such an enterprise. He opposed it in part because he suspected that Lord Shelburne, a friend of America but a political rival whom he disliked, was its prime mover. More important, the marquis distrusted the City men, who he felt were rash. A protest would be useless unless it came from "men of rank, character & fortune in this country"—persons like himself. Rockingham was not disposed to take any step that might enhance the influence of the City or might seriously disturb his own very satisfactory situation, so he advised Portland to give Sayre an answer that did not commit the Rockinghams to vigorous action. Portland and Rockingham informed Sayre that they thought it desirable for the enemies of the North ministry to work together, but they insisted upon retaining freedom of action.[13]

Apparently they did not classify Sayre as a mere City man. Afterward, Sayre asserted that the marquis and others in his following went so far as to promise to arrange for Sayre's election to the House of Commons, but that he declined to take advantage of their pledge. There may have been an undertaking to act in his behalf when opportunity offered, and it was within their power to secure a seat for him.

Sayre did not wait for them to move, however. Instead, realizing that it was then impossible to mobilize against the North ministry and that the near future in England for him was not promising, he left for the

13. Ross J. S. Hoffman, *The Marquis: A Study of Lord Rockingham, 1730–1782* (New York, 1973), 337–38; Sayre, *A Short Narrative.*

Continent to continue to do what he could for himself and for his own country. Becoming an open rebel, he committed himself to the cause of American independence.[14]

Had Sayre remained in England, it is altogether likely that Rockingham, Burke, and their allies would have done something for him, although probably not enough to make him happy. After the North ministry fell from power in 1782 and was replaced by one under Rockingham, with Edmund Burke as a chief dispenser of patronage, Nicholas Nugent at last secured compensation for the abuse he had suffered and was made a baronet.[15] Much later he encountered financial disaster. The *Gentleman's Magazine* announced the death on October 21, 1811, "in the Fleet Prison," of "the once gay, gallant, and fashionable Sir Nicholas Nugent."[16]

What reward Francis Richardson received for his efforts in behalf of Britain remains unknown. Informers do not win affection, and at least some of his fellow officers in the Guards must have concluded that he was either a liar or a fool, or both. But his military career was not ruined, and he eventually achieved the rank of colonel in the Guards.[17]

14. *American State Papers. Documents, Legislative and Executive . . . Commencing March 4, 1789, and Ending March 3, 1823* (Washington, 1834), IX, 81.

15. Nugent's title passed the Privy Seal on August 13, 1782. George Edward Cokayne, *The Complete Baronetage* (Exeter, 1887–88), V, 409–410. The Rockingham ministry collapsed shortly before the formal issuance of the patent, in consequence of the death of the marquis. The successors of the Rockinghams, led by Lord Shelburne, presumably had no reason to oppose the appointment.

16. *Gentleman's Magazine*, LXXXI (1811), Part II, 490. Nugent's death is also recorded in the *European Magazine*, LX (1811), 319. His title was not inherited.

17. Watson, *Annals of Philadelphia and Pennsylvania*, I, 560. A contemporary analysis of the Nugent and Richardson pamphlets in the *Monthly Review*, LIV (1776), 337, suggests that Richardson lost popularity in the army and praises Nugent. "How far Mr. R.'s reputation will yet stand immaculate, in the opinion of men of that nice and scrupulous honour which is so laudably characteristic of a soldier, is a matter which time alone can ascertain: in the mean while, his *zeal* for the *safety* of the King—God bless his Majesty! has not, if we are rightly informed, passed unrewarded." As for Nugent, "he has been tried . . . with the strictest impartiality in *our* court; and we have found him *guilty* of obstinately refusing, in utter defiance of his superiors, to *violate the honour of* FRIENDSHIP, *and the confidence of* PRIVATE CONVERSATION." The magazine expressed the opinion that "the world is all before him," and hope, unfounded in fact, that newspaper stories reporting promotion of a Captain Nugent to a lieutenant colonelcy referred to him. That Richardson suffered, so far as his career is concerned, is unlikely. He was a colonel by 1789. *Gentleman's Magazine*, LVII, Part II (1789), 961.

7

The Amateur Envoy

HEN THE Second Continental Congress declared the United States of America to be independent, it was only too plain to a majority of its members that their infant nation might survive only briefly without assistance. Accordingly, the Congress appealed for help at many courts of Europe, especially those where Britain was disliked or hated and where there was military or economic power that might be directed against her. So it was that Benjamin Franklin, having entered his seventies, made the eastward crossing of the Atlantic for the fourth time. He landed in France before the end of 1776. Franklin was one of three commissioners—the other two being merchant Silas Deane of Connecticut and Dr. Arthur Lee—assigned the task of securing all possible aid from the Bourbon king of France, Louis XVI, and other European rulers and states. In Paris the three strove to secure formal recognition of American independence, a military alliance, and French intervention in the struggle against Britain. Under the direction of the Congress, they also did what they could to get help at Madrid, Berlin, Amsterdam, Florence, and St. Petersburg.

The presence of the "militia diplomats" in Paris attracted Stephen Sayre to that city, where he felt there ought to be a high place for him in the employ of his native country. From London Dr. Edward Bancroft, who would serve both Britain and America as secretary of the three commissioners and as a British spy, wrote on March 4, 1777, to William Carmichael, also a less-than-devoted servant of the three, that "Mr. Sayre is now out of confinement and desirous of some kind of employment outside of England; probably he will pay our friends a visit. He regrets that Prince Arthur has left France." In other words, Sayre intended to go to Paris to ask for an appointment and regretted that "Prince Arthur" Lee had departed from that place for Madrid. Lee would, presumably, act as his friend and sponsor. Sayre could not expect a warm welcome from Franklin, with whom he had never been cordially associated, nor from Deane, whom he had probably never met.[1]

The former banker did recklessly go to Paris. In fact, Sayre left England before the end of February. If his prospects were dubious in England, he still had important connections there and property—at least property rights—that would be endangered by his entrance into the service of the American rebels. Besides, he did not have in the Congress even one advocate who would insist upon his splendid merits and upon recognition of his great qualities. He was out of touch with Francis Lewis, a member from New York who was favorably disposed toward him. Arthur Lee and William Lee had two brothers, Richard Henry and Francis Ludwell, in that body to speak in their behalf. Moreover, Richard Henry and Francis Ludwell Lee were allies of Samuel and John Adams in the Congress. Virginia and Massachusetts were thus aligned behind Arthur and William Lee, and so it was that Arthur was named one of the three commissioners and William was appointed as an American commercial agent at Nantes while Sayre was still involved in bankruptcy proceedings. In May, 1777, Congress assigned William to Berlin and Vienna. Sayre's good and younger friends were thus well established in the diplomatic service of the new nation before he sought a place in it. Was he in desperate need of money? He reported afterward that he had command of an income of five hundred pounds per annum when he was freed from bankruptcy proceedings.[2] If so, it would seem that a shocked and humiliated man who had twice been incarcerated in England, becoming ever more aware that he was an American, chose to cast his lot with the rebels striving for freedom beyond the Atlantic despite personal risks, for doubtful gain. He did not possess cold sagacity.

Sayre reminded Franklin that he had Chatham's confidence. It was well known that Frederick the Great retained a very high opinion of Chatham founded on the steady and generous assistance the Englishman had supplied to Frederick in the dark days of the Seven Years' War, when

1. Isham (ed.), *Deane Papers*, III, 443–44; Sayre to John Adams, February 21, 1799, in Adams Family Papers, Massachusetts Historical Society, Boston.

2. Sayre to Isaac Sears, August 25, 1778, in London *Chronicle*, August 12–14, 1779.

the warrior king was almost surrounded by enemies. Arthur Lee, having failed to secure attention in Spain, was to go to Berlin to solicit aid from Frederick. Franklin therefore consented to the appointment of Sayre as Lee's secretary, with a salary of one thousand pounds per annum. According to a later statement from Sayre, both Franklin and Deane expressed high regard for him at that time. Lee advanced Sayre two thousand livres.[3]

In Paris, Sayre came under the scrutiny of the British secret service, which was anxiously watching the courts of Europe wherever the Americans sought aid. In mid-May Paul Wentworth, an American-born British agent, reported to his superior, the earl of Suffolk, that Lee and Sayre were about to leave for Berlin. Lee would travel in an English post chaise "painted deep green, & with A. Lee in a cypher. Sayre goes with him as a companion only—& talks *gravely* of going on to Petersburgh to make a conquest of the Empress, who loves he says handsome men & may have a curiosity for an American gallant." Catherine the Great was remarkably fond of men and had already enjoyed a long succession of lovers. Her habits were well known, but Wentworth seems to have failed to recognize an American joke. Suffolk certainly did not perceive that Sayre had playfully deceived Wentworth, and he wrote to Hugh Elliot, the British minister in Berlin, to inform him about Lee and Sayre: "I have only to add, with respect to Mr. Sayre, that he is a man of desperate fortune, but with the disposition rather than the talents to be mischievous. His personal vanity is at the same time so great that he talks of going forwards to Petersburgh in order to try the effect of his address & figure at that court." Other reports that Suffolk received from Paris were more accurate. Lee and Sayre had been unable to secure passports from the Prussian minister there, though they hoped to obtain permission from Frederick for American privateers to use his port of Emden on the North Sea and to obtain military gear.[4]

3. Monsieur D'Aubarede to comte de Vergennes, November 15, 1777, in Benjamin Franklin Stevens (ed.), *Facsimiles of Manuscripts in European Archives Relating to America, 1773–1783* (London, 1889–95), XIX, No. 1741 (this report about the appointment is obviously derived from Sayre but appears to be substantially correct); *American State Papers*, IX, 82; Sayre to Isaac Sears, August 25, 1778, in London *Chronicle*, August 12–14, 1779; Lee, *Life of Arthur Lee*, I, 350.

4. Stevens (ed.), *Facsimiles*, VII, No. 694, 696, XV, No. 1454, 1538.

The two Americans proceeded to Berlin—inconspicuously, they fancied. They traveled by way of Munich, Prague, Vienna, and Dresden, and Sayre used the name of Stevens or Stephens. On June 4, they established themselves at the Corsica Inn in Berlin. Their arrival created "noise" in the Prussian capital, and Hugh Elliot, who lived in the same inn, immediately began to watch them. Frederick the Great was absent on military maneuvers. Elliot believed the American emissaries would not accomplish much. Soon, however, Elliot began to suspect that the Prussians were conferring with the Americans, as was indeed the fact. Frederick was hostile to Britain and had not permitted Hessian troops to march across his territory en route to service with the British forces in America. His aides—he had ministers only officially—listened to the two emissaries, and there was talk of barter of American tobacco for Prussian clothing and weapons. In the end, however, the only things of substance that soon came from the efforts of Lee and Sayre were contracts for the purchase of cloth and nine hundred defective muskets.[5]

Berlin was dull for Elliot, an energetic young man, and he may not have been sorry to have the task of contending with the Americans. Because of him, the Lee-Sayre mission, despite its lack of important gains for the Patriots, achieved international notoriety. The Americans were in the habit of dining in the country, leaving their papers at the inn. They dined so as usual on June 26, with a Monsieur de Launay. While they were away, Elliot, apparently with the help of a servant whom he had bribed, secured access to the papers. He was able to copy some of them and make brief digests of others before the return of Lee and Sayre. Elliot sent on the information gained from his coup to London. When the Americans discovered Elliot's action, they protested to King Frederick, who had by then returned to Berlin. Elliot had misbehaved—he had abused the hospitality of the king. He was reprimanded by Frederick, who referred to him as that "goddam Elliot," and also by the earl of Suffolk. But the scolding from Suffolk was only a formality, and the earl quietly rewarded the young spy. Actually, possession of the papers brought no great benefit to Britain, because there was no vital secret in them.[6]

5. Frederic Kapp, *Friedrich der Grosse und die Vereinigten Staaten von Amerika* (Leipzig, 1871), 27; Stevens (ed.), *Facsimiles*, XV, No. 1455, 1470.

6. Lady Minto, *Memoir of the Right Honourable Hugh Elliot* (Edinburgh, 1868), 108. There are several accounts of this amusing affair. See Stevens (ed.), *Facsimiles*, XV, Nos.

But the coup did in all likelihood hurt Stephen Sayre. Tension had been building between him and Lee, and Sayre afterward told Franklin that "it was with infinite difficulty, that I restrain'd myself from an open rupture" with his fellow countryman while they were in Berlin. "I conceive," declared Sayre, "he did us infinite prejudice there tho' he might have done great & essential service. I found myself too weak to support an opposition to him & too delicately circumstanced, even to complain." How much a better man than Lee could have achieved, one cannot say. He was inordinately suspicious of other men, and he ascribed too much virtue to himself—actually, it is surprising that Sayre remained Lee's friend for a decade or more. The theft of the documents made Lee appear ridiculous, and he may have placed the blame for it upon Sayre. The two men quarreled. Did Lee know that Congress had appointed his brother William to the post held by Sayre? Leaving Berlin, he informed Sayre that he was discharged. So doing, Lee exceeded his authority, since Sayre had been employed by the three commissioners. George III, reading a report from Paul Wentworth, received the news that Sayre had been dealt another blow.[7]

Sayre stayed on in Berlin. He explained afterward that, "having no expectation . . . that the most humiliating attendance at Paris would give me any employment, I chose to remain at Berlin, where I could live more at ease & at less expence." He proposed to stay there until answers came to letters he wrote to America asking for employment. But such replies never came, and he could not be quiet. According to Hugh Elliot, "he talks of going to Petersburg, sometimes of entering into the service of His Prussian Majesty." Elliot reported on July 12 that Sayre must still be, despite his quarrel with Lee, in American service. Ten days later, the British minister wrote that Sayre had gone to Potsdam, presumably to convey proposals to Frederick through the king's reader, Monsieur Catt. Sayre had indeed become a self-appointed emissary of the United States. Lord Suffolk declined to worry about the intrigues of the American: "If Mr. Sayre's Prussian projects carry the same proportion of folly & indiscretion with those which have thus far influenced his whole

275, 1467, and 1468, and Sayre's narration, written long afterward, in the Arthur Lee Papers, Houghton Library, Harvard University. Kapp, *Friedrich der Grosse und die Vereinigten Staaten*, 41, reports Frederick's condemnation of Elliot.

7. Sayre to Franklin, March 21, 1779, in Benjamin Franklin Papers, American Philosophical Society, Philadelphia; Stevens (ed.), *Facsimiles*, II, No. 182.

conduct, in his own affairs, they are not likely to engage much attention in so wise a cabinet as that of Potsdam." He was confident that Prussian manufacturers would furnish no goods to the rebels without cash payment.[8]

On August 24 Sayre wrote from Berlin to Paul Wentworth, reporting that he had on the carpet a bargain whereby Prussia would give immediate assistance to Congress in return for American purchase of East Indian goods from a monopoly established at Emden. Sayre also claimed that Frederick had written to him no fewer than four letters in his own hand and that the king had promised to consider the proposal seriously. Where the Prussians would get the tea and other goods for the monopoly Sayre seems not to have explained. Wentworth offered an estimate of the American that must have pleased Suffolk: "Mr. Sayre is very vain, credulous & ignorant." Or was the American obviously lying about the letters from the king and sending on foolishness to a man he knew, or suspected, to be a British spy? Sayre did propose a joint whaling enterprise to be established at Emden—not an utterly impractical scheme if ships were obtained. He also suggested that Frederick should seek to acquire a free port in the West Indies from which Prussia could trade with the United States. By using an indirect route, Prussia and America could circumvent the British naval blockade. How such a port was to be gotten and kept, Sayre did not explain. It is not to be doubted that the self-chosen spokesman for America was prolific in devising plans or that they were often chimerical. But everyone did not see him as a mere conceited fool. Caron de Beaumarchais, a subtle diplomat, reported to the French foreign minister, the comte de Vergennes, that Lord Chatham had received two important letters from King Frederick through the agency of Sayre.[9]

The self-appointed representative of the United States might move in such lofty circles as Berlin afforded—except for meeting King Fred-

8. Sayre to Mr. Adams, June 15, 1778, in Franklin Papers, A.P.S.; Stevens (ed.), *Facsimiles*, XV, Nos. 1470, 1475, 179.

9. Stevens (ed.), *Facsimiles*, II, No. 195, XX, No. 1770; John R. Sellers *et al.* (eds.), *Manuscript Sources in the Library of Congress for Research on the American Revolution* (Washington, 1975), 213. For a fuller account of the adventures of Arthur Lee and Sayre in Prussia from a German point of view, see again Kapp, *Friedrich der Grosse und die Vereinigten Staaten*, 27–77.

erick—but he was in worse trouble than when he left England. In addition to the two thousand livres advanced by Lee when the two men left Paris, Lee had paid their expenses until his departure from Berlin. On leaving that place Lee had cut Sayre off the American payroll. After his return to Paris, Lee wrote to Sayre to repeat that his former intimate had been discharged. Sayre appealed to Franklin for justice. He must "think it is indeed very hard for me to be left to the necessity of returning to England to the mercy of my enemies, who are also the enemies of public liberty, after having compromised myself, by openly declaring for the cause of America, to the extent of losing my liberty and risking my life." Franklin was a "man of honour"; accordingly, declared Sayre, "I expect that you will exercise the influence which you must have over your two colleagues, so that I may not be forced to abandon the cause of America to which you know too well that I have sacrificed everything except my attachment to that same cause." Were Sayre to return to England, it would seem "as if I had abandoned those principles which have hitherto guided me in all the actions of my public life, and will dishonour me in the eyes of those whom I most esteem." In the event that Franklin could not help him, Sayre wished his letter to be "a protest against the horrible injustice which I experience" and "a justification of my honour and my conduct." He urged Franklin to send him money. The Philadelphian would not or could not act to assist Sayre, who was informed that the commission washed its hands of him and that "his assuming a public character" after Lee left Berlin was "unwarrantable." Sayre was ordered never to do it again.[10]

That decision was not shaken by an appeal to Vergennes by Monsieur d'Aubarede, who had become a friend of Sayre in England. According to the Frenchman, it was Franklin who had arranged to send Sayre to Berlin with Lee. D'Aubarede insisted, no doubt correctly, that Sayre, "the most gentle and amiable man I know," was not responsible for the quarrel between the two Americans in Berlin, and he informed Vergennes that Sayre desired an appointment as secretary of the commission at a salary of one thousand pounds per annum. Were Sayre forced to return to England, d'Aubarede believed, the American cause would be dishonored.

10. The letter of dismissal by the commissioners was prepared by Lee. Stevens (ed.), *Facsimiles*, XIX, No. 1732; Lee, *Life of Arthur Lee*, I, 350.

Sayre had "many friends in England and America, and all those who know him will never be persuaded that he is in the wrong, and will accuse the cupidity of the deputies." Franklin declined to discuss Sayre's affairs with d'Aubarede. If Vergennes intervened, he did not act with sufficient force to change the decision against Sayre. Shrewd in the ways of men, he probably chose not to intervene in a squabble among the Americans. Sayre was subsequently informed by the commissioners that it would be "criminal" for him to pose as an emissary of the United States.[11]

It is possible that Vergennes, seeing potential benefits to France from the activities of the disowned American agent, quietly encouraged Sayre to proceed with gifts of money. Early in December, the news reached Paris that the British army under General John Burgoyne, which had marched southward from Canada, had laid down its arms at Saratoga. Vergennes then persuaded his fellow ministers and King Louis XVI that the time had come for France to enter the war as an ally of the United States and to bring the detested English to their knees. Sayre might be able, at very little cost, to create troubles for Britain at neutral capitals in northern Europe. Since Sayre did secure money, did proceed to Denmark and Sweden, and remained remarkably active, he may have received some aid from Vergennes. Sayre did borrow four hundred pounds from Isaac Panchaud, a Paris banker of Swiss and Dutch descent, a very intelligent, liberal, and enterprising man who had links with the government of France. Conceivably Vergennes recommended the loan. However, Sayre may well have become connected with Panchaud at an earlier time, since the banker had lent money to both John Wilkes and John Reynolds.[12]

Sayre left Berlin before the end of November and traveled to Copenhagen. From that place he wrote to the three commissioners on

11. Stevens (ed.), *Facsimiles*, XIX, No. 1741; copy of letter from the Commissioners to Sayre, n.d., in Benjamin Franklin Papers, Library of Congress, Washington, D.C. The letter was probably sent to Sayre in November.

12. Robert Bigo, *La Caisse d'Escompte (1776–1793) et les Origines de la Banque de France* (Paris, n.d.), 26–52; Robert Lacour Gayet, *Calonne* (Paris, 1963), 56, 70, 76, 81, 112–14, 130; Bleackley, *Life of John Wilkes*, 242. That Sayre became an agent of Vergennes is suggested in Amandus Johnson, *Swedish Contributions to American Freedom* (Philadelphia, 1953), I, 558. The loan was repaid at the end of the war, as will appear.

Christmas Day that he had intended to go to Paris by way of Hamburg and Rouen. However, at Hamburg, from which place he had planned to proceed to France by sea, he saw "more propriety" in turning toward the Danish capital. He thought that he would spend the winter there, take passage "by the first spring ship" to St. Croix, and voyage from the Danish island to some American harbor. There was a hint of a season's present that the commissioners could not have desired. "As far as I have been able to learn the disposition of the court here, it is extremely favourable to the States of America but of this I will inform you fully in a short time. I beg the favour of your correspondence." The Danish minister in Paris, Sayre said, would forward mail to him.[13]

Less than a week later, Count Bernstorff, the Danish foreign minister, reported that Sayre had come to Copenhagen to propose "un plan de commerce" between Denmark and the United States.[14] Then, for many months, there was no direct contact between Sayre and the American emissaries in Paris. According to Sayre, Franklin refused to answer his complaints and even declined to forward letters to Sayre from America. Sayre had sent more than one hundred letters across the ocean but had not received even one after his departure from England. The treatment he had been accorded by the commissioners, he complained, "is more than any gentleman ought to bear. No title or situation from the commonwealth of the United States, can make any man above answering my letters—for it is the duty of a gentleman, and cannot be dispensed with." He could not account, he said, for Franklin's behavior. While Franklin may have been neglectful, he could not, of course, act to assist the overly active Sayre without the consent of Arthur Lee and Silas Deane. When Franklin learned, late in 1778, that he had become minister to France—when he had power not shared with Lee and Deane—he displayed a disposition to aid Sayre.

WHAT DID Sayre do in Copenhagen, where he lived for more than a year? He was as ingenious as ever in devising schemes for personal kudos

13. Lee, *Life of Arthur Lee*, II, 365; Sayre to the Commissioners, December 25, 1777, in Lee Papers. The British secret service had it that Sayre had obtained a credit of five hundred pounds and that he intended to buy an estate on St. Croix. Stevens (ed.), *Facsimiles*, IV, No. 489.

14. Adolph B. Benson, *Sweden and the American Revolution* (New Haven, 1926), 42.

and national profit. The losses and humiliation he had suffered in London rankled, and he wished it to be known in England that he had been an important person there. Learning of the death of Lord Chatham in May, 1778—an event that produced an outpouring of praise for Pitt—Sayre arranged for the publication in English newspapers of three letters he had received from the great statesman which demonstrated that the two men had been intimate immediately before the onset of the American war and had striven together to prevent it.

He also arranged for the printing of a remarkable note in which Sayre had recorded statements made to him by Chatham at that time concerning men and events during the last years of the reign of George II and the first years of the rule of George III. The note reflected unfavorably upon Lord George Germain, who was managing the British war effort from the Colonial Office and was a favorite target for enemies of the North ministry. It condemned Pitt's colleagues in the cabinet as plotters who had sabotaged his efforts to win the Seven Years' War, praised George II, and discredited his grandson. Germain had several times declined to obey orders, for a reason or reasons still unknown, to lead a cavalry charge against the French in the Battle of Minden and had been cashiered for cowardice; he was often denounced as the "Minden man." Chatham is reported to have said that he knew that Germain's failure to obey "was not from impressions of fear; I could prove it in a court of justice; it was the operation of that faction in the cabinet, who did more to pull me down, than they would have done to ruin all the enemies of England. He was one of them. Much advantage was lost, which would have attended a complete victory." Chatham is said to have asserted that the faction also made sure that "a grand secret expedition" against the French coast, which he had planned, would fail. He was quoted as declaring that "while the late King lived, they could not displace me; when he died, it remained only in a question with them, at what time it should be done." If publication of the documents brought Sayre any credit, it aroused at least one Englishman to fury—William Cole, the well-known antiquarian and friend of Horace Walpole. Reading them in the Cambridge *Chronicle*, Cole commented that Sayre was acquitted of treason "by the restlessness of the American faction," that he lived in Denmark "*or any where* to do his *friends in America service*. Mr. Sayer, I say, his correspondence was, *without disguise, published in every paper in the* kingdom, to *poison* the *minds* of the *people*, & rouse them into rebellion." [15]

But the attention of Sayre was not primarily directed toward English politicking. It was turning toward the sea. In the summer of 1778 he wrote to his friend Isaac Sears, urging that Sears come a-privateering to the North Sea and the Baltic in 1779. Sears could profitably sell the ship in which he crossed the ocean and could use an infinitely superior one planned by Sayre to raid British commerce. There could be a profit of £100,000 from the enterprise, he was promised. Sayre claimed that merchants in Copenhagen were building a model of his vessel, which would carry more sail before the wind, sail much nearer the wind, and be safer in heavy weather than others currently in use. It would be cheaper to construct, and "no ball, unless by very great chance," could tear a hole in it. Moreover, its rigging, if damaged, could easily be repaired. This marvel of navigation upon the stocks was to sail to Virginia. Were it not that he had promised friends on St. Croix to remain at the Danish capital as a merchant, Sayre declared he would go in the ship to the Chesapeake and enlist in the infant American navy. "I would have been with you long since," he wrote, "but for the great danger of being taken, and in consideration of laying ignominiously in an English jail during the war." He was thinking of sending a model of the vessel to Congress. In the meantime, he would be pleased to serve as an agent for Congress in Denmark—then including Norway—to secure naval supplies for the Patriots and to assist American privateers. [16]

In September Sayre sent off a letter in a similar vein to Francis Lewis, who was disposed, even eager, to act in his favor. In 1777, Lewis as a member of Congress had proposed appointment of Sayre as a commissioner to one of the European states, but he had been informed by the

15. The letters and the note, taken from the Cambridge *Chronicle*, together with the comments of Cole, are in Add. MSS. 5823, fol. 236, British Museum. It is possible that publication of the documents was independently executed by a friend of Sayre, but he had the letters in his possession many years later. He had them printed in *A Short Narrative*. It may be significant that the widowed mother of Bartholomew Purdon married a William Cole.

16. Sears independently went on a privateering expedition and was captured by the British.

Committee of Correspondence of Congress that the post given Sayre with Arthur Lee was "a bar" to putting Sayre in "another department." Failing to receive any message from Sayre during the three years that followed the Declaration of Independence, Lewis had ceased to act in behalf of his fellow New Yorker. Sayre feared that he had lost Lewis' friendship and claimed that he had written to Lewis at least seven times. Did Lewis think him "unworthy a correspondence, while unengaged in the glorious defence of my country? Alas, I am miserable under my present state of inactivity, and ardently long to share the danger, the burden, and the glory of the day." He expatiated a second time upon the wonders of his model ship, a plan of which he proposed to send to Congress. Lewis ought, along with Sears, to invest in building it. Sayre confessed that he had a "natural love for every thing respecting a ship"; he wished to build his splendid vessel and carry hemp and cordage in it across the ocean. Thus he could evade British capture and "effect my purpose of getting into America; my wife too will come along with me." [17] After arrival in America, he wished to enter Patriot naval service, since he expected that the war would continue for several years. Britain might be ready to concede American independence by 1780, but the Patriots ought to persevere in the struggle until the British abandoned all of their possessions in North America to the new nation.

The two letters to Sears and Lewis were intercepted by the British on the Atlantic and were published in a Loyalist newspaper in New York in the early summer of 1779. Sayre apparently received no response from either Sears or Lewis. In any case, Lewis, who had been dropped from the New York delegation to Congress in November, 1778, could not exert much influence in behalf of Sayre. Many months afterward, six other messages from Sayre reached Lewis, who by that time had become a member of the American Admiralty Board. Lewis responded with a long letter in which he expressed interest in establishing commerce between Denmark and America. Carried by Henry Laurens, who had been sent to Europe on a diplomatic mission, it did not arrive at its destination, for Laurens was captured by the British and imprisoned in the Tower of London. [18]

17. Obviously, Sayre was in touch with his wife. Evidence that she was with him in Copenhagen at the time has not been found, but it is clear that he desired her company.
18. The letters to Sears and Lewis appear in Rivington's *Royal Gazette*, June 23,

On November 7 Sayre wrote about his new projects to Franklin, asking why Franklin had ceased to answer his appeals, since Sayre had done "nothing to injure that good opinion of me which you have always allowed me to deserve." Sayre proposed in behalf of Copenhagen merchants an exchange of naval stores desired by the Patriots, for tobacco sought by the Danes, at the Danish Caribbean island of St. Thomas. Such a trade, enabling the Americans to obtain supplies without crossing the Atlantic, would be useful, of course, as a means of thwarting the British blockade of the Thirteen States, since American ships engaged in it would be exposed to seizure only between the island and North America.

Sayre emphasized the wonders of the new ship, which incorporated improvements devised by Captain Gardiner, a draftsman in the service of the Danish king, Christian VI, who was "a genius of the first rank" and had been acquainted with Franklin in London before the war. The ship, a frigate, "just now off the stocks," would carry eighteen or twenty guns and would sail faster than any British craft. The building of such vessels would make the British navy "*almost useless,*" Sayre believed, and would give "inconceivable advantage to our rising navy." An earlier version of one of Gardiner's ships had easily outsailed British vessels on voyages to St. Croix. To prove that many more such voyages could be made, Sayre suggested that arrangements be made for the ship to carry Danish goods to Virginia or Maryland and to return to Denmark with tobacco. He wished to serve as its supercargo to America. Exchange of goods in the West Indies would require time to establish, but a trip to the Chesapeake could easily be managed with Franklin's help. Sayre informed Franklin, as he had told Sears and Lewis, that he wished to seize "an excellent opportunity of getting safe to America." He intended to enter the Patriot navy immediately after reaching the Chesapeake. "I am well acquainted with every part of navigation . . . it has always been the most pleasing amusement of my life." He hoped to "share some part of the glory of defending the great cause of liberty of America."

In that November there was one American who declined to admit that Sayre was infallible regarding ships and sailors, Captain John Paul

---

1779. For the relation between Sayre and Lewis see also Frank Moore (ed.), *Materials for History* (New York, 1861), 147–54.

Jones. Informed that Sayre had criticized his handling of the *Ranger* in the waters around the British Isles, the hotheaded and quarrelsome Jones attacked Sayre in a coffeehouse in Nantes and slapped Sayre in the face. In a struggle that followed, Jones did not fare well, since he was much smaller than Sayre. Accordingly, Jones picked up a cane to resume the fight. Neither man suffered great damage. Jones had to promise to keep the peace in order to satisfy the authorities of Nantes. [19]

Having received official notice of his appointment as minister to the court of Louis XVI, Franklin pondered Sayre's new appeal for help. The New Yorker had indeed received shabby treatment because of Lee's enmity. Sayre had stood forth for American rights in England, before Lee, at least as early as Franklin himself. He had been injured in England by the government of Lord North. He had doubtless behaved unwisely. Still, ought not something be done for him? Sayre was certainly familiar with ships and sailing—perhaps even more than Franklin knew, for a boyhood on the south shore of Long Island entailed knowledge of the ocean and of vessels traversing it. That ship about which Sayre wrote just might have possibilities, and he might be useful as a naval officer. In a letter of December 25, Franklin informed Sayre that he was interested in the projected voyage to the Chesapeake.

Franklin's reply came too late, Sayre claimed in a letter of January 13, 1779, to be of service. The Danish minister had sent word back to Copenhagen that Franklin would have nothing to say about the proposals. The projected voyage was abandoned for lack of American interest in it, and the ship was sold for "the India trade." How unfortunate, lamented Sayre. The government of Denmark had been the real owner of the vessel, with a prominent Danish merchant, Conrad Alexander Fabritius de Tengnagel, serving as the ostensible proprietor. Well, anyway, commented Sayre, he had been instrumental in persuading the Danish ministry to make the island of St. Thomas a place of deposit where the Americans could trade for the European goods and gear they needed. He was much pleased to be in correspondence with Franklin, but he was still unemployed. He would "probably set out for Stockholm next week, for I am made to understand that a good deal may be done there—perhaps my coming may be requested—if so I mean to make the

19. Sayre to Franklin, November 7, 1778, in Franklin Papers, A.P.S.; Augustus C. Buell, *Paul Jones* (New York, 1906), I, 137–38.

journey; and tho' I am fully sensible America can do very well without the good will of any more European powers, yet that is no reason why any thing should be neglected." "A modern Don Quixote, going about to protect & relieve the virtuous in distress," he hoped that "the ardour of knighthood will not do me real prejudice in your opinion." He indulged in a bit of name-dropping—to which Don Quixote would not have resorted—and informed Franklin that letters would be forwarded to him by Fabritius and also by Frédéric de Coninck, another wealthy Copenhagen merchant, one much engaged in surreptitious trade with the Americans by way of the West Indies. Sayre also said that Francis Lewis had pledged to use his "utmost interest" to help him secure an appointment in Europe—with the implication that Franklin would do well to try to please Lewis.[20]

The mysterious reference to a journey to the capital of Sweden must have aroused Franklin's curiosity, a curiosity that was not removed by another letter from Copenhagen of March 10. Sayre had returned from Stockholm. "I am well pleased at the disposition of that court," he wrote, "& have good reason to believe it will soon show itself friendly to our cause. I not only had the honor of several conferences with the first minister, but with the King in person." He continued, mysteriously, that "perhaps I am warranted in supposing, that thro' Sweden, Russia might be wrought upon to change her conduct with her opinions. I wish I could be explicit; but you would condemn me were I to commit the subject matter to the hazzard of the post." He was hinting that he had effectively stimulated King Gustavus III of Sweden to solicit the help of Catherine the Great for the defense of the rights of neutrals on the high seas against Britain.[21] A common front of European neutrals against naval searches of their vessels and seizure of those carrying military materials to the enemies of Britain would have seriously embarrassed the British war effort, it is true, but Sayre's bland assumption of authority and the claim of great success at the Swedish capital could not please in

20. Sayre to Franklin, January 13, 1779, in Franklin Papers, A.P.S. There are sketches of Fabritius and Coninck in the *Dansk Biografisk Leksikon*.

21. Afterward Sayre claimed that the king had solemnly promised to do all that he could to form a league of neutrals and that the king had urged him to go to St. Petersburg to solicit the help of Catherine the Great. Sayre to Washington, October 15, 1790, in Department of State, Miscellaneous Letters.

Paris. Sayre also reported that he was soon to leave for Amsterdam, from which place he would sail as soon as possible to the Dutch West Indian island of St. Eustatia, thence to the American mainland. Rather, he would leave unless Franklin—he labored under the false impression that Franklin had become "the sole representative" of America in Europe—offered him a post. He hinted that with the recall of members of "a certain family"—the Lees—Franklin could do something for a man who had suffered at their hands. Sayre wished to align himself not only with Franklin but with Silas Deane, who was engaged in a furious controversy with the Lees that would convulse Congress.[22]

A chilly reply went from the new minister to Sayre. Franklin was pleased to learn that the court of Sweden looked at America with friendly eyes, but he wrote to Sayre, "I saw in the newspapers that a deputy of Congress was in Stockholm; did you obtain the audiences you mention by assuming that character?" He continued, "I am not as you have heard, the sole representative of America in Europe. The commission of Mr. A. Lee, Mr. Wm. Lee, and Mr. [Ralph] Izard, to different courts still subsists. I am sole only with regard to France. Nor have I power to give you any employ worth your accepting."[23]

That cold rebuke was written at the end of March and did not reach its apparently desperate recipient until after he had sent off another appeal to Franklin, dated March 21, still from Copenhagen. Franklin must have wondered whether Sayre was quite sane, for he wrote about his improvements in naval architecture in even more extravagant language than before. To the many virtues of his superior vessel he now added invulnerability in battle: "*She cannot be taken by any ship now in use of any burden or denomination whatever—But shall with certainty ruin the first rate ships in the world, in a very few moments*—nor is there the least probability of losing a single man in the engagement." Making use of her, America could ruin the existing British navy and force Britain to build a new fleet. Sayre had revealed some of his discoveries in Copenhagen but had preserved important secrets. Would Franklin pay the expenses of the inventor to Paris so that he could confidentially describe his achieve-

22. Sayre to Franklin, March 10, 1779, in Franklin Papers, A.P.S. Condemning the Lees, Sayre even suggested that they might sow "fatal seeds" of division in the emerging American nation.

23. Smyth (ed.), *Life and Writings of Benjamin Franklin*, VII, 274.

ments in person? If not, would the minister give him a letter of recommendation to a French official in the West Indies? For, alternatively to
employment in Europe, he would go to the islands and try to "recover an
estate I had in Dominica" en route to the United States. Would France be
willing, he asked, to put Dominica, exposed to capture by the British,
under the protection of Sweden? So doing, France would gain the help of
Sweden, and Dominica would virtually serve as an American port. "I am
now in correspondence with the prime minister of Sweden, on a subject
somewhat of this nature," wrote Sayre. Understandably, Franklin did
not answer.[24]

From Copenhagen came another letter to Franklin, of April 13, in
response to the request for more information regarding Sayre's activities
in Sweden. He had been for many days "confined to my rooms with the
blind piles," had "suffer'd intolerably," but was recovering. His illness
probably resulted from his journey to Stockholm, because of "travelling
night & day without rest." His illness was only part of a remarkable
story. Watching military maneuvers in Copenhagen in the summer of
1778, Sayre had been approached by Swedish onlookers. They had heard
about him—the affair of the theft of the letters by Hugh Elliot had made
the names of Lee and Sayre familiar in the courts of northern Europe. The
Swedes, like many other people, assumed that Sayre might still be an
American agent, and he had neither admitted nor denied that he was
such. Since a secret emissary could not be expected to admit his identity,
his silence was interpreted as proof that he was still in the employ of
Congress. Obviously, Sayre could have convinced them that he was not
an American agent, but he permitted them to deceive themselves. They
had urged him to visit Stockholm, telling him that King Gustavus
would not object. At Stockholm the American had been a guest at a
social assembly, a masquerade attended by many members of the royal
court. "I was order'd to wear a pinck colour'd ribbon in my hat at the
masquerade—to answer a signal &—I was consequently conducted" to
the king's box. There he had "a conference of about half an hour alone"
with Gustavus. The following day, by arrangement of the king, Sayre
conferred with the prime minister and the royal treasurer. There was a
general agreement that Sweden would profit from acquisition of an

24. Sayre to Franklin, March 21, 1779, in Franklin Papers, A.P.S.

island in the Caribbean Sea and that Sweden would act to secure one, short of a rupture in relations with Britain. However, observed Sayre, the prime minister was venal and had made no effort to keep the American in Stockholm for further discussions. Little was said in these meetings about Russia. Once more Sayre declared his intention to make his way to America by way of the Caribbean, departing from a port in Norway.[25]

Such is the background for the claim later advanced by Sayre that he was the originator, or one of the founders, of the League of Armed Neutrality of 1780, of which more will be said later. He was in Denmark, where it originated, at the appropriate time. So far as is known, Sayre did not mention his dream ship to the Swedes. There was, in any event, hardly time for discussion of this subject. It is therefore unlikely that Sayre stimulated Gustavus' interest in naval invention. The Swedish monarch afterward bought a ship devised by a Scottish genius, which had five masts that could be lowered in case of need, a false keel, and wheels under its bow to propel it during calms. Just how the wheels—paddlewheels?—were to be moved does not appear. The vessel became known as "the sea monster." Sayre seems to have had an affinity for individuals interested in naval architecture and engineering as well as hush-hush politicking.[26]

Word of the extraordinary ships crossed the Atlantic and reached General Washington, who was confronted by superior forces of British troops. If those forces could be deprived of reinforcements in men and supplies—if they were denied the help of the British navy—his task would be enormously lightened. "I know not how to think of the invention of Mr. Sayer," he wrote. "It appears a very extraordinary one. I can only wish that the thing may be practicable, and that we may have it in our power to be the first to give it patronage, and to profit by what it promises." Curiosity was rising on both sides of the Atlantic.[27]

25. Sayre to Franklin, April 13, 1779, in *ibid.* Elsewhere Sayre said that he did not act in accordance with the suggestion that he visit Stockholm until an inquiry at the Swedish capital offered evidence that he would be welcomed there.

26. John Brown, *Secret Memoirs of the Courts of Europe: The Courts of Sweden and Denmark* (Philadelphia, 1897), II, 225–26.

27. John C. Fitzpatrick (ed.), *The Writings of George Washington* (Washington, 1931–44), XVII, 225.

Sayre was constantly about to leave Europe, but he did not go. He arrived in Amsterdam on May 17 and immediately wrote to Franklin, again asking for a letter of recommendation that he could carry to the French West Indies. The letter was not forthcoming, and Sayre bombarded the minister with pleas for aid, bringing forward old projects, urging a new one, and offering himself for any suitable service that Franklin might desire in Holland. He had cash or credit. Wrote William Lee, "Mr. Sayre is at Amsterdam which is all I hear of him, except that he had the command of as much money as he chose. How he obtained this I know not." Much of it was apparently lent to Sayre by the Dutch firm of Delalande & Fijnje, who supplied much of the means for building his ship, which he later undertook in partnership with some Russians.[28]

If Sayre was not in immediate financial distress, his future remained clouded. He continued to beg Franklin for help in developing the ship. He now said that parts of it normally made of oak could be constructed of cheaper pine. The military secret that would make it virtually invulnerable he would convey only to Congress, but he wished to show Franklin a model of the vessel. At Sayre's request, two American merchant captains, Alexander Coffin and Joseph Cordis, inspected a model and wrote to Franklin that they endorsed all of Sayre's claims for his craft. The novel scheme that the ingenious Sayre brought before Franklin would from another person have been rather startling. Spain was entering the war as an ally of France. The British navy would be hard pressed, and the garrison forces in Ireland were small. According to Sayre, friends in England had suggested that a small squadron from abroad carrying commissions for Irish leaders could stimulate a successful rebellion, provided that the ships bore an American leader whom the Irish could trust—of course, Sayre himself. Moreover, conquest of England was quite feasible—there were few redcoats there, and the English militia would not fight for George III and his associated oppressors. Would, could, Franklin arrange to provide the necessary fleet? There was an anxious, even desperate note in Sayre's pleas for assistance: "Can your Excellency see the propriety of my services in any manner while I remain here? Am I doom'd to receive no countenance from the country to which

28. Sayre to Franklin, May 17, 1779, in Franklin Papers, A.P.S.; Ford (ed.), *Letters of William Lee*, I, 657; Dávila (ed.), *Archivo del General Miranda*, V, 396.

I sacrifice all private considerations? Others are supported, I know not how, after accusations that, if true, ought to hang them." [29]

Franklin at length permitted Sayre to come to his headquarters at Passy near Paris to display a model of his ship and to apply in person for appointments. The American minister received in late summer a French translation of a letter to Isaac Sears in which Sayre had described his invention—the letter had been intercepted by the British and published in New York and London newspapers. At the end of the description was a note in French that said, "It seems that the Americans have profited by the device of Sayre for seven of their vessels have arrived this summer at Amsterdam and nine others are expected." [30] Sayre might just possibly have a valuable secret or secrets. Sayre also wished to talk to Franklin about a possible invasion of Britain—specifically Ireland. More realistically, he sought letters of marque that would permit him to use his ship as an American privateer. Sayre went to Passy in August, returning to Holland in mid-October.

While waiting for Franklin to act, Sayre was busy in the Dutch capital. Sir Joseph Yorke, the British ambassador, kept an eye on "the noted American agent," who was soon striving to negotiate a loan to the American patriots. Sayre proposed that Dutch investors lend money to Congress, which was in dire need of cash and credits, receiving as security certificates, each of which called for a grant of one hundred acres of land in the interior of the central states. The scheme failed to loosen the purse strings of the prosperous Dutch. Moreover, Sayre was openly received at first only by the merchant Jean de Neufville. However, he stirred friends of America in the Netherlands to action. They were led by Baron Joan Derck Van Der Capellen, who had heard, of course, of the ci-devant sheriff of London and found him to be a man with a heart and a head, frank, open, and formed to manage great affairs. Adherents of the House of Orange favored England as against America, but Dutch people who sought to reduce the power of their dominant family rallied behind Van Der Capellen in behalf of the new republic. Van Der Capellen urged

29. Sayre to Franklin, June 7 and June 9, 1779, Joseph Cordis and Alexander Coffin to Franklin, June 27, 1779, Sayre to Franklin, June 9, 1779, all in Franklin Papers, A.P.S.

30. London *Chronicle*, August 12–14, 1779; "Lettre intéressante imprimée dans les papiers anglois du 16 Août 1779," in Franklin Papers, A.P.S.

that Congress appoint an emissary to The Hague. Congress complied, and John Adams at length appeared. More and more help was extended to the United States by the Dutch republic. Sayre was also busy in a shipyard at the Texel, near Amsterdam, for he was building a "little frigate." Rather, it was being constructed under his direction.[31]

The contemplated invasion of Ireland, so far as Sayre was concerned, faded away. Its chances of success diminished after Britain prepared to meet the new challenge posed by the entrance of Spain and the Spanish fleet into the war. The French waited too long, said Sayre. He regretted the loss of "an honorable employment with the army" because his health was uncertain—was he troubled by hemorrhoids?—but he "would have attended the expedition, tho' under the surgeon's hands." Nor was Franklin carried away by enthusiasm for the naval inventions of his fellow American. The minister inspected a plan of the revolutionary vessel and rather doubted that it would assure the success of the revolution in America. He did consent, however, to give Sayre a commission to go a-privateering with his little frigate—provided that Sayre could supply bond for two thousand pounds against law suits that might arise from privateering (Congress required such a bond to protect the United States against claims). The night before he left Paris, Sayre learned of another possibility. John Paul Jones had brought H.M.S. *Serapis* into Dutch waters after his famous capture of that warship with the *Bon Homme Richard*. Pierre Landais, the French captain of the *Alliance*, had not only failed to assist Jones against the *Serapis*, but had actually fired a few shots into the *Bon Homme Richard*. Sayre was told that Landais would be discharged. From Valenciennes, on his way to Amsterdam, he wrote to Franklin, "If that event should take place, I should think myself happy to succeed him in the command of her. I hope your Excellency can have no apprehension that I should in any shape, or under any circumstances, disgrace the American flagg."[32]

---

31. Friedrich Edler, *The Dutch Republic and the American Revolution*, Johns Hopkins Studies in Historical and Political Science, Series XXIX, No. 2 (Baltimore, 1911), 80–81. The loan plan is published in W. H. De Beaufort (ed.), *Brieven Von En Aan Joan Derck Van Der Capellen Van De Poll* (Utrecht, 1879), 154–57, 106.

32. De Beaufort (ed.), *Brieven*, 157–58; Sayre to Franklin, October 10, 1779, in Franklin Papers, A.P.S. Sayre believed that Franklin was prejudiced against the naval invention by the opinion of his friend in Holland, Charles G. F. Dumas, who was

Pierre Landais was a very strange man. He was unbelievably cross-grained, at least half-mad. He should have been superseded, but he kept his command. Sayre must have been keenly disappointed. At least he had the consolation that his enemies, the Lee brothers, had been discharged by Congress and that Arthur went home on the *Alliance*. Richard Henry Lee had resigned from his seat in Congress, and without his support his siblings could not keep office in Europe—Arthur Lee had done his best to make life miserable for Franklin as well as Sayre. It is to be suspected that as commander of the *Alliance* Sayre would have found Arthur Lee impossible in forced intimacy at sea and would have meditated dropping him overboard. On the *Alliance* that quarrelsome American engaged in a nasty altercation with the sullen Landais, and the French captain gave evidence of his displeasure with Lee and the world by letting his ship drift idly for five days off Newfoundland. Eventually, the ship did deposit Arthur Lee in Boston, and soon thereafter—at last—Landais' follies led to his discharge.[33]

Nor did Sayre secure his letter of marque from Franklin, and he asked for it again in a letter of November 21. "Your grand son[34] made a memorandum to forward it by the next post after my departure." The letter of marque was denied because Sayre had not offered proof of financial responsibility. He had offered the names of two Paris bankers, one of them Isaac Panchaud, for securities, but neither man agreed to sponsor Sayre.[35]

Sayre felt it was unjust to ask for evidence of such responsibility from a man who could not supply it, who had suffered bankruptcy because of

---

stigmatized by Sayre as a "shoemaker." It was a little odd that the son of a Long Island villager who made and repaired shoes should sneer at another man who began life in that same economic activity.

33. Samuel E. Morison, in *John Paul Jones: A Sailor's Biography* (Boston, 1959), 253–54, mishandles Sayre's situation. He believed that Sayre, because of his quarrel with Arthur Lee, "retained from that association a bitter hatred for Franklin and all his works." Morison also found Sayre guilty of "impudence" in seeking to replace Landais. Sayre evidently had little other direct contact with Jones. There is an account of the bizarre incident aboard the *Alliance* in Potts, "Arthur Lee: American Revolutionary."

34. William Temple Franklin, who acted as secretary to his grandfather.

35. Sayre to Franklin, November 21, 1779, in Franklin Papers, A.P.S.; Franklin to Charles Dumas, November 8, 1779, in Francis Wharton (ed.), *The Revolutionary Diplomatic Correspondence of the United States* (Washington, 1882–89), I, 616.

his devotion to the cause. There had been so many applications, so many rejections. At last Sayre turned momentarily and venomously against Franklin. Sayre was in touch with the Lee brothers before the departure of Arthur, and it is to be suspected that he imbibed the ugly suspicions the lawyer had long harbored with respect to his colleague. Arthur Lee went so far as to question Franklin's loyalty to the American republic, a preposterous notion. There were, to be sure, several British spies in Paris who had infiltrated the American service, one of them a secretary of Commissioner Lee. More plausibly, Lee accused Jonathan Williams, an American purchasing agent, of cheating the United States. But Lee also then charged Franklin with the same crime, because Williams was a grandnephew of Franklin. Sayre repeated that charge in a letter to Baron Van Der Capellen in December, 1779. The story had it that Williams cheaply bought thousands of French muskets that had been condemned as unfit for use and charged the United States a high price for them. Said Sayre rhetorically, "They were sent to America to defend the most glorious cause the sun ever saw—the unhappy men who used them, had hearts but no arms, & of course were sacrificed. The French officers in America who saw & knew the arms, will tell you the story now, with tears in their eyes." But, Sayre continued, Williams "is, more than ever, now patronized by that great villain, who is his uncle." It had become clear to Sayre that Franklin would not willingly do anything in his behalf. This letter, however, was written when he was afflicted by a fever.[36]

Later, in tranquillity and with perspective, Sayre declared that Franklin was the only truly qualified diplomat in the service of Congress during the War of Independence—a defensible judgment, despite the praise heaped by admirers upon John Adams and John Jay.

In an 1803 letter to William Duane, Sayre amusingly estimated some early American diplomats often praised for their sterling performances:

God knows; the ministers we have sent to Europe (Mr. Franklin & Jefferson excepted) have, till of late, made us appear very contemptible, as far as they have been seen & known. One sent us bad arms—another spent his time, & the public money, in coarse embraces of common prostitutes—another

36. William Graham Sumner, *The Financier and the Finances of the American Revolution* (New York, 1891), I, 219; De Beaufort (ed.), *Brieven*, 162–63.

immersed himself in a hutt of 50 dollars a year to save his salary of £2000, & his other perquisites of £2500 sterling per an: allowed him thro' family intrigue. . . . Another, mistaking the patience of his guests for approbation talked always of himself. Another pressed important business to issue when it was clearly in our interest to delay it—his double salary would have been better earned had he slept till his return. Another was a teacher of music to little girls, and admitted to a gentleman's table when little Miss might ask it as a favor. Another was kept at a distant court at £1500 sterling per an: to learn the French language. I do not mean to call in question the fitness & talents of Mr. Lawrence [Henry Laurens]—having been made a prisoner, he had no opportunity for exertion—nor do I dispute the qualifications of Mr. Gouverneur Morris—he is a man of the world—speaks the French language with ease & accuracy—but his appointment was unfortunately ill-timed—his hardy front would grace the levee of Bonaparte or the Great Mogul, but it did not accord with the taste of the sans coulottes.

Jonathan Williams was the man who sent bad arms, Arthur Lee the person who should have slept, William Lee the miser, and Francis Dana the man paid for learning French.[37]

The little frigate also brought disappointment to the unhappy Sayre. Late in October, he expected that it could be launched at the beginning of November and that it could go to sea about two weeks later. His contractor was even planning to build a second vessel. But ships seldom leave the ways on schedule. In mid-December he had a crew, chiefly Americans, and the naval marvel was to sail with the first fair wind. But he was worried: "The carpenter, contrary to my plan, took it into his head to put six-pieces of timber runing upwards & downwards on the inside, instead of planking her on the outside from head to stern. I fear those timbers are not sufficient to hold the ribs together, for if they seperate she will leak." Messrs. Delalande & Fijnje had permitted the carpenter-builder to have his way despite repeated orders from Sayre to plank the vessel. There were delays in construction until ice prevented launching, and the builder refused to rectify the error that Sayre perceived. Then the fever that had plagued Sayre returned. He had hoped that he would be able to sail to Philadelphia, that Captain Coffin would follow him across the ocean with a larger version of the superior ship. He

37. Sayre to William Duane, August 4, 1803, in Duane Papers.

proposed that Baron Van Der Capellen emigrate to the New World. Then it became apparent that "his construction did not answer." The ship did not go to sea, nor did Sayre cross the Atlantic. Instead, he turned eastward, leaving behind him a debt owed to Delalande & Fijnje. He was in St. Petersburg before the coming of spring.[38]

38. De Beaufort (ed.), *Brieven*, 158, 162–64, 170–71, 240; Dávila (ed.), *Archivo del General Miranda*, V, 396.

8
The Wanderer in Russia

ATHERINE the Great, a widow, ruled the Russian empire with a firm hand after her husband was murdered—it was believed that there was blood of the recent tsar upon that hand. The German-born tsarina was intelligent, bold, unscrupulous, and more or less enlightened in comparison with most of the European rulers of her time. Passing her fiftieth birthday in 1779, she was notorious for her robust charms and a long list of lovers. Utterly cynical, she had taken a slice of Poland in the first partition of that unhappy country.

Catherine had contemptuously refused to sell the services of Russian troops to Britain for use against the American rebels. She possessed a fleet of sorts, as well as an army, and, like other European rulers, was vexed by interference with Russian maritime commerce by the British navy. On February 28, 1780, Catherine formally announced that an armed Russia would insist upon the rights of its neutral citizens and ships upon the seas as against other nations at war—in effect, against Britain. For the British were doing what they could to choke France, Spain, and the American rebels by use of their navy, and they were accustomed to deal roughly with neutrals who tried to carry arms, masts, spars, and other military materials to their enemies.

A few weeks after Catherine's announcement, Stephen Sayre turned up in St. Petersburg and began to build ships. Catherine did not intend to go to war against Britain, nor did she expect to be forced into hostilities, but who could say that such a war would not come? She had been enlarging her fleet, and she obviously would not be offended if ships superior to those of the British could be launched under the Russian flag. Consequently, she did not drive the inventor away from Russian harbors. As usual, Sayre did not toil only at ship architecture. He once more sought to arrange for a free port in the Caribbean through which America could secure supplies—this time with the free port under Russian control.

If Catherine sought to alarm Britain, she succeeded. In the summer of 1780, Christian VI and Gustavus III joined Catherine in a League of Armed Neutrality. Other European rulers joined it later. The British had reason to be watchful at St. Petersburg, and they were. Sir James Harris, the British ambassador at Catherine's court, was an able, devoted, and determined diplomat. He was, moreover, the brother-in-law of Hugh Elliot—not a favorable augury for Sayre. On April 17 Harris reported in a letter home: "There arrived here about a week ago an Englishman by the name of Smith. From his language, way of living, and behavior, there are strong suspicions of his being either an American or a rebel agent." Sayre pretended to be a resident of one of the Caribbean islands, said Harris. The British envoy may not immediately have identified the newcomer as the former sheriff of London and secretary of Arthur Lee, but he knew enough about him to be suitably on guard. He soon discovered that "Smith" was Sayre. The chevalier de Corberon, the French chargé d'affaires at the Russian court, also soon became aware of the real name of the briefly mysterious new resident of St. Petersburg.[1]

Harris sent fascinating reports back to London concerning the newcomer. "No Englishman is known to him. He has called on the French charge d'affaires, who does not choose to trust him." Early on, Harris believed that "as he meets with no encouragement anywhere, I flatter myself he will depart without my giving him consequence by ministerial interposition." The Englishman continued to write in similar vein:

> Sayre, after having employed various methods to gain importance and to excite curiosity, seems at last resolved to leave us. He said before one of the persons I had set about him that he was sent on a fool's errand; that he had succeeded in nothing, and was only making himself ridiculous by staying here. It does not appear that he was in any shape accredited by the Congress, or come with any other view than to try the ground. I am told that he is

1. This account of Sayre's adventures in Russia, except as otherwise indicated, is based on Griffiths, "American Commercial Diplomacy in Russia," 384–89. For the report of Corberon, see L. H. Labande, *Un Diplomate Français à la Cour de Cathérine II, 1775–1780* (Paris, 1901), II, 307–308.

plausible, impudent, and indiscreet, with better parts than judgment, enterprising in forming a bold project, but unequal to its execution.

Said Harris, "He bears every feature of a rebellious adventurer, but is without those qualities requisite to obtain the confidence even of his own party. I am convinced had he remained here no inconvenience would have attended it; but it is known that he departs disappointed and dissatisfied."

The judgment of Sayre formed by Harris was not entirely unsound. The British minister also related that Sayre made an effort to secure help from the duchess of Kingston, who happened to be at St. Petersburg in the spring of 1780. She was declassée in England, where, once upon a time, she had appeared in public wearing a gown so diaphanous above the waist that she had shocked even British aristocrats not easily disturbed by the misbehavior of one of their class. The duchess had also married a second time while still legally bound to her first husband, and had escaped imprisonment only because of her rank and a legal technicality. Probably she still had money. Had Sayre known her in England? He tried to borrow money from her but did not succeed.[2]

Was Sayre actually downhearted? Did he intend to leave Russia, as Harris believed? Sayre would have been discouraged had he paid sufficient attention to a decree of the tsarina that forbade Russian merchants to serve as formal owners of vessels that actually belonged to foreigners. But the atmosphere in St. Petersburg was Byzantine in more than religion—what Catherine wanted, Catherine might seem to oppose. Her two principal ministers were ostensibly at odds on policy, with Count Panin disposed to favor America, Prussia, France, and Spain, and Prince Potemkin, once a lover of Catherine, pretending to be a friend of Britain. The empress did not arrange to grant Sayre an audience—an act that would have given Britain cause for protest—and his jest regarding conversion of the empress into a friend of America by use of his masculine charms remained a pleasantry. But Catherine did nothing immediately to interfere with his activities, and he believed that she would not prevent them from succeeding.

Sayre became busy soon after his arrival. He had, Harris was told, the verbal and financial support of Van Brienen, the Dutch resident in St.

2. Wharton (ed.), *Revolutionary Diplomatic Correspondence of the United States*, I, 617.

Petersburg, and he received financial assistance from Delalande & Fijnje.
He was before long proposing that Catherine establish a colony—and, of
course, a free port—on an uninhabited island near the Dutch territory of
Surinam. Russian hemp and sailcloth could be exchanged at the colony
for American rice and indigo, and it would also be possible for Russia
profitably to secure sugar, cotton, and coffee through possession of the
island. The scheme was presented to Catherine through one of her
economic advisers, A. R. Vorontzov, president of the College of Commerce. The empress rejected it disdainfully and contemptuously, learned
Harris. Even so, Sir James did not relax his vigilance. "Unless I saw here
every day fresh and unheard of extravagances," he said, "I should not
think his ridiculous plan deserved a moment's attention." But Catherine
was indeed wary of committing ships and money to a venture more likely
to bring British wrath than rubles, francs, or Spanish dollars. She might
take another slice or two of Poland or think of driving the heathen Turks
back into Asia Minor, but she would not undertake risky adventures in
distant seas, eastern or western, by Sayre in partnership with a Russian
army officer named Arseniev who had been an aide to the head of the
imperial navy—this even though, according to Sayre, he had the support of Prince Niswitzky and General Borodin.[3]

The chevalier de Corberon was not impressed by Arseniev and considered him vivacious rather than sound. It is possible that Arseniev had
also been earlier a Russian partner of Sayre in Holland. In any case, the
two men received the consent of the Russian admiralty to establish a
shipyard on the banks of the Neva River, and they leased ground from a
brewer who lived nearby and began to erect their works. Then, according to Corberon, an Englishman approached the brewer, who was in debt
and had signed notes that were due. The brewer was told that he must
either break the lease or pay the notes immediately. He could not meet
the obligation, and he was threatened with financial ruin. The brewer
asked the partners to abandon their lease, but they refused. Suspecting
that their works were menaced, Sayre and Arseniev employed guards to
protect their shipyard. However, a few days later, during the evening
of June 28, both the brewer's house and the shipyard were destroyed
by fire.

3. Sayre to Washington, October 15, 1790, in Department of State, Miscellaneous
Letters; Sayre to John Adams, October 21, 1780, in Adams Family Papers.

Sayre and Corberon were convinced that Harris had arranged the conflagration. Count Panin could hardly believe that Harris would so grossly abuse his diplomatic privilege. Sayre appealed to the empress for redress. Through Count Potemkin, Sir James protested his utter innocence. He opened a counterattack, describing Sayre "in his true colors" as a speculator and a spy. Panin asserted that the fire was begun by English sailors. Van Brienen and the Prussian envoy declared that the charge of incendiarism was justified, and the belief that Harris was guilty spread through the Baltic world. Then a different explanation was brought forward—that the fire had come from the shop of a neighboring blacksmith. The empress assured Harris of her belief in his innocence— the charge spread by the American made no impression upon her, "*ils ne font aucune impression sur moi*"—and she declined to take formal notice of the accusation from Sayre. Did Catherine know that Harris was the brother-in-law of Hugh Elliot, or that Sayre had been claiming to be able to make great improvements in sailing ships, so that it might be worthwhile to interrupt his labors?[4]

Arseniev and Sayre would not let Harris or the fire stop them. They began their shipyard anew, and they laid the keels for two vessels, employing a Russian ship carpenter who had acquired expertise in England. Harris consoled himself with the belief that the enterprise could not succeed, that the facilities for launching the vessels were inadequate, and that they would not go to sea. The empress pleased Harris by a formal warning to Arseniev that he could not have both Sayre as a partner and the protection of the Russian flag. There was indeed a danger that Russia would become embroiled with Britain if the partners were allowed to proceed.[5]

The empress found another reason to be concerned about the American. She received an intercepted letter written at Archangel from an

4. Sayre to John Adams, October 21, 1780, in Adams Family Papers; Earl of Malmesbury (ed.), *Diaries and Correspondence of James Harris, First Earl of Malmesbury* (London, 1844), I, 327–29.

5. Afterward, as will appear, Sayre often magnified his own importance. There is a splendid example of his boasting in a letter he wrote to Albert Gallatin on June 30, 1801, in the Albert Gallatin Papers, New-York Historical Society, New York. Among other very dubious statements, Sayre claimed that Harris reproached Count Panin for permitting a dangerous agent of Congress to remain in St. Petersburg.

"Englishman" named "Alexander Bell" and addressed to Benjamin Franklin, which mentioned the building of a ship for the American cause.[6] "Alexander Bell" was, of course, Sayre, trying to reopen correspondence with Franklin. Catherine warned her governor-general in Archangel that it would be illegal to build a ship that would aid the rebels against George III—and perhaps against other rulers. What was Sayre doing in the far northern port of Archangel in the summer of 1780? A vessel could rather easily elude the British navy by sailing through the broad waters north of the British Isles. Was he, by any chance, thinking of using Archangel as a base for whaling? Whatever his motivation, he did not long remain on the shores of the Arctic. Perhaps frigid Archangel cooled even Sayre's ardent and speculative spirit.

Moreover, it turned out that the empress meant what she said when she asserted that she would not permit Arseniev and "Smith" to operate their vessels under the Russian flag. In consequence, Sayre was compelled to let the ships become the property of Arseniev. Afterward, Sayre declared that he had hoped to sail in one of them for America but had not dared to undertake the voyage while the war continued, for fear of capture by the British. He did complete two vessels of 1,200 tons each and sent them with cargoes of hemp, masts, and other materials to France in 1782. The ships made other later voyages to France and also to India. It is likely, as Sayre later indicated, that he was trapped by the Russians, cheated, and forced out of a profitable enterprise. He came out of the venture owing money to Delalande & Fijnje.[7]

SAYRE also sought, and failed, to secure an appointment as an American emissary to the court of St. Petersburg. John Adams became one of the American commissioners in Europe in 1778 and was temporarily entrusted with the task of making peace with Britain in September, 1780. Adams had been toiling in Amsterdam in an effort to get Dutch aid when he received a proposal from Sayre to circumvent the British

6. Catherine to Aleksis Petrovich, December 9, 1780. A translation of the letter has been supplied by Ronald D. Landa, with a citation to *Iaroslavskie Gubernskie Vedomosti* (1874), No. 23. Franklin apparently did not receive the letter.

7. Dávila (ed.), *Archivo del General Miranda*, V, 396–97; Sayre to Washington, December 10, 1793, in Department of State, Miscellaneous Letters; Sayre, *A Short Narrative*.

naval blockade by developing a trade between the United States and Russia via an island in the West Indies. "I make no apology for troubling you with a letter," wrote Sayre on October 21,

> because your Excellency must know me by reputation, & because the purport of it is of a public nature. As to myself, I trust, you must be persuaded, there is not an American now in arms, more ardent in our cause—I am sure none can have more reason to detest the British government. When I left Great Britain, I did it with a full determination of risqing my life in service, either by sea or land. Unfortunately, those gentlemen who directed our affairs on the Continent could not agree how I should be employ'd—nor did they give me any reason to hope for release, should I have been made prisoner on my way to America. The hazard at that time was extremely great and I well know that if once I fell into the hands of the English my treatment must have been fatally cruel.

Accordingly, Sayre continued, he resolved to do all that he could for America in Europe. Forced to act as a private citizen, he had made many friends for his own country while engaged in commerce. His Russian friends, the prince and the general, had been promised the protection of the Russian navy by the empress herself for mercantile voyages to France. Could Adams act to enable the sending of Russian naval stores from France to American waters?[8]

Adams sent a reply that committed him to nothing whatever. He agreed that a trade between Russia and America by way of the West Indies would be valuable to the new republic, but he wondered why the empress did not insist upon a direct exchange—even if a challenge of the British blockade led to war between Russia and Britain. Sayre indicated that Catherine might go so far as to let his ships go to France with the secret understanding that they would then proceed with the blessing of France to North America. Would Adams move to secure French assistance? The indolent Franklin would do nothing to obtain it, Sayre believed, unless Adams urged him on. Indeed, nothing much could be achieved in Europe, said Sayre, without action by Franklin. "I have always found such coldness in application, & such insupportable negligence, as to every matter I proposed to him, as to discourage me from all

8. Sayre to John Adams, October 21, 1780, in Adams Family Papers.

future intercourse." He had received no encouragement from Franklin, even though the British had arranged to burn his ship and to attack him in every way possible. "I have been an evidence of the unbounded corruption of that abominable court of Great Britain for many years. No wickedness or villainy stands in their way—they are profligate & abandon'd from the King to the doorkeeper." Harris followed "strictly the system of his court, therefore I have everything to dread. I am obliged to have a guard & 4 sentinels constantly on the watch. I am obliged to go perpetually arm'd, for I am hourly inform'd that I must expect every mischeif that money and hate can effect." Sayre indicated that he expected to be in Amsterdam in June of the following year and to spend some time thereafter in Bordeaux. If Adams believed that Sayre could be of service to America in St. Petersburg, Sayre was willing to return there as a commercial agent. He was also prepared to remain in Bordeaux until Congress could act upon a recommendation from Adams for such an appointment.[9]

Sayre was not able to leave the Russian capital until the following autumn. Nor did Adams do anything for him. Adams did arrange to place an American emissary on the banks of the Neva, but the man who appeared there was his secretary and protegé, young Francis Dana of Massachusetts, who traveled eastward in the following summer accompanied by an even younger Adams offspring, John Quincy. John Adams prided himself upon his virtue, but he looked after his own. Dana arrived in St. Petersburg in August, 1781. He wrote in a letter of October 22 to the older Adams that Sayre, who was to set out the following day, would deliver the epistle in Amsterdam. "He knows nothing from me about my business or affairs," reported Dana. He had had little to do with Sayre, who had been "unfortunately confined by sickness almost the whole time I have been here." Dana also naïvely remarked that Sayre had failed to perceive that the Russian empress was friendly toward America—presumably Sayre had tried to warn him not to be taken in by sweet words from her and her ministers. Dana would soon learn that Catherine was cold-blooded so far as the making of policy was concerned. Sayre afterward pointed out that Dana was not fitted for his post: he had

9. Sayre to Adams, December 30, 1780, in *ibid*. Sayre perceived the enormous economic possibilities of Russia.

had little worldly experience, and he was compelled to take lessons in French after his arrival in St. Petersburg. Sayre, on the other hand, had acquired at least a smattering of the language of diplomacy before he went to Russia.[10]

Something more should be said about the lack of intimacy between Sayre and the empress. Her amours were the talk of Europe. In 1787 the London *Times* published a remarkably ribald squib concerning her fondness for men, and it will be recalled that Lord Byron's Don Juan was a fictional lover of the mistress of all the Russias. Several years after Sayre's departure from St. Petersburg, his friend Francisco de Miranda, the South American revolutionist, visited Russia and created a very favorable impression upon Catherine. She gave him generous presents, and she instructed her envoys to do everything possible to smooth Miranda's journeys in Europe. The lady was at that time approaching the end of the fifth decade of her life, but there was much speculation in various quarters regarding the relationship between the Latin American and the empress. In 1806, Tom Paine reported concerning a conversation with Miranda that the revolutionist did not mention "his affair with old Catharine of Russia nor did I tell him that I knew of it." It is therefore no cause for astonishment that Sayre had comment to make. Miranda was comely enough, quite dark in color, hazel-eyed, about five feet, ten inches in height. Sayre wrote in June, 1789, from London to Samuel Ogden, a prominent New York merchant, for the benefit of their mutual friend, General Henry Knox, as well as Ogden himself, that "Miranda dined with me two days since & the day after his return from Paris. His prejudices are still the same against the French nation, & their manners. He has, however, travel'd to great advantage—nothing has escaped his penetration—not even; the Empress of all the Russias, as I believe—a mortifying declaration for me to make, who was 21 months in her capital without ever making my self acquainted with the internal parts of *her extensive & well known dominions*." Sayre had an excuse for his failure to make a conquest of the empress: "My vanity furnishes a reason for this superior good fortune. He speaks French well—I spoke it ill. I do not admit his figure, or his address, where a woman is to decide, to be very clearly on his side. But seriously, he has such letters, to all her ambas-

10. Adams (ed.), *Works of John Adams*, VII, 468; Sayre to Washington, October 15, 1789, in Department of State, Miscellaneous Letters.

sadors, as no other man ever received from a crown'd head—they command every thing he may wish or desire. He talks of returning to Russia." Sayre continued, "I would never have left it, under the same circumstances, for I am fool enough to get in love, where I get into favour." [11]

There was another and amusing repercussion from Sayre's sojourn in Russia. Mercy Otis Warren, writing her well-known history of the American Revolution, exhibited spleen against John Adams. Sufficiently solicitous for appointments to office of his kin, Adams did little to reward the Otises and Warrens who had helped him up the political ladder. Mrs. Warren would have it that Francis Dana was not ideally suited for his mission in St. Petersburg: he was a person of sterling worth but did not possess a very pleasing personality—like Adams himself. She said that he accomplished nothing in the Russian capital and that even at the time of his appointment "it was thought that he had not either the address, the penetration, the knowledge of courts, or of the human character, necessary for a negotiator at the court of a despotic female at the head of a nation of machines, under the absolute control of herself and her favorites." She asserted that distinguished talents as well as a pleasing address were peculiarly necessary in St. Petersburg "both from the character of the nation and the monarch." The Baltic had been opened to neutral shipping, despite British complaints, before Dana reached Russia.

That hostile assessment of Dana was accompanied by faint praise of Adams himself. He performed very well in Holland among unsophisticated Dutchmen, Mrs. Warren claimed, but he was not of much use in Paris because he was "deficient in the *je ne sais quoi*, so necessary in highly polished society." Adams, ever jealous of his own repute, became furious. Did he think she was familiar with bawdiness? He wrote to Mrs. Warren, protesting that she was unfair to him and also to his young friend. Dana was a worthy envoy, and it was not his fault that Catherine refused to receive him as American minister—no European ruler received an American envoy until independence was assured. (Adams apparently did not know that Gustavus III had talked at least briefly to Sayre.) He went on to condemn Sayre without naming him. It was true,

11. Virginia *Argus*, April 11, 1806; Sayre to Samuel Ogden, June 29, 1789, in Knox Papers.

he said, that "the grand autocratice" had "an animal weakness," such
that, it was believed, "she had sometimes conversed with strangers from
other motives than curiosity or policy, but not publicly." She had never
"that we hear or read of, acknowledged the independence of a new nation
for the sake of such interviews. I blush for my country too. A certain
native of America, who had been, as he thought, a great man in Europe,
and who thought himself, and was thought by some others, to be the
handsomest man in the world, both in face and figure, as well as the man
of the most polished manners and irresistible address,—this gentleman
made a voyage or a journey, or both, to Petersburg, in hopes of obtaining
an audience of the autocratice *for the benefit of his country*." But, wrote
Adams, "neither the face nor the figure nor the address could procure a
glance or an ogle from her." The nasty and unfair comment upon
Sayre—Adams would perhaps have been less hostile to personal beauty
had he possessed more of it himself—puzzled Mrs. Warren. She sent
him a stiff reply. What in the world was Adams talking about? She had
not the faintest notion; she knew nothing about the gentleman so much
criticized; she was merely weighing the merits of Dana in Russia. Did
Adams blush? She gave him further cause for unhappiness—she bluntly
accused him of a display of ingratitude toward the Otises and Warrens.[12]

It is likely that Adams cared no more for Sayre in 1781 than he did
twenty years later. Adams had great respect for his political allies,
the Lees, and had doubtless imbibed some of their hostility toward the
New Yorker.

Sayre should have reached Amsterdam in November—did he go
there in part in order to explain to Delalande & Fijnje that returns from
their investment in him would be delayed? Certainly he did not stay long
at the capital city of Holland, because he was in Paris early in February,
1782. Wrote Mrs. Ralph Izard from Paris on February 10: "Mr. Sayre
called on me about a week ago. I have not seen or heard of him since."[13]

12. Mercy Warren, *History of the Rise, Progress and Termination of the American Revolution* (Boston, 1805), II, 301–305, III, 176–77; Charles Francis Adams (ed.), "Correspondence Between John Adams and Mercy Warren, Relating to Her 'History of the
American Revolution,' July–August, 1807," *Collections of the Massachusetts Historical
Society*, 5th Ser., IV (1885), 445, 454–56.

13. "Letters from Mrs. Ralph Izard to Mrs. William Lee," *Virginia Magazine of
History and Biography*, VIII (1900–1901), 22.

Sayre must have learned before that time of the surrender of Lord Cornwallis and his British army at Yorktown. Before long, it became apparent that the war was winding down in America and that the Patriots had won their independence. The royal forces were dwindling beyond the Atlantic, and England could raise no more troops to replace losses. Parliament solemnly pledged to look upon anyone in government as a traitor who should urge offensive operations against the Americans, and at last Lord North and his cabinet fell. Patriot emissaries in Paris, where peace negotiations began, could hardly fail to obtain independence upon favorable terms.

Franklin, John Adams, and John Jay were the principal spokesmen for the United States, and they were compelled to consider many proposals. Franklin received one that may have seemed bizarre to him. Sayre was a guest at a great party given by the duchesse de Grammont to celebrate the victory over Cornwallis, where Franklin was enthusiastically acclaimed by the guests.[14] Ought not something to be done for another Patriot who had sacrificed much more than the Philadelphian, without reward? Presumably Sayre learned then, earlier, or later that the dean of the American emissaries was not a thoroughgoing rascal. He wrote to Franklin on June 12, proposing that a free port be established in Puerto Rico. Would not appointment of Sayre as governor of the island—a Spanish possession not likely to become the property of the United States—be suitable? Franklin may not have replied to the appeal for office.

Sayre must have considered returning to England, the more so in that his wife was with him in Paris in the early autumn of 1782. Apparently they were separated until the war began to die down, with Elizabeth remaining in England while her husband roamed about the Continent for five years. She was living with him in the Rue de Richelieu when Frederic Reynolds, son of Sayre's lawyer and friend in London, a young man then still under eighteen years of age but afterward a very successful playwright, went to the Continent in August to try to secure payment of a debt owed by Lord Grandison to the attorney. Succeeding in his mission at a spa in Belgium, young Reynolds sent the money back to his father and traveled on to Paris to see the sights. With little money to

14. Reynolds, *Life and Times of Frederic Reynolds*, I, 231.

spend, he hoped that Sayre would assist him. His confidence was justified. He received from Sayre "a most kind and friendly reception.
Though his stocks were then, nearly as low as mine, he lent me five
guineas; at the same time, reminded me, that he owed my father, nearly
as many thousands. I dined with him, and Mrs. Sayre, to whom he was
'rather married.'" In the evening Sayre took young Reynolds to the Fair
of St. Lawrence, an amusement place. Frederic Reynolds, like so many
people, commented regarding Sayre upon "the remarkable handsome-
ness of his person." He was "a most conspicuous personage," even when
he was in rather awkward circumstances. Sayre also arranged for the safe
return to England of young Reynolds, who had come away without a
passport. An American, Elkanah Watson, was in Paris, about to leave for
London. Sayre arranged for Reynolds to travel as a servant with Watson
in his coach, a device that proved successful. In his later years, Reynolds
remembered Sayre as "my kind friend."[15]

If Frederic Reynolds recorded in his diary that Sayre was "rather
married"—that he was henpecked—one must recall that the presence of
the young man reminded Elizabeth Sayre of her husband's sojourn in the
Tower and of his bankruptcy. She could not but feel a revival of memory
of those humiliating events. Did she wish that he would return with her
to England, where she still had inherited property rights?[16] Moreover,
the political situation had changed. Lord Rockingham and then Lord
Shelburne, men not hostile to Sayre, followed North as prime ministers.
Sayre could return to London, if not as a conquering hero, at least as a
man associated with victors, however disliked they might be in some
English quarters.

Sayre's ties with the American republic brought him profits of one
sort or another, but they were psychic rather than monetary. Moreover,
they had entailed disappointment and grief. So far as influential personal
connections were concerned, they might turn him toward England

15. I have seen no reference to Elizabeth Sayre from 1777 to 1782. She could hardly
have accompanied her husband on all his adventures on the Continent. *Ibid.*, I, 174,
218–19, 227–30, 243–45; Elkanah Watson, *Men and Times of the Revolution; or,
Memoirs of Elkanah Watson*, ed. Winslow C. Watson (2nd ed.; New York, 1856),
164–66.

16. John Nichols, *Literary Anecdotes of the Eighteenth Century* (London, 1812–15),
VIII, 660, mentions that the heirs of Judge Noel still owned a large house in Stamford.

rather than America. He had no intimate friend in a position of power beyond the Atlantic, and his acquaintances there had dwindled during an absence of fifteen years. Besides, his mother died on June 5 at the age of eighty-nine. Several of his siblings were still alive, and he had many nieces and nephews in the United States. His older brother Matthew, after serving as a lieutenant in the American army, lived until 1819.[17] The Sayres and closely allied families—Howells, Hallocks, and Halseys—were multiplying, but Stephen's experiences in the great world had taken him far from the simple life of eastern Long Island and its ways of thought and behavior. He might prefer life in England for its comforts and luxuries.

However, Sayre hoped that his services to the new nation would be rewarded by men in power in America more appreciative of his merits and sacrifices than had been her emissaries in Europe. Besides, there might be political and economic opportunity in his native land for a gifted man still in his forties, still ambitious. In the upshot, Sayre chose once more to cast his lot with the United States, and he apparently parted again from his wife. He sailed for America without her, and they were separated for more than two years—at least, no record has been found of her presence in the New World during that period. It may be that she refused to go to America.

Sayre encountered one more disappointment before the war officially ended. As the year 1782 drew toward its close, he was in Bordeaux preparing to sail for America with Captain Hallet on the *Minerva*, a British vessel that had been captured by John Paul Jones. Learning that the Patriot emissaries had secured a preliminary treaty, signed on November 5, which guaranteed American independence, Sayre wrote twice to John Jay, a fellow New Yorker, to ask for a copy of it. If he could not have a copy, could he have a statement from Jay as proof that the document had been ratified? He told Jay that he did not submit his request to Franklin because Franklin would not reply. Sayre wished to have evidence that the war was ending so as to ward off possible British recapture of the *Minerva* on the ocean. There was still, he feared, a possibility that he would enter upon a second residence in the Tower if he fell into British hands. But Sayre also desired the privilege of carrying

17. Banta, *Sayre Family*, 53, 88.

the splendid news to Congress. Jay replied that the war would not come to a close until all the parties engaged in it consented to arrangements for peace, and he declined to supply the terms of the preliminary agreement.[18] Sayre could report that it had indeed been endorsed, and he could say that independence, though not formally acknowledged by Britain, had been achieved. But he did not come home as a conquering diplomatic hero when he landed in America in 1783.

18. Sayre to John Jay, December 10, 1782, in Henry P. Johnston (ed.), *The Correspondence and Public Papers of John Jay* (New York, 1891), III, 5, 8.

9

The Prisoner for Debt

HE AMERICA to which Stephen Sayre returned in 1783 was not the America he had left seventeen years earlier. The emerging nation had its war wounds. Its distant future, at least to a perceptive observer, was bright; for the time being, however, it was in disorder. British forces remained in New York City until December, 1783. Commerce was restricted and confused by the expenses of war, and inflation added to trade woes. Because of lack of money, Congress was barely able to offer enough in the way of pay and other rewards to persuade its troops to disband and go home. Congress itself wandered from Philadelphia to Princeton to Annapolis to Trenton and then to New York; it barely secured a quorum at Annapolis in the spring of 1784 permitting final signature of the treaty of peace.

Waiting for a suitable opportunity to ask Congress to reward him, Sayre settled in New York City. Before the end of 1783 he was admitted to a "Dancing Assembly" there with Colonel William Stephens Smith, Francisco de Miranda, and various gentlemen. He soon made many other new acquaintances, among them General Henry Knox, William Duer, Chancellor Robert R. Livingston, John Stevens, Alexander Hamilton, and Samuel Ogden, and he renewed his friendship with Isaac Sears. Establishing himself as a merchant, Sayre was one of forty charter members of the Chamber of Commerce, formed in April, 1784. But it was already obvious that repercussions from his English bankruptcy would hurt him in America.[1]

Chancellor Livingston liked Sayre. A leader of the Livingston clan

---

1. Dávila (ed.), *Archivo del General Miranda*, V, 262; James G. Wilson, *Memorial History of the City of New York* (New York, 1892–93), III, 15–16, IV, 535.

and a potent politician, the chancellor was of a sanguine and speculative bent, as were almost all of Sayre's new friends. It was well known in New York that the Bank of North America, founded by the financier Robert Morris in Philadelphia, was prospering—Morris' financial ruin was still in the future. A similar institution ought not only to be profitable in New York for its principal founders but should promote the prosperity and growth of the city, then smaller than Philadelphia. Accordingly, Livingston, his brother-in-law John Stevens, a merchant, and Sayre undertook to create a Bank of the State of New York. Sayre, as a man experienced in managing such an institution, supplied leadership among the men of business; Livingston sought a charter for it from the state legislature.

At first they had the support of Isaac Sears and lawyer Alexander Hamilton, already a power in the city as the son-in-law of Albany magnate Philip Schuyler and as the hero of a charge against the British at Yorktown. But Hamilton turned against the Livingston-Sayre-Stevens scheme and came forth in support of a rival combination seeking a charter for a Bank of New York, headed by General Alexander McDougall, another war hero, a self-made man who had acquired learning and polish to accompany a native courage. Sears also rallied behind McDougall. Sayre and Stevens held a coffeehouse meeting on February 24 to push their proposal, but McDougall served as chairman of a larger meeting two days later that launched the Bank of New York. It is to be suspected that many investors preferred to follow the leadership of the worthy and well-known McDougall and the clever Hamilton rather than accept that of a man, however experienced and charming, whose bank in London had collapsed. Besides, the proposals of the chancellor and Sayre were less attractive in that they emphasized loans upon land rather than the creation of a sound currency for circulation in the city. Livingston and Hamilton, fighting for a charter in the state legislature, momentarily canceled each other's efforts. In the end, however, the Bank of New York carried the day. It opened its doors, and it was still in existence almost two hundred years later. The Bank of the State of New York remained—a project.[2]

2. There are good accounts of the struggle between the two groups in Henry W. Domett, *A History of the Bank of New York* (3rd ed.; Cambridge, Mass., 1884), 3–15, and George Dangerfield, *Chancellor Robert R. Livingston of New York, 1746–1813* (New York, 1960), 201–203.

Another Sayre enterprise of that year remained only a project. In the late summer and autumn he was in the region of Chesapeake Bay, doubtless seeking tobacco for export to Europe. From Georgetown on August 20 he wrote to George Washington, who was relaxing at Mount Vernon after his long service in the War of Independence. Washington had long been interested in opening a channel of trade between the Chesapeake and the Ohio Valley—he owned many thousands of acres of land in the upper valley of the Ohio that would increase in value if the Potomac River, which was blocked by falls and rapids, could be opened for use toward the distant interior. After inspecting the river, Sayre informed Washington that those impediments could be surmounted without resort to expensive locks by using chains and balancing boats going in opposite directions. His devices developed for those purposes were not ideal and would probably require money to execute. Sayre proposed two ways to get the necessary money, tolls and the tontine—the latter not an ideal method of extracting cash from the public. Washington was busy preparing for a journey over the Appalachians; he acknowledged the letter and urged Sayre to give his ideas to the public. Did Washington remember the ship design that Sayre had predicted would ruin the British navy, and was he cool in consequence? He was probably not much affected by the fact that Sayre signed his letter with "all possible respect & veneration"—the Father of His Country was becoming accustomed to adulation.[3]

Sayre wrote again from Georgetown on October 15. He planned to be in Annapolis toward the end of November—Congress was to meet in that town, and Sayre obviously intended to push his claim to a reward for his services in Europe—and he wondered if Washington would be there for a discussion of the devices, which Sayre believed would replace the use of locks everywhere. Sayre hoped that the states of Virginia and

3. Sayre reported on his scheme to an unnamed English friend, whose reply was published in the Virginia and Alexandria *Advertiser* of December 16, 1784. The friend was probably Lord Mahon. He agreed with Sayre that locks should be avoided and condemned George III. He informed Sayre that the French were planning to build a canal from the Atlantic to Paris and that the English ought to open a water route from London to Portsmouth. Mahon, a speculative and impractical man, was much interested in canal building. See the sketch of him in the *Dictionary of National Biography*. Sayre to Washington, August 20, 1784, in George Washington Papers, Library of Congress, Washington, D.C.; Fitzpatrick (ed.), *Writings of Washington*, XXVII, 465–66.

Maryland, which were quarreling over navigation of the Potomac, would adopt his contrivances at Washington's urging. The general invited Sayre to dinner at Mount Vernon, but he did not offer his endorsement of the project.[4]

Nor was Sayre's appeal to Congress for recognition and reward of his efforts in Europe on behalf of the new republic remarkably fruitful. On February 15, 1785, he presented a petition to that body asking for salary and expenses as an official American agent and also as a self-appointed but very effective one. In support of the petition he gave oral testimony to John Jay, who was serving as the secretary for foreign affairs. Sayre claimed that the three American commissioners in Paris had sent him to Berlin, that they had promised to recommend him to Congress for other appointments, and that he was employed by the commissioners while he was in Berlin and Copenhagen. Unable to offer proof of those assertions, he claimed that letters from the commissioners that would have confirmed his relationship with them had been captured on the ocean by the British in 1777. Admitting that he went to Sweden without official status, he declared that he had played an important role in laying the foundation for the League of Armed Neutrality.[5] To emphasize his sacrifices as well as his services in the American cause, Sayre supplied certificates of his good character; mentioned his activities in England in defense of America; said that his bankruptcy, so costly to him, proceeded from British persecution; claimed that he had been promised a seat in the House of Commons and a government appointment by the marquis of Rockingham if he would stay in England until Rockingham returned to power as prime minister; and asserted that he had abandoned a bright future in England by choosing instead to serve the United States.

Congress was hard pressed at that time for money, and it was obvious that Sayre sought more than minor return for his services. In accordance with a recommendation from Jay in April, Sayre was asked to supply additional proof from Arthur Lee and Benjamin Franklin. Congress was

4. Sayre to Washington, October 15, 1784, in Washington Papers; Sayre to Washington, October 15, 1790, in Department of State, Miscellaneous Letters.

5. Sayre made this claim in one form and another many times. Two scholarly studies of the League of Armed Neutrality do not even mention his name. See Paul Faucille, *La Diplomatie Française et la Ligue des Neutres de 1780* (Paris, 1893), and Isabel de Madariaga, *Britain, Russia, and the Armed Neutrality of 1780* (New Haven, 1962).

then meeting in New York, and Lee was in town. Sayre humbled himself, asked the Virginian for a helpful statement, and was refused. It was useless, he saw, to approach Franklin. In any event, he would not have received much cash. A congressional committee proposed that his services in Berlin were the only ones deserving additional reward and suggested $1,055 as an appropriate sum.[6]

Sayre also tried in New York to get the support of Congress for the building of one of his invincible warships in the spring of 1785. He submitted the project with a mysterious "A. Almiras" as a partner. General Henry Knox, as secretary of war, did not denounce the scheme when it was submitted to him for an opinion, and a committee agreed that Sayre should be rewarded—if he and Almiras could construct such a vessel.[7] The scheme languished.

Other associations into which Sayre entered in New York were much more pleasant. Henry Knox, enormously fat and jolly, extravagant and venturesome, was cordial. Much closer was the relationship between Sayre and William Duer, at that time a seemingly prosperous businessman. Duer, ten years younger than Sayre, was the younger son of a wealthy English merchant. After military service in India, he had settled in New York in 1768 and had married a daughter of the so-called earl of Stirling. He and his wife, "Lady Kitty," were pillars of society. Duer was of a sanguine and speculative temperament, a man after Sayre's own heart. So agreeable to each other were Duer and Sayre that they entered into a special pledge of enduring friendship. Another new intimate of Sayre was Colonel William Stephens Smith, who had served on Washington's staff. He was a tall, dark, slender man of good figure who had earned a reputation for bravery. Smith was utterly devoted to liberty, not merely for the United States, but he was not remarkable for financial integrity—Washington afterward refused him an army commission because he had borrowed money twice upon the same security.

Most exotic of the new friends was Francisco de Miranda, a native of Caracas, Venezuela, then in his middle thirties. Miranda was a scholar and linguist, a pursuer of women, and a visionary. Dismissed from the

---

6. *American State Papers*, IX, 81–82, 226; Sayre to James Madison, June 9, 1801, in Madison Papers; Worthington C. Ford *et al.* (eds.), *The Journals of the Continental Congress, 1774–1789* (Washington, 1904–37), XXIX, 530–31, XXIII, 73n, 91, 241, 363.

7. Ford *et al.* (eds.), *Journals of the Continental Congress*, XXIII, 364n, 379, 390, 395.

Spanish army for misuse of money, he was an impulsive and attractive man then beginning his long-continued efforts to overthrow Spanish rule in Venezuela and all of South America. To Duer, Knox, Smith, Alexander Hamilton, and Sayre, Miranda was fascinating, and they were disposed to assist him in his struggle against the arbitrary Spanish monarchy. There was some talk of ways and means, and a plan of sorts for action. When Miranda went to Europe in search of assistance, Duer supplied him with money to make the journey. Duer and Sayre undertook to correspond with Miranda in cipher and to assist each other in all enterprises. Duer also furnished the South American with a letter of introduction to his brother-in-law, George Rose, an official in the British treasury, and Sayre recommended Miranda to John Reynolds. Sayre sent a farewell note to Miranda, who was embarking at Boston. "Good voyage, & health to you," he wrote. He asked Miranda to send him from England the Abbé Raynal's history of America so that he could learn more about Latin America, "and the political magazines." He signed his letter with fervor, "yours forever."[8]

New York City was remarkably full of colorful personalities immediately after the War of Independence. Among them was a striking couple who were to be most important to Sayre, the baron and baroness Poellnitz—the baroness being by birth Lady Anne Stuart, daughter of the earl of Bute, once the beloved prime minister of young George III. The history of Poellnitz is curious; that of Lady Anne, as she was commonly known even after her marriage to the baron, is romantic.

Lady Anne, Bute's third daughter, was born in 1746 and in her youth was acknowledged to be intelligent, charming, and possessed of a delicate beauty. In July, 1764, in London she married Hugh, Lord Percy, an army officer, the son and heir of the first duke of Northumberland and Mary Wortley-Montagu. The union was, on paper, an ideal one, but it soon began to collapse. Percy had engaged in amorous adventures before the marriage—Casanova relates that he exchanged mistresses with the nobleman at Turin—and resumed them before many months had passed. Lady Anne also sought happiness in an extramarital union. In the *Town and Country Magazine*, a London periodical that published scandalous accounts of prominent persons, she is described as "The Paphian Votary," "a meteor among the reigning toasts of the age," whose "eyes made captives at every glance." Their "darts were irresistible." The fortunate man, "The Successful Gallant," was a Mr. Bird, reported the magazine. Actually, the first of her adulteries, according to a more reliable source, was with a Sir John Hippisley, who was visited by Lady Anne in his quarters in the Temple. "Percy Bird," however, received the credit, or discredit, that should have gone to Hippisley. At length, in March, 1779, Lord Percy received a divorce from Lady Anne by act of Parliament, and she obtained from him an annuity of £1,600. In 1780 she married Poellnitz, described unfavorably by a diarist as a "sort of companion or butt" for the humor of Frederick the Great.[9]

Friedrich Karl Hans Bruno Poellnitz was, in more polite language, chamberlain at Frederick's court. He had inherited the office from his father, a witty libertine who was expelled from Russia because of bad behavior, wandered about Europe, and was twice imprisoned for failure to pay his debts. The father, who published his memoirs, was, according to the English *Annual Register*, rather a silly man who was never accused "of a violent passion for the fair sex." He was converted to Roman Catholicism and sought an office in the cathedral church of Courtrai, France, despite his having fathered at least one child. He was also accused of attempted blackmail. The son also displayed quirks of behavior, and it ought not to be assumed that he was a youthful innocent

9. One may consult "Northumberland" in *The Complete Peerage* about the marriage and titles of Lord Percy. His illegitimate half brother, James Smithson, was the benefactor of the Smithsonian Institution. The account of Lady Anne's escapades is in *Town and Country Magazine*, X (1778), 345–48. She was also the subject of an amusing pseudo-epitaph, published in 1780, when she was very much alive. It ran: "Tread lightly, gentle Passenger; Perhaps lost in the Raptures of Joys she wishes to eternize, She only sleeps. The once lively Lady P. .cy, shrouded in the Vest of cold Mortality, Subverts our Maxims, or appalls our Senses; Enforces our Reflexion, or encourages our Disbelief Eternally disunited from the Nobleman she injured, her Ladyship offered a very cogent Claim to Mr. B---'s Affections, but without success. Piqued at the Affront, and tired of an unsettled Life, she gave her hand to the Earl of ----, who had just been divorced from the Partner of his Bed, and died on the Wedding Night. Depart with Caution, lest, even now, she seduce you to her Embraces." Sir Herbert Croft, *Abbey of Kilkhampton* (London, 1780), 73–74. Frances Bickley (ed.), *The Diaries of Sylvester Douglas (Lord Glenbervie)* (London, 1928), I, 361–62; Charles Durnford and Edward Hyde East, *Term Reports, in the Court of King's Bench* (New York, 1834), I, 5.

cozened into marrying Lady Anne. He was born in 1734, had had two wives and one divorce, and was burdened with a brood of four children.[10]

The Poellnitzes did not stay in England. They had agreed that they would emigrate to America, and soon after their marriage they appeared in Paris and introduced themselves to Benjamin Franklin. They went on to Bordeaux. From that port the baron wrote to Franklin to announce that he had resigned his appointment as chamberlain to Frederick the Great and that he wished to be looked upon as one of the free men of America. He and his family would embark for North Carolina or Maryland as soon as the coming of peace permitted passage without the dangers of war at sea.[11]

They sailed before the end of hostilities to North Carolina, in the spring of 1782 deposited the children there under the protection of James Iredell, a connection of Lady Anne, and moved on northward. They were in Richmond in June, 1783. From that town the baron condemned war: "Peace don't soot rogues witch like to fish in trouble water. Whereas war witch was first invented by highwaymen soots better their disorderly passions than peace does, which reveives law and good order in society, and keeps them in awe!"[12] Arriving at length in New York in 1784, the couple settled down in a house that the baron bought on Bowery Lane.

They did not remain in it long. He left for London to face lawsuits, leaving his wife to arrange matters in New York, then follow him to England. Sayre assisted her with business, arranging for General Knox to lease the Poellnitz house. The baron did not wish Sayre to act as his agent, to receive rent from Knox or other income for the Poellnitzes. He questioned Sayre's financial integrity and believed that Sayre's bank scheme was a swindle, but the baroness insisted on employing him. Did

10. *Annual Register*, VIII (1765), 64–69. Unless otherwise indicated, data concerning the baron are derived from Charles S. Belsterling, "Baron Poellnitz of New York City and South Carolina," *New York Genealogical and Biographical Record*, LXXX (1949), 130–41.

11. A. Minis Hays, *Calendar of the Papers of Benjamin Franklin in the Library of the American Philosophical Society* (Philadelphia, 1908), II, 248, 340, 460. In 1788 the baron offered to give Franklin the benefit of his special ability to deal with the stone. *Ibid.*, IV, 366.

12. R. Don Higginbotham (ed.), *The Papers of James Iredell* (Raleigh, 1976), II, 347, 349, 357, 369, 393, 399, 419.

Poellnitz suspect that she might become too friendly with Sayre? Lady Anne also took passage for Europe, but not for Portsmouth or London. She sailed on the French packet *Le Courier de New York* for l'Orient on April 30, 1785. Sayre escorted her aboard the vessel.[13]

The baron afterward related a tale of woe. Assuming that his wife would soon follow him, he went to London to defend himself against numerous lawsuits for debts amounting to £18,000 contracted by her before their marriage. According to the baron, the suits were malignantly instigated by Earl Percy, who did not wish to pay debts contracted by his former wife after the divorce but before her second marriage. The German allowed himself to be arrested and was imprisoned. He also lost a legal struggle when an English court ruled that he was indeed obligated to pay the debts.[14]

But the baron had a defense—that the divorce had been obtained by collusion. He threatened to prove that such was the fact, and he urged his wife to come to England to offer evidence. She wrote him tender letters; she wrote to her mother and to her sisters expressing fondness for him. But she did not appear, and the baron at first believed that she must have been lost at sea. Learning that she had gone to France, he asked Percy to resume payment of the annuity. Percy refused. The baron then discovered that Percy was giving it directly to Lady Anne, that he was the victim of a plot, that she had deceived him, that Sayre had connived with her and with Percy, and that she had joined Sayre in France. The plot, said the baron, was the work of Lady Anne. It had been arranged in New York between her and Sayre that she was to go to France and remain incognito for six months. Sayre would settle his affairs and sell the Poellnitz property in New York, which was in her name. Then, "in his tour of Europe," Sayre was "to provide in Spain a retired place where they intended to live." Percy meanwhile was to pretend that she had died but

13. Baron Poellnitz to Henry Knox, August 3, 1785, in Knox Papers. *The Pennsylvania Mercury and Universal Advertiser*, May 6, 1785, reported her departure as a bit of social news.

14. One of the suits, *Corbet v. Poellnitz*, is recorded in Durnford and East, *Term Reports, in the Court of the King's Bench*, I, 4–9. Corbet was Andrew Corbett, husband of Lady Augusta Stuart, Lady Anne's sister, who was no longer living. He is mentioned in Steele, *Memoirs of Mrs. Sophia Baddeley*, I, 37, 67, II, 2–27, III, 81, as a man who vainly sought the favors of that lady, while Percy's father is listed as a successful suitor.

continue surreptitiously to furnish her annuity. Poellnitz claimed that she even at one time denied that she was married to him, that he had lost an income of £2,000 per annum. He reported that Sayre was later arrested for debt in London, with Lady Anne. Lady Anne, he wrote in 1788, "is nothing more to me in this world."[15] Did he obtain an annulment or a divorce? He eventually settled again in New York, buying a house owned by Andrew Elliot, a brother of Hugh Elliot. In New York he denounced Negro servitude. Later, he moved to South Carolina, married a fourth time, and acquired Negro slaves before he died.

The baron was not remarkably shrewd. While he was in London, the ballooning craze spread from France to England. He listened to a Frenchman who assured him that a balloon carrying passengers could be propelled through the air, using an "artificial" wind when necessary. Poellnitz applied for a patent for such a craft but was not able to demonstrate that he knew how to move it. The attorney who heard his request for a patent suggested that he required the services of a physician rather than those of a lawyer.[16] Nevertheless, his sorrowful relation, so far as Sayre is concerned, is largely true. Sayre did follow Lady Anne to France, he went to Spain, and she was with him in jail in London in 1787, doubtless because she had failed to settle her debts.

Meanwhile, failing to receive pay from Congress for his past services, Sayre sought an appointment as secretary of legation in London, but his friend Colonel Smith, recommended by Washington, obtained the post, which earned a salary of £1,200 per annum. The appointment would have enabled Sayre to return to London in at least modest triumph, so he must have been much disappointed. To his credit, Sayre conceded that Smith deserved the job.[17] The colonel proceeded to London, and there he married Abigail, the daughter of John Adams, who had become minister of the United States to the Court of St. James in June, 1786.

Sayre secured a consolation prize of sorts—letters of recommendation from five members of Congress, including Elbridge Gerry of Mas-

---

15. Higginbotham (ed.), *Papers of James Iredell*, II, 22.
16. Reynolds, *Life and Times of Frederic Reynolds*, I, 258–59.
17. Dávila (ed.), *Archivo del General Miranda*, VI, 213.

sachusetts, Rufus King of New York, and James Monroe of Virginia—which he could carry to Adams and to Thomas Jefferson, who had succeeded Franklin as minister to France. The congressmen said that they could not nominate Sayre for an office that he would accept. They urged the ministers to send our "worthy friend" on a mission to the emperor of Morocco and other rulers on the Barbary Coast. They declared that his services and sufferings had earned him preferment and that "his knowledge of mankind, his polite address, his commercial, and political accomplishments, and above all, his sense of honor, and integrity, cannot fail of insuring you as great a degree of success, as the qualities of any other person you can employ in that department." [18]

Sayre had another reason for turning toward southern Europe. He had formed a partnership with William Duer in a small ship, and with the help of the merchant house of Gardoqui of Bilbao, the two friends hoped to sell two shiploads of masts and other naval stores to the Spanish government. By August 25, 1785, Sayre was almost ready to sail from New York. Had he still other motives for leaving America? He said afterward that considerations of honor dictated his decision: he wished to pay, at least to reduce, his debts in Holland and England. Therefore, he proposed to establish himself once more as a merchant in London. He disposed of all his American assets before taking ship for the Old World. Moreover, with Duer and Robert R. Livingston he was commissioned to try to secure payment from the British government of claims for goods supplied to the British army during the War of Independence. [19]

In mid-September, 1785, Baron Poellnitz went from London to Paris in search of his wife. He was in France for almost three months, but he could not find the lady. Where was Sayre during that period? He landed in England in October, too late to take part in the North African enterprise. The emphatic recommendation that he carried from the American lawmakers profited him nothing—Matthew Lamb had already been chosen to head the mission. Jefferson was willing to send out Sayre as second to Lamb, provided that assignment was not already

18. Edmund C. Burnett (ed.), *Letters of Members of the Continental Congress* (Washington, 1921–36), VIII, 138; Adams (ed.), *Works of John Adams*, VIII, 316–18.

19. Sayre to John Adams, August 25, 1785, in Adams Family Papers; Dávila (ed.), *Archivo del General Miranda*, V, 396.

filled, but Sayre was not interested in the minor post, feeling it beneath the dignity of a man who had consorted with British prime ministers and a Swedish king.[20]

Had Sayre led the mission, he could not have accomplished much. The piratical rulers of North Africa were accustomed to receive bribes, even from Britain, for all her naval power, in exchange for promises not to seize merchant vessels and crews of unbelievers. The promises were not always kept. The beys, deys, and bashaws apparently could be taught the ways of civilized traffic in the Mediterranean only by gunfire, and the United States then had no cannon to discharge in the harbors of Algiers or Tunis. Lamb did eventually manage to secure a pledge from Morocco to permit American vessels to plow the Mediterranean, but otherwise he won no glory.

Sayre apparently spent that autumn in France. He was in Paris on December 8, uncertain whether he would go on to Madrid. He did reach that city in January, 1786, then he went south to Cádiz, where he was able to sell the two shiploads of naval stores to the Spanish government.[21]

Did Sayre and Lady Anne enjoy an idyllic interlude in the autumn of 1785 while the baron vainly searched for his errant wife? The records do not say. Did the two adulterers—they would doubtless have found that word objectionable or irrelevant—spend the early months of 1786 exclusively with each other? Again, no answer can be given. But it is not to be doubted that Lady Anne came to prefer the comely and charming Sayre, who knew the ways of English society, to her husband, who remained Germanic.

IN THE summer of 1786 London newspapers frequently reported the activities of Sayre, Lady Anne, and their connections, assuredly to the discomfort of the couple. On Tuesday, June 6, Lord Percy's father died, and he became duke of Northumberland, with an enormous income

20. Julian Boyd (ed.), *The Papers of Thomas Jefferson* (Princeton, 1950–), VIII, 525, 572–73, IX, 85, 90–91, 115, 250; Dávila (ed.), *Archivo del General Miranda*, V, 376; Colonel Smith was in Bordeaux in May, 1787. He reported, along with indignities suffered by Sayre on account of debt, that Lamb was "about to embark from Minorca with a load of jack-asses for America. *Sic transit gloria mundi.*" Boyd (ed.), *Papers of Thomas Jefferson*, XI, 366.

21. Dávila (ed.), *Archivo del General Miranda*, V, 376.

estimated at £50,000 per annum. Did Lady Anne regret, at least briefly, her divorce from that peer? A few days later Lord Macartney, who had married a sister of Lady Anne, fought a duel, was wounded in the shoulder, but survived.[22]

The London *Times*, a publication that was by no means stuffy or staid in its early years—on one occasion it bluntly and vulgarly referred to Catherine the Great's preferences with respect to male anatomy—struck hard against Sayre and Lady Anne, especially against him. Was Alexander Bicknell by some chance writing for that newspaper? On July 15 it announced the death of Sophia Baddeley in Edinburgh and declared that Perdita Robinson had assisted Mrs. Baddeley when she lived "in Chelsea in the most deplorable and wretched condition that helpless woman could be in—having the cravings of nature, without the means of supplying them, added to the pangs of labour, and all the horrors of an outcast and forlorn wretch to combat." The following day the *Times* connected Sayre with Mrs. Baddeley and Lady Anne in most unflattering language. "The once gay fluttering Perdita is no more, and many of her favored swains [are] doing repentance. The wanton Baddeley is also consigned to her native earth—that form which has inspired the sprightly circle of midnight revelry, is now food for worms, and scarce a remembrance of her beauty remains. . . . Mr. Garrick always gave the most ample testimony of her merits. As a singer, whenever pathetic expression was necessary, she stood unrivalled." The *Times* referred to "the beauty of her person" and "the elegant implicity of her performance." The newspaper went on to record her triumphs and her pathetic end at the age of thirty-seven as the object of the charity of fellow actors.[23] Then, without intervening news, the *Times* reported that "Lord Bute's eldest daughter is arrived from America, where she has resided for some time," and that "Mr. Sayre is also returned from the Continent with his family." Elsewhere in that issue, the newspaper, presumably upon the basis of information derived from Sayre, announced that William Lee was dead—he had left democratic America for another country, perhaps Hell. By innuendo Sayre was connected with Mrs. Baddeley, as he would be openly not long afterward when the memoir of the actress by

22. London *Chronicle*, June 6–8, June 8–10, June 10–13, 1786. The duke lived until 1817.

23. London *Times*, July 14, 1786.

Elizabeth Steele and Alexander Bicknell was published. Moreover, innuendo would have it that Lady Anne came back to London with Sayre and "his family." On August 8 the *Times* struck again at Sayre, reporting that "a roach who sailed from hence to America with a *fair* lady lately married, in crossing the Atlantic Ocean, back, it is said, on her business, has been made a gudgeon, to reward him for his attention." The gudgeon, or dupe, was Baron Poellnitz.

The *Times* was not the only London newspaper that assailed Sayre. The squib associating him with Lady Anne actually appeared first in the *Morning Chronicle and London Advertiser* on July 14, and it was reprinted by the London *Chronicle* in its issue of July 13–15. The daily prints contained other news that could hardly have pleased the American. At the time of Sayre's return to England, former Sheriff William Plomer was Sir William Plomer, Lord Mayor of London. It must have occurred to Sayre that, had he avoided enthusiastic politicking in behalf of America, he might have become Sir Stephen, Lord Mayor, or Sir Stephen, M.P. Nor can he have rejoiced to read in the London *Chronicle* in November that his old enemy Lord Mansfield, soon to retire, was "the handsomest, wisest, and (happily for his country) the healthiest man of his age in Great Britain, and probably in Europe." [24]

Sayre did not succeed in restoring himself as a man of business in London in the latter half of 1786. In November, a London newspaper reported that he was in Madrid, serving as a special envoy for the United States. This interesting news was sent home by the Spanish ambassador. [25] However, Sayre did not go to the Spanish capital in an official capacity.

Early the following year, Sayre was in prison in England for debt. On January 12, 1787, the London *Times* gleefully reported that "a certain gentleman, confined in *Banco Regis*, on an *attachment*—but not an attachment to his wife,—employs himself daily in the exercise of drawing the *long bow*, at which he is remarkably *adept*." The reader was expected to know that Sayre was confined in the court of the King's Bench and that his property had been attached by a creditor or creditors. The reader would also know, or seek to find out, what person he preferred to his

24. *Ibid.*, November 9–11, 1786.

25. Maria Francisca Represa Fernandez *et al.* (eds.), *Documentos Relativos a la Independencia de Norte América Existentes en Archivos Españoles* (Madrid, 1976), II, 603.

Elizabeth. Inquiry would reveal that Lady Anne was with him in prison. A week later, the *Times* sardonically published another squib at Sayre's expense. "We hear," announced the newspaper, "that Stephen Sayre, Esq. formerly Sheriff of this metropolis, and late Minister from the United States of America to the Court of Spain, has formed an extensive commercial connection in several of the sea-ports of France."[26]

Sayre remained in jail for more than twenty months. In May, 1788, he related a sad story to Miranda.

> I have now to state a serial of misfortunes & treachery that you will hardly credit. . . . When I came here, it was my intention to have settled a house . . . I therefore brought over all the money & property I could command. . . . A fatal confidence led me to place it in the hands of a lawyer— one Reynolds, who had shown me friendly attention, about the time of my ruin by government in 1775—too late I found he was in desperate circumstances, for I did more than deposit my money—I gave him bills on Bilbao & other aids, so as to involve myself beyond my ability—the rascal, on my requiring justice & my property has sworn a false debt of £7,000 & upwards against me—arrested me for that sum—too large to get bail.

Sayre related that he was confined by Reynolds to the King's Bench, "where I have now been, near 16 months fighting him thro all the tricks of law, to get my own property—above £1,200 in money & near 20,000 in dollars in Congress certificates—also above £3,000 cash of a friend's who thro' my connections he got hold of & keeps."[27]

In October, 1788, Sayre related his tale of woe a second time for Miranda's benefit. "On my coming to England, I had some hopes of doing something toward repaying Delalande & Fijnje, and all others to whom I was indebted. I was joint agent with our friend Duer & Mr. Livingston to recover claims on this government—mostly for supplies to the army during the late war—this to the amount of near half a million sterling—our commission was from 5 to 25 per cent." Sayre asserted that William Pitt, the younger son of Chatham who had become prime minister, "promises to take all such claims under consideration, as soon as the finances enable him to satisfy them." But this dream of easy wealth

26. London *Times*, January 19, 1787. The squib was copied in the London *Chronicle* of January 18–20, 1787.

27. Dávila (ed.), *Archivo del General Miranda*, V, 376–77.

had been shattered by Reynolds, "who had formerly, shown me some instances of good will & friendship—I thought him an honest man—he has proved himself the worst of rogues—not only refusing to return my property, but swore a debt of £7500 against me—shut me up, since January 1787 in this prison." Apparently, Delalande & Fijnje were also demanding payment from Sayre.[28]

The narratives sent to the Spaniard did not tell the whole story. One would not know from these little histories that Reynolds had been a close and loyal friend of Sayre, or that Sayre had owed him money ever since the solicitor had lent him £5,000 after the collapse of Sayre & Purdon. But Reynolds was indeed at least partly responsible for the incarceration of his old friend. The solicitor was in financial trouble, to a degree because of an unfortunate investment in an estate in Dominica, when Sayre's property was put in his hands. Apparently Reynolds withheld it from Sayre in order to force him to repay the old loan, or at least part of it. Unable to meet his current debts, the American was seized on January 10, 1787, for nonpayment of a debt of £2,200 to one Elizabeth Piper, a widow. He was committed to the Fleet Prison two days later for want of bail. Other creditors, to whom he owed several thousand pounds, descended upon him. It seems that he satisfied all the claims by April. But then another group of creditors brought forward new claims, including one for £5,000 by Reynolds, and Sayre was sent to the Marshalsea Prison for debtors on the south side of the Thames. It appears that he was transferred back to the Fleet early in 1788. In any event, he did not regain his freedom, except perhaps for a few brief hours between legal processes, until more than twenty months had passed.[29]

It was possible at that time for a creditor to keep a debtor in jail indefinitely by paying fourpence a day for his maintenance. Charles Dickens afterward, in *Little Dorrit*, described the dismal half-life of poor wretches locked up because they could not or would not meet their obligations. But it was possible, as Dickens related, for an incumbent, if he had money or credit, to live quite comfortably in private quarters, being denied only freedom to leave the precincts of the prison. It may be assumed that Sayre had his own rooms, and for a time at least Lady Anne

28. *Ibid.*, V, 396–97.
29. Reynolds, *Life and Times of Frederic Reynolds*, I, 326, 373; P.R.O., Prisons, Ser. 4, Bundle 10, p. 25, Bundle 11, pp. 103–104.

was with him. Dr. Michael Lort wrote from London on April 9, 1787, to a friend in Ireland, Bishop Thomas Percy, a connection of the duke of Northumberland: "Lady Percy, that was, is now in the King's Bench Prison, gallantly attending her paramour, the noted Sheriff Sayre."[30]

Lady Anne was accustomed to scandalous writings concerning her amours. She could hardly have been shocked by the appearance of *The Memoirs of Sophia Baddeley*, so hostile to Sayre. But that publication could not have failed to injure the feelings of Elizabeth Sayre, who had suffered enough because of the troubles of her husband. If she did not mind gossip about his supposed affair with the actress and various unflattering comments about him in the book, she must have resented statements in it that she was old when he married her, and that he had married her only for her money. She could derive little satisfaction from the news that Mrs. Steele, hunted as a debtor and then as a forger, wretchedly ended her life as a fugitive from justice in a London tavern in November, 1787. Nor could she have been pleased by the report in the *Times* of the arrest of her husband.[31]

In his distress Sayre appealed for help to the younger William Pitt, but the prime minister ignored his plea. Thereupon Sayre wrote to Lady Chatham, Pitt's mother. Would she please tell her son that Sayre was a

30. John B. Nichols, *Illustrations of the Literary History of the Eighteenth Century* (London, 1817–18), VII, 483. There is no good reason to doubt the presence of Lady Anne with Sayre in prison. She was not incarcerated for debt, and her name is not among those listed in the prison records as held for nonpayment. The London *Times* of January 15, 1788, declared that "a certain affected Morning Print, remarkable for its incautious, groundless and calumniating assertions, has turned its misrepresenting from the dead to the living. Mr. O'Kelly had never been a chairman or a marker at a billiard table; nor is *Lady Percy* a beggar, or the paramour of a King's Bench prisoner. But the *World* is a lying World." Evidently it had been forgotten at the *Times* that the story regarding Sayre and Lady Percy had been published in its own columns a year earlier. The denial of Lady Percy's situation is erroneous: the relationship between Sayre and Lady Percy cannot be described precisely, but it was certainly intimate. It is likely that Sayre learned about and chuckled over the plight of John Walter, publisher of the *Times*, who was sent to Newgate prison in 1789 for libels against the sons of George III. Walter complained bitterly because prisoners of the King's Bench could have their own quarters, servants at all times, and visitors until 10 P.M., while he was treated as an ordinary criminal at Newgate. For Walter's plight, see James Hutton (ed.), *Selections from the Letters and Correspondence of Sir James Bland Burges* (London, 1885), 156–58.

31. London *Chronicle*, February 22–25, November 15–17, 1787; *European Magazine*, XII (1787), 436.

friend of his father and that he deserved help? She replied that she would mention the old friendship to the prime minister, but he did not act to assist the prisoner.[32]

Sayre's residence in prison was longer than it need have been because he refused to resort to bankruptcy, a step that would have made it impossible for him ever to engage again successfully in banking, at least in England. At last he regained his freedom by a counterattack against Reynolds. Threatened by imprisonment for his own debts—persons searching for him on behalf of Sayre could not find him—the lawyer fled to France in the fall of 1787, taking with him, according to Sayre, all the Sayre property in his possession. He did not return to England until three years had passed, and thereafter he lived quietly under an alias until his death. Somehow Sayre managed to satisfy his Dutch creditors. Friends came to his assistance with money, but because of legal technicalities he did not secure his release from jail until the fall of 1788. He wrote to General Knox on October 3 that he had just been released from "my long, & illegal confinement—have drove my adversary out of the country, or into some corner, where he must have changed his name for his security. It is now my turn to act upon the offensive, if ever I can find the malignant villain." He continued, "It has cost me above 500 guineas to defend myself, so as to prevent him fixing me for life in prison." He had not dared, he said, because of "the practice of the courts in this country," to seek redress against Reynolds in them. He hoped that America would not be plagued by lawyers.[33]

One of the persons who supplied money to Sayre in his great need, Miranda, was traveling about in Europe. Through Colonel William Smith, Sayre established contact with the Latin American. Sayre told Miranda that he had supplied a part of the five hundred dollars that Duer lent to Miranda when that officer left for Europe in 1784. Would Miranda, now in good financial condition, return the money? The traveler arranged for Sayre to receive the money. Expressing profound gratitude, Sayre wrote in July, 1788, to Miranda: "I hope we shall have many

32. Lady Chatham to Sayre, September 6, 1787, in Sayre, *A Short Narrative*.

33. Dávila (ed.), *Archivo del General Miranda*, V, 377, 397; Reynolds, *Life and Times of Frederic Reynolds*, II, 15, 95–96; Sayre to Washington, October 15, 1790, in Department of State, Miscellaneous Letters; Sayre to Henry Knox, October 3, 1788, in Knox Papers.

opportunities of gratifying our mutual expectations, *and in matters of high import"*—presumably arrangements for a rebellion in Spanish America. A month later Sayre wrote again to his friend about the future. He was "perfectly sure" of paying his Amsterdam creditors "if I live some five or six years under common events." He intended to resume banking on Oxford Street, where he would be supported by "many rich & solid men." "I made a capital mistake in leaving England, & persisted too long in it," he asserted, "otherways I might now have been exceedingly rich, with weight & influence." He would turn over to his supporters his claims upon the United States, certain to be paid when Washington, as was to be expected, became the first president. Sayre averred expansively that "on my going down to Virginia, I made him my sincere friend." "We may yet live," he declared, "to accomplish our designs."[34]

Sayre wrote in much the same vein to Henry Knox and doubtless to William Duer. He was still a vigorous man with great schemes, and he put forward old projects and some new ones. He still claimed to have a naval invention—he now called it "the love"—that might "on some critical occasion, decide the fate of any nation who may adopt it." He could sell his secret to Britain or France, but he preferred to let America have it—for a suitable reward. Would Knox sound out Washington? "Don't imagine me degraded because I have been oppressed—my spirit is yet pure from corruption—my mind yet above a base action—my resources are not yet annihilated—my ambition, my expectations, & my resolution, are the same. If I remain still longer in this country, it is with a good ground of hope to make myself independent—without which I shall not be respected even among the virtuous sons of America—here there is opportunity of acquiring wealth—there the door is shut against the utmost exertions." America had been guilty of ingratitude. "I have already experienced that neglect in the American government, which takes place in all other states—had I remained quiet in England during the late contest I had gone over with the weight of riches I could have acquired by such conduct. I should have been better treated." Aware that the new republic had not rewarded the sacrifices of its soldiers and its sailors, Knox could not have denied that Sayre had a well-founded

34. Dávila (ed.), *Archivo del General Miranda*, III, 327, V, 377–78, VII, 95, 107, 116–17.

grievance. "I do not intend to make a second mistake," asserted Sayre. "If I am not invited over, on some sure foundation, or early provided for in that line of employment in Europe which I know I deserve, & which I am able to fill; my resolution is, to make the same establishment, which I formerly made in this city. As the first succeeded beyond my most sanguine expectation—I conclude a second must succeed also—I have now more experience of a sort, too, that must be of the utmost use."

Did Sayre actually believe that he could successfully engage in banking in London a second time? While he tried to make a new start, he settled down for some months in a house on Parliament Street, close to the centers of executive and legislative authority in Britain. During that period he planned to make a journey to France. He made no progress in England, and early in 1789 he wrote again to Knox. On the assumption that Knox would be asked for a decisive opinion if the American government chose to consider "the love," he proposed to supply Knox with the secret. Since there was no necessity for his early appearance in America, Sayre asked the fat general to recommend him as consul in London, should it be decided that one was needed. It would be cheaper for the United States to appoint him rather than to send a man across the ocean.[35]

In the summer of 1789 Sayre wrote gaily to Samuel Ogden for the benefit of Knox about the amorous activities of Catherine the Great. He then reported that "I am once more a banker in my old situation in Oxford Street. I repent ever having left it. Yet my own country is dearer to me than to half those who profess so great a love for it. If I have opportunity, I will give proofs of this assertion"—one of the "proofs" would lie in giving America first chance to acquire "the love." But he sent his letter to Ogden for relay to Knox because the general had failed to respond to his pleas: "*I am still disposed to consider myself worthy reply*—holding the rank of gentleman entitles me to one. I hope he will deign to converse with the President on the subject of my former letters, & that I shall, at last, be honor'd with a decisive answer."[36] As secretary of war, responsible for both land and sea forces in the cabinet of President Washington in the new government established in 1789 under the

35. Sayre to Henry Knox, October 3, 1788, January 3, 1789, in Knox Papers.
36. Sayre to Samuel Ogden, June 29, 1789, in *ibid.*

Constitution, Knox acquired power and influence. But it would be some time before that government would have money to spare, especially for a secret invention. Knox did not respond for many months, nor did a petition for action from Sayre to Washington quickly produce a result.

In his letter to Ogden, Sayre mentioned that their mutual friend Miranda had just come from France and that he had been Sayre's guest at dinner. The two men had talked about France; Miranda was prejudiced against the French, Sayre said. The two could not have foreseen that the Revolution getting underway across the Channel would lead them into extraordinary adventures.

The outlook for Sayre meanwhile remained bleak. His new bank, despite his successful struggle against bankruptcy, did not live more than briefly, if it appeared at all. In the summer of 1789 he hinted to Miranda that he needed a loan, but Miranda replied that he was not able at the moment to lend money. Early in September Sayre forthrightly asked to borrow from the South American; Miranda should have no fear regarding repayment, for Sayre had "resources, tho' not at command." Miranda again failed to respond to the call for help. Later he asserted that he would have done so had he realized that Sayre was in dire need, as was the case. "I had then due to me many considerable debts," Sayre explained to his friend, "from those who had it in their power to pay me— more small ones—but not a single man could be persuaded to do so. I have been compel'd to arrest all of them." Before the middle of October, however, Sayre was able to report to Miranda that he had received "large remittances—*my wants are at an end*."[37]

Sayre received another shock when his wife died on November 29. The London *Chronicle* announced that "on Sunday last died, Mrs. Sayer, wife of Stephen Sayer, Esq. Banker, Oxford-Street." The death of his marriage partner must have disturbed him, even though there is some reason to believe that the Sayres had become estranged in consequence of the scandals arising from his connection with Lady Anne Stuart and the publication of the Baddeley *Memoirs*, despite the fact that extramarital affairs were quite common in her circle of English society in her time. Her patience must have been tried by the adventures and wanderings of her husband. That she had turned against him, that at least she did not

37. Dávila (ed.), *Archivo del General Miranda*, V, 426, 428.

trust him with property, is indicated by the fact that she left a will in which her niece, Mrs. Morgan, was named as executor. Afterward, Sayre referred to property rights in England that he hoped to establish; it may be that he was thinking of property that had belonged to his first wife. Shocked though he may have been, he married another Elizabeth within a year. [38]

38. London *Chronicle*, December 3–5, 1789. Other announcements appeared in the *European Magazine*, XVI (1789), 471, and *Gentleman's Magazine*, LIV (1789), 1151. See also notation upon the will of Judge William Noel, in P.R.O., Wills. Efforts to locate the will of Mrs. Sayre have been unsuccessful.

10

The French Revolutionary

T HE EBULLIENT and venturesome Mr. Sayre was tamed for a part of the year 1790. There is even a hint that he considered self-destruction. But he recovered his spirits, married a second time, engaged in business in Paris, and played an interesting role in the great French Revolution as a citizen of France, America, and the world.

In the late spring of 1790 the widower described his situation bleakly to General Knox and twice appealed for help. He had not received answers to letters to William Duer and Knox—"Insignifancy as to myself may have been the cause, why you did not make me a reply." He still sought appointment as consul in London with the rank of resident. As such, he could act in behalf of American sailors impressed by the British; besides, the appointment would give him diplomatic immunity and protection against creditors. "I am even now harass'd by a rascal," he said. He had obtained a house for his bank but had decided not to open it. To be sure, he wrote on May 10, there were "other & greater objects" before him. One possibility, he hinted, lay in a crisis developing between Britain and Spain. British merchant vessels had been seized by the Spanish off the western side of Vancouver Island, and there was determination in London to demand redress and recognition from Madrid of British ownership of the island and neighboring territory. Spain might refuse; if so, there would be war, and England would assist Francisco de Miranda, who was still in London, to foment rebellion in Spanish America.

Therein lay opportunity for Sayre and Duer. America and France might be drawn into the conflict, and as partners the two men might reap very large profits from supply contracts recommended by Miranda in Britain and America. Duer was indeed interested in that possibility, and he informed Sayre that Knox would be a third partner. On June 15 Sayre wrote again to the secretary of war. There was the matter of that ship: Sayre had asked his influential "old friends" Ralph Izard and William Floyd to recommend it to the American government, and he asked Knox to do likewise. *"As I am not to live always* (if I may form my opinion by the sample of other men)," said the importunate Sayre, "I do not mean to lose the present moment to benefit myself." Sayre also wrote directly to President Washington about his ship and supplied information about it.[1]

Miranda—who was dreaming of the creation of a great Latin American state stretching from the Mississippi to Cape Horn and headed by an Inca who would rule with a bicameral legislature—was indeed approached in the crisis and received a subsidy arranged by William Pitt. At the end of August, Sayre believed that war was imminent. From Honfleur in France, en route to Paris, he urged Miranda to propose that his friend Sayre be employed by Britain to buy supplies *"honestly"* for an army, even that he be appointed commissary general for both the army and the navy on an expedition against the Spanish (British commissaries in the American War of Independence had been remarkable for grafting). If Miranda's influence did not extend so far, would the South American use Sayre as his secretary? "You may, in this situation, serve me very importantly . . . in case of success—If we are disappointed we have philosophical minds superior to the issue, be what it may." Should England abuse Miranda, Sayre would be pleased to use his papers to inform the world that his friend had been badly treated. However, there was no war—Spain gave in to British demands.[2]

Before that bright prospect faded, Sayre asked Jefferson, about to become secretary of state, for a job in language that could hardly fail to offend. At Le Havre, Sayre learned that Jefferson was about to leave France for New York, and he reminded the Virginian that he had brought letters to him in 1786 "recommending your appointing me to the place, which *I found so honorably* fill'd by Mr. Lamb." The reference to

1. Sayre to Henry Knox, May 10 and June 15, 1790, Henry Knox to Sayre, September 24, 1790, all in Knox Papers.

2. Dávila (ed.), *Archivo del General Miranda*, VI, 77.

Lamb's failure hardly strengthened Sayre's application for "some employment in Europe if I may be thought worthy of it." It would seem that Sayre sought to injure Jefferson's feelings rather than to secure an office.[3]

Henry Knox did respond to Sayre's appeals. The secretary of war discussed "the love" with President Washington and reported in the fall of 1790 that "the magnitude and astonishing qualities of your plan were such that he could give no explicit answer thereto. Every effort of genius, capable of demonstration and which will either directly or indirectly promote the power and interests of the United States is justly entitled to reward." But there was that matter of "demonstration"—could Sayre supply it sufficiently to persuade Congress to act? Knox was sure that the lawmakers, if they believed in Sayre's work, would be liberal. Through his brother William, who went to England that autumn, Knox sought to secure information about the activities of both Miranda and Sayre. On November 3 William Knox reported to the general that Sayre was in Paris.[4]

If Sayre received the invitation to arrange a display of his ship in New York, he did not quickly respond. France was turning up frequently in his correspondence (Dennis De Berdt held letters for him in London during his absences across the Channel), and at the end of August Sayre announced that he intended to go from Honfleur to the French capital and expected to remain there for some time. Ultimately he would stay in France for almost three years, except for one journey to England. It may be that he was initially attracted beyond the Channel by Lady Anne, since his liaison with her had not ended, and she may have preceded him to France. It is to be suspected that his troubles in English society and his failure to secure recognition and employment from the republic across the Atlantic enhanced the fascination that the continuing French Revolution exerted on him, but he was also seeking economic opportunity. He was in Paris in mid-October. In November he was in Le Havre, trying to establish himself there as a merchant.[5]

3. Boyd (ed.), *Papers of Thomas Jefferson*, XVII, 421.

4. Henry Knox to Sayre, September 24, 1790, William Knox to Henry Knox, November 3, 1790, both in Knox Papers.

5. Sayre to Knox, May 10, 1790, in *ibid.*; Dávila (ed.), *Archivo del General Miranda*, VI, 78.

After settling in France, Sayre wrote no fewer than four letters to President Washington asking for a diplomatic appointment. On October 15, recounting his unfortunate experiences in England and on the Continent, he asked for an appointment as consul general in France, England, Holland, or Sweden, alternatively as minister to one of the less-important European nations. He had arranged for recommendations from Ralph Izard, who had returned to America, and from William Floyd, an influential New York politician. His application would probably have failed in any case, since it was marred by condemnation of Lamb, Dana, John Adams, and the Lee brothers. From Le Havre Sayre asked to be made secretary to the minister at Paris or London; he received no reply. In July, 1791, reporting that he had become a manufacturer of snuff in the French capital, he asked again for the post of secretary there, writing, "This is the last time I ever mean to trouble you with importunities." Three months later, he proposed that Washington sell part of his extensive landholdings west of the Appalachians through the agency of Colonel William Blagden, a friend of Sayre, to Frenchmen interested in migrating to America. It is likely that Washington suspected that Sayre lacked good judgment and therefore declined to make use of his services. He referred the applications for jobs to Secretary of State Jefferson, who did not choose to do anything for Sayre, having no reason to befriend an enemy of the Lee family and Vice-President John Adams.[6]

In the meantime, Sayre not only became a tobacco manufacturer and merchant in Paris, but acquired a second wife and a measure of economic stability. On November 9, 1790, he went to call upon Gouverneur Morris, the new American minister to France, a one-legged New Yorker distinguished for aristocratic leanings, social polish, intelligence, *savoir-faire*, and a propensity for engaging in amours. On November 27 Sayre signed a prenuptial agreement in Paris before two Roman Catholic clergymen, stipulating "previous to my marriage with Mrs. Eliza Dorone that all the property she now has, or may have hereafter by gift, will or other ways from her brother Stephen Dorone of the island of Jamaica, or from James Boswell, Esq., her brother in law, shall be still her own, for her own proper use holding it separately and independently of me, or

6. Sayre to Washington, October 15, 1790, November 20, 1790, July 2, 1791, September 10, 1791, all in Department of State, Miscellaneous Letters.

any of my creditors, in trust." The trustee was to be "Jacob Parayra" while the bride-to-be remained in France. The ceremony was doubtless performed shortly afterward. The second Mrs. Elizabeth Sayre apparently was a widow, although possibly a divorcee, and she had a son. Born and bred in England, she was an heiress to lands in Jamaica. She was, it would seem, much younger than Sayre. Evidently, at the age of fifty-four, he still retained appeal for women.[7]

Obviously relieved of major economic worries by his marriage, Sayre was successful in business in Paris. "Jacob Parayra" was Jacob Pereyra, a Jew and a native of Bayonne, born about 1743, a partner with one Laborde and Sayre in a tobacco factory at the Bonnet de la Liberté on the rue St. Denis. Whether the business was established before or after Sayre's marriage is not clear, but the partnership came to an end in 1792—an event that may have arisen in part from political dispute, for Pereyra surpassed even Sayre in his devotion to the French Revolution. Pereyra soon became an extremist among extremists in French politics. He continued in the business on the rue St. Denis and was eventually guillotined. Sayre established a new factory with another partner, Marie Jean Baptiste Benoist Beaupoils, formerly a French army officer, at Number 7 in the Passage des Petits Pères, near the Place des Victoires.[8]

Before the firm of Sayre & Pereyra ceased business, Sayre at last paid off his debt to John Reynolds, who had remained in France until 1790 and then returned to England to avoid revolutionary tumult. He was still alive in 1816. Frederic Reynolds visited Paris in the spring of 1792 and amiably consorted with Sayre. The bitterness that had existed between his father and Sayre seems to have vanished. When the son penned his autobiography, so often cited in these pages, he said nothing about the clashes between his father and Sayre in the English courts. Consult-

7. Gouverneur Morris, *A Diary of the French Revolution*, ed. Beatrix C. Davenport (Boston, 1939), II, 53; Banta, *Sayre Family*, 89; Sayre to William Duane, August 4, 1803, in Duane Papers. In a letter to William Duer, June 19, 1794, in the William Duer Papers, New-York Historical Society, New York, Sayre refers to a "1500 dollars—not my own property, but my wife's son's, she holds in trust." Banta, *Sayre Family*, 90, indicates that Mrs. Sayre had a sister Mary born in 1759.

8. John Goldsworth Alger, *Paris in 1789–94: Farewell Letters of Victims of the Guillotine* (New York, 1902), 80, 352; *Réimpression de L'ancien Moniteur*, XVI (Paris, 1854), 17–20, 40.

ing a diary kept in his youth, Frederic Reynolds portrayed Sayre as a superlatively attractive, kindly, and good-humored gentleman.[9]

How would Sayre appear, were a journal kept by Lady Anne to be found? She was in Paris that spring, apparently still on terms of intimacy with him. A London banker wrote meaningfully to Sayre on March 13, "I have to acquaint you that Lord Bute died last Saturday." Did Sayre have the task of informing Lady Anne that her father had died? At the end of that month the same banker sent Sayre a draft that Lady Anne had written upon Dennis De Berdt, which had not been honored. Presumably she had no money in De Berdt's hands and no credit with him. No further reference to her, except for one, has been found. That one, however, is curious. In her will, written in 1818, the second Mrs. Sayre mentions an annuity of one hundred pounds per annum that she had bought from Lady Anne, to be paid during the lifetime of the noblewoman. All that reasonably can be inferred from this fact is that the Jamaica heiress and the reckless daughter of the prime minister were at one time not remarkably hostile to each other. Were these two women both in the Sayre ménage in Paris after his second marriage? If so, the arrangement did not endure indefinitely. When Sayre and Elizabeth went to America, Lady Anne remained in Europe. It appears that she died about 1819, in complete obscurity.[10]

The Sayre family did not soon leave for America but occupied quarters for many months in the Passage des Petits Pères, where the Sayres were residents in White's Hotel, sometimes called the Hotel d'Angleterre because it was a home and rendezvous for Englishmen and Americans who came to Paris. There, according to an advertisement inserted by Sayre in the *Journal de Paris* on May 25, 1792, retailers of tobacco could buy superior smokeweed of such high quality that a small amount could be mixed with inferior tobacco to make a satisfactory product—an appeal to the pocketbooks of the thrifty French that was

9. N. Tanner to Sayre, March 13, 1792, in Duane Papers; Reynolds, *Life and Times of Frederic Reynolds*, II, 95–96, 137, 151; Cecil Price (ed.), *The Letters of Richard Brinsley Sheridan* (Oxford, 1966), III, 181, 243–44. Wrote Sheridan to Frederic Reynolds in that year, "I hope my old valued friend your father is well."

10. N. Tanner to Sayre, March 13, 1792, March 30, 1792, in Duane Papers; Banta, *Sayre Family*, 90; Bickley (ed.), *Diaries of Sylvester Douglas*, I, 362.

doubtless peculiarly effective in that time of economic distress.[11] Had Sayre become at last content to be merely comfortable, he might have avoided new adventures, but he continued to wish to play a larger part in the affairs of the world.

Actually, White's Hotel became a hotbed of politics, for the Englishmen and Americans who sojourned there and made use of its facilities were devoted to the cause of liberty, none less so than Sayre. The humiliations he had thrice undergone in monarchical England had made him a radical indeed, and he sympathized profoundly with the Frenchmen who wrecked the Bastille in 1789, attacked the arbitrary power of their monarch, and sought to destroy the privileges of a vicious aristocracy and corrupt national church. Sayre was the senior member—senior at least in age—of a group of determined reformers who gathered at White's in loose imitation of the famous French clubs, such as the Jacobins, and were disposed to support drastic change in France in order to renovate a sorry world. Among the English habitués of White's were James Watt, son of the great Isaac, and Sir Robert Smith; from Scotland came John Oswald; Ireland supplied Lord Edward Fitzgerald; the poet Joel Barlow was an American; England and America furnished Tom Paine; from Italy came the adventurer and author Count Alphonse Giuseppe Emmanuel Balthazar Gorani, who was an admirer of Sayre.[12]

The senior member of the coterie was not content with supplying oral stimulus to the cause of liberty. Becoming friendly with Jean-Frederic Perregaux, a Swiss Protestant who was a highly respected banker in Paris, Sayre began to develop, early in 1792, a seemingly grandiose scheme for the financial benefit of America, France, and Stephen Sayre. By that time the absolute monarchy of France had been replaced by a constitutional one, with King Louis XVI still theoretically upon his throne. The country was in disorder. Many thousands of nobles and clergymen had fled to other lands to seek refuge from reformers and mobs determined to destroy privilege, and the emigrants clamored for military action by European rulers to put an end to the French tumult. The

11. Alger, *Paris in 1789–94*, 352.

12. *Ibid.*, 88, 324–29; François V. A. Aulard (ed.), *La Société des Jacobins* (Paris, 1889–97), IV, 346; David F. Hawke, *Paine* (New York, 1974), 257, 279, 283; Marc Monnier, *Un Aventurier Italien du Siècle Dernier: le Comte Joseph Gorani* (Paris, 1884).

king and Queen Marie-Antoinette also hoped for foreign rescue from passionate enemies. Nearly bankrupt at the beginning of the revolution, France had resorted to a new paper currency, that of the famous assignats, which was rapidly losing value. Sayre and Perregaux worked out a complex scheme whereby the American national debt, part of it owed to France, would be refinanced in London and Amsterdam to the benefit of both nations, America obtaining a lower interest on the debt, France securing gold and hard money. There would be commissions for those who arranged the refinancing—Sayre, Perregaux, and an English banking firm (which would not have been interested in the scheme except for the participation of Perregaux).[13]

Whatever possibilities the plan possessed, it was not developed in time to secure serious consideration in Europe. On April 15 the rulers of Austria and Prussia declared war on France. As their troops advanced toward Paris, a frantic uprising overthrew the monarchy and led to the imprisonment of the king and queen. Amidst scenes of terror and horror in Paris, France became a republic, and its troops checked the advancing Prussian and Austrian armies. Even so, when Gouverneur Morris saw it in October, the republic seemed doomed to early extinction. That cynical gentleman would not in any event have knowingly assisted a rabble of envious and bloodthirsty commoners against their betters. So, although a committee of finance of the new French regime might favor Sayre's refinancing scheme, Morris would have nothing to do with it. Had he endorsed it, the arrangement would hardly have aroused uncontrollable enthusiasm in Philadelphia, the temporary American capital.[14]

But if the appearance of the French republic destroyed whatever chance of success Sayre and Perregaux had, it also offered Sayre an opportunity that he did not fail to seize. The new regime was confronted abroad by Austrian and Prussian armies and by threat of war with Spain, and it was detested by a large minority at home. It could and did raise huge armies, partly by conscription; it could replace aristocratic officers

13. Perregaux's career is described in J. Lhomet, *Le Banquier et Sa Fille, la Duchesse de Raguse* (Paris, 1926).

14. N. Tanner to Sayre, March 13, 1792, March 30, 1792, [Stephen Sayre], "Proposals for the consideration of the Committee of Finance," with note regarding the behavior of Morris, August 24, 1792, in Duane Papers; Morris, *Diary of the French Revolution*, ed. Davenport, II, 53.

with French sergeants and foreigners, including Miranda. But it needed weapons desperately. There were muskets to be had in England, which was as yet neutral, so the republican leaders decided to send an agent across the Channel to buy as many of the guns as possible. Several men asked for the assignment, and Sayre was chosen because of his familiarity with England and English ways of doing business. Presumably his employers also saw in him ability, energy, and zeal. Under the instructions of Joseph Servan de Gerbey, the minister of war, and Charles-François Lebrun, the minister of foreign affairs, Sayre set off for London. Afterward he said that he was also instructed to do what he could to assure that England would not join the enemies of the republic.[15]

In England it was vigorously brought to Sayre's attention that a very large segment of the population detested the French republicans and all their works. Those in England who valued their positions and privileges—aristocrats, bishops, merchants, and propertied folk in general—were alarmed lest the revolution spread across the Channel. The killing and disorder that accompanied the birth of the republic created and exasperated enemies of a France that had been a foe in many wars, and the massacre of hundreds of prisoners in Paris on September 2 horrified many persons in England.

Sayre arrived in London almost simultaneously with the news of the slaughters and discovered that, as an agent of the government responsible for the massacre, he was none too safe in the country that was once his home. Even his old friend John Wilkes was hot against the terrorists. Sayre looked up another old friend, Colonel William Smith, who warned him that there was reason for Sayre to believe he was in danger. So, on or before September 8, Sayre asked Thomas Pinckney, who had become American minister to Britain, to give him American diplomatic status. According to Sayre's later recollection, Smith endorsed the request, perhaps thinking that the interests of France and the United States were identical.[16]

Pinckney dealt with the remarkable request like a true diplomat—he

15. J. Bénétruy, L'Atelier de Mirabeau (Paris, 1962), 413–15; Lebrun to Sayre, September 19, 1792, Sayre to William Duane, August 4, 1803, both in Duane Papers. There was talk in Paris in 1791 that Sayre would accompany Talleyrand on a diplomatic mission to London. Alger, Paris in 1789–1794, 352.

16. Ghita Stanhope and G. P. Gooch, The Life of Charles Third Earl Stanhope (London,

sent it across the ocean to Secretary of State Jefferson for consideration. Jefferson eventually and stiffly answered, assuring Pinckney that he had been "perfectly right" in "refusing [Sayre] the protection of an appointment under you, a protection due to those only who are bona fide employed in the mission of the U.S. which it would be wrong to extend to any other, and might compromise our honour & good understanding with the British Court were they to refuse to admit it." Meanwhile, Sayre asked Lebrun to give him formal French diplomatic status and to supply money. Lebrun arranged to provide 400,000 francs but said that Sayre should be safe as a person charged with the business of the French republic.[17]

Did Sayre give out that he came to England to buy grain for the French army, and was he menaced by his former enemy, or enemies, at the London *Times?* On October 3 that newspaper printed a disconcerting suggestion for agents of the new republic: "There are several persons now in this country, who are come for the purpose of *purchasing corn for the French army.* We hope they will receive every *proper attention.*" By that time Sayre was safely back in Paris.

Through various more-or-less concealed bargainings, including an effort to obtain British army weapons stored in the Tower of London, Sayre did secure muskets for the French—ten thousand of them, he claimed. He was not content with that substantial achievement, however. Colonel Smith, who detested George III as much as Sayre did and referred to that pudgy monarch by his German title of the Elector of Hanover, devoutly hoped "for the success of France & the ruin of despotism." He suggested to Sayre that the French troops, for lack of muskets, might use pikes and swords instead, provided they did not fight in formal array that exposed them to fire from cannon and small arms. As fertile as Sayre in bizarre notions, Smith also suggested that the United States could furnish all the muskets and cannon France needed from American arsenals at West Point and Springfield, Massachusetts. Thus

---

1914), 120; Colonel William Smith to Sayre, September 23, 1792, in Duane Papers; Sayre to William Duane, August 4, 1803, in Duane Papers; Jefferson to Pinckney, November 13, 1792, in Thomas Jefferson Papers, University of Virginia Library, Charlottesville, Virginia.

17. Lebrun to Sayre, September 19, 1792, in Duane Papers.

the United States could pay part of its debt owed to France for aid in the War of Independence.[18]

In the midst of his hectic stay in England, Sayre considered the suggestion from Smith and combined it with a scheme that he had formed with Jacob Pereyra, who had been a partner in more than the making of tobaccos. The plan called for an attack by France upon Louisiana, then held by Spain, in the event that war broke out between the two countries. From London and again immediately after his return to Paris, Sayre wrote to Miranda, who had become a volunteer lieutenant general in the French army. Sayre assured his old friend that "we have nothing to expect from this Court but hatred, hypocriscy, injury & war," and suggested that Miranda should consider the use of pikes. Far more important, with Spain on the verge of waging war against France, the time was coming to strike for the freedom of the Latin Americans, Sayre urged. He was eager to go out to America on the French packet for October, provided that he had the blessing and support of France. He doubted that he could secure access to American arsenals—Gouverneur Morris and Robert Morris, the financier, would probably persuade President Washington to keep them closed to the French—but he would be able to proceed across the Appalachians and to gather Americans and Frenchmen in the settlements beyond the mountains for a successful descent upon New Orleans. Sayre predicted that France would give Miranda another commission as lieutenant general as soon as hostilities began and would send him across the ocean to assume command. And, wrote Sayre, "if things go no further, France may always keep possession of this most valuable country." However, if the independent Latin American nation desired by Miranda came into being as the result of the efforts of the republicans, Sayre asked that Miranda use his influence in that new nation to secure Sayre's appointment as its first minister to the United States.[19]

Miranda received the letters and pondered. In the one penned in

18. Colonel William S. Smith to Sayre, September 23, 1792, in Duane Papers; Stanhope and Gooch, *Life of Charles Third Earl Stanhope*, 120.

19. Frederick Jackson Turner, "Genêt's Attack on Louisiana and the Floridas," *American Historical Review*, III (1898), 661; Dávila (ed.), *Archivo del General Miranda*, VI, 200–206.

London there was a statement by Sayre that "I love the French and am one of the citizens of France." Then just how much devotion was there in Sayre to the cause of Latin American freedom? Miranda must have suspected that Sayre was merely trying to use him and was seeking to profit from either of the two attacks upon Spanish America. Miranda did not reply for several weeks; when he did, in a letter that has been lost, he denounced Sayre as an "adventurer"—a word that was, of course, also applicable to Miranda, an officer cashiered for misuse of Spanish army money. Sayre defended himself in a long autobiographical statement sent from Paris on November 1 that tells somewhat more about him than he intended and exaggerates some of his achievements:

> Upon due reflection, I am sincerely disposed to thank you for your candour—you give reasons for having kept me in the shades—as these reasons were weighty in your mind. I shall be submit & be silent, as to every thing past. The object of this letter is, to furnish you with a reply, if ever you are, hereafter told, that I am an *adventurer*. It is in the power of the worst of men, to call the best rogues, rascals, & Read the following outlines of my life, & judge, whether such an epithet can be apply'd to me.
>
> I was bred at New Jersey College—received a Bachelor's degree; and that of Master of Arts at Cambridge.—At the age of 21 years, I commanded a company in the 2nd battalion of the New York forces, on the Lakes—my conduct was such, that the Governor, the next year offer'd me a Major's commission, tho I was one of the youngest captains of the two battalions.—Forseeing the certainty of a speedy peace—I refused it—went into business as a merchant—went to the island of St. Croix, with an unlimited credit, on the first house in London drew bills, at discretion, but never abused their confidence—I am now possessed of their letters, which prove what I say—upon my coming to London, offer'd me a co-partnership—I accepted one—served the house, effectively, as such, till the death of the principal, who was an agent for the then colony of Massachusetts.—Upon his death I became a banker, in company with a gentleman, who had a landed estate of £1,500 sterling per an: I married a woman of one of the first families in England—She had money & landed property. I have now a right to two estates there—but am kept out of possession, by my partner's creditor—not by my own—for I had quitted the bank, long before its failure.—had lent him £10,000—but the fangs of the law—rather the practice of roguery was

not—withstanding all this—extended to my other estates. My commitment to the Tower, was meant to ruin me—it did not succeed—but the lawyers found means under pretense of a partnership, to effect it.

In 1777 I left England—came here—the American commissioners named me their secretary, & sent me to Berlin, with one of them—I received only 3,000 liras tho I remain'd there 6 months—went from thence to Denmark—from thence to Sweden—laid the foundation of that great confederacy, call'd the arm'd neutrality—tho M. Vergennes, has assumed the credit of it—this I did, with my own credit, on Mr. Panchaud who I have since fully repaid with interest as Mr. Perregaux, will at this instant testify—for soon after Lee came from Berlin, the commissioners never could agree upon any one thing—they supply'd me with no more money—and Congress owe me about 10,000 dollars. Sensible of this but unable to pay me, when last in America—it was a question between Colon Smith & me, who should be sent to England—his strong recommendations, from the commander in chief added to his own merit & services prevail'd.

A committee, was then named to hear my complaints—there was no money—but I obtain'd letters to Jefferson & Adams, requesting them to send me to Algiers, to make a treaty—when I arrived here, they had appointed a trader in mules, who had once been in Algiers for a cargo—this was his only recommendation.—But before I left New York, I had powers of attorney, to make claims on the English government to the amount of near £200,000—In this, I was not employ'd as a stranger—but they were my countrymen, when I was born. I will give you no farther trouble, than to ask you—do these things accord, with the character of an *adventurer*? P.S. About £1,200, will clear my estates in England of every demand—they may be let at £650 per an.[20]

Why did not Sayre borrow the £1,200, Miranda must have asked himself. Sayre and Miranda did not meet again for thirteen years.

Menaced as they were, the French republicans failed to make good use of Miranda. They continued to employ him in Europe, and when he performed ineptly at the Battle of Neerwinden he was accused of treason—failure was commonly equivalent to treachery in the minds of the men of the Convention and its Committee of Public Safety, which

20. Dávila (ed.), *Archivo del General Miranda*, VI, 211–13.

ruled France in the early years of the Republic. Miranda was imprisoned and put on trial; he was fortunate to be acquitted. Eventually, in 1798, he was expelled from France and turned once more to England for help in securing Latin American freedom. Nor did the French move rapidly in the Mississippi Valley. France did not go to war with Spain until after the guillotining of Louis XVI in January, 1793, and the year was well under way before steps were taken to set men in motion down the great river.

Before that year opened, Sayre entered upon diplomatic maneuvers that reflect more credit upon him, doing what he could to keep England out of the war. In September he had vainly tried to establish contact in London with the most prominent champion of the French republicans in England, his old friend Lord Mahon, who had become by inheritance Earl Stanhope. The marriage of that nobleman to the daughter of the great Chatham had long since been dissolved by her death, but Stanhope was intimate with her brother the prime minister, who was not yet committed against the new regime in Paris, although the normal communications between Paris and London had collapsed. The earl could be relied upon to act in the cause of liberty and progress. Long-faced and long-nosed, he was intellectually gifted and devoted to reform. A canal-builder and an inventor of devices used in printing, he sought to improve sailing vessels and to find means to propel ships by other than uncontrollable winds. He was the head of a Constitutional Society dedicated to the principles of the Glorious Revolution of 1688 that overthrew the would-be tyrant James II. Stanhope was disturbed by the wholesale killings in France in September, but he nevertheless approved of the new republic.[21]

On October 28 Sayre wrote to Stanhope, expressing regret that he

21. No evidence has been found that Sayre sought to make use of a tenuous connection with Sir James Bland Burgess, an undersecretary in the British Foreign Office. Burgess married an Elizabeth Noel, a cousin of the first Mrs. Sayre, but she died only two years after the marriage, long before the outbreak of the French Revolution. There is a sketch of Burgess in the *Dictionary of National Biography*.

A surprising number of people associated with Sayre were interested in ship design. In 1753 the Academy of Sciences at Paris offered a prize for discovery of means other than wind to move a ship. Various suggestions were made, but no one proposed using steam power. Among those who discussed the problem was one Jacob-Rodrigues Pereire. Théophile Malvezin, *Histoire du Commerce de Bordeaux* (Bordeaux, 1892), IV, 6. Pereire could have been the father of Sayre's partner.

had been unable to confer with his old acquaintance in September, for he had been entrusted with matters of far greater importance than buying muskets, but the news of the "massacres" had rendered useless any attempt at that time to bring up those matters. Now, said Sayre, he wished to come to London to speak for "a great and powerful nation, a more formidable republic than the Romans at any period." Would Stanhope, "as a friend of mankind," sound out Pitt and Lord Grenville, the British foreign secretary, to discover whether, if Sayre came to London, either of them would enter into "a cool and friendly deliberation" with him in an effort to avoid another Anglo-French war. The republicans "would meet you on the most friendly ground; but they are not to be intimidated." "I have more to offer," said Sayre, than might be supposed. "A private interview may lead to public arrangements, peace and happiness." According to Sayre's later recollection, Stanhope replied that any negotiation should be public, thus ruining the scheme. Sayre sent Stanhope a second message on November 12 in another attempt to stave off hostilities: "I wish your Lordship could come over here for some ten or twenty days, after seeing the proper people; I cannot venture to write upon the matter to be thought of and considered. . . . I have a part of White's Hotel, his first floor is yet unoccupied. As I wish to see you often without appearing to do so, let me engage the apartments for you. You will be well received here by all the leading characters, you will return with accurate information, may meet Parliament with advantage and confidence, and render service to the world." Stanhope failed to seize a last chance to ward off a clash.[22]

Was Sayre even more active in French efforts to stave off war with Britain than has been indicated? Afterward, Augustus W. Miles, who served as an intermediary between France and Britain and who also sought to avert war, related that an unnamed party, whom Miles referred to only as "*****," approached him in London in September on behalf of the French republicans and that this person sought an interview with "the minister," presumably Pitt. Miles distrusted the Parisian sponsor of "*****" and refused to comply. Lebrun, of course, had more than one

22. Stanhope and Gooch, *Life of Charles Third Earl Stanhope*, 120–21; Sayre to William Duane, August 4, 1803, in Duane Papers. Sayre also claimed that he had been in the confidence of General Dumouriez, Lebrun's predecessor in office.

agent in England at the time. Even so, "*****" may well have been S-a-y-r-e. If he was, Sayre initiated a last great effort on the part of France to secure the neutrality of Britain, for the discussions between Miles and "*****" led to the appearance in London of Hugues-Bernard Maret as a special emissary from Lebrun (of course, the French could not entrust such vital negotiations to an American). Maret conferred with Pitt in December and again late in January, 1793, but to no avail.[23]

On November 18 White's Hotel was the scene of an extraordinary dinner arranged by fifty of the foreign friends of the new France—including Sayre—who were accustomed to gather at that place. One hundred men attended. With James Watt presiding, they drank toasts to French armies that had driven back the Prussians and Austrians, to the destruction of all tyrants, and to the abolition of all hereditary honors. Lord Edward Fitzgerald and Sir Robert Smith announced that they were abandoning their titles. The gathering sang an English song to the tune of the *Marseillaise* and sent an address to the Convention that ruled France which lauded the nation for its gallantry and praised France for its struggles in behalf of reason and truth. "Let us hope," said the address, "that the victorious troops of liberty will lay down their arms only when there are no more tyrants or slaves. Of all these pretended governments, there will soon remain only a shameful memory." The address also expressed the wish that the French, English, Scottish, and Irish would unite "to ensure entire Europe for the enjoyment of the rights of man and establish on the firmest basis universal peace." It is likely that Sayre was the author, or one of the authors, of that remarkable document.[24]

The men who frequented the hotel agreed to establish a formal club, which would meet there to foster the cause of freedom. It did not long endure. The French republicans, having discovered that Louis XVI encouraged other European rulers to come to his rescue by military force, executed him in January, 1793, and they disturbed Britain by aggressive

23. [Augustus] W. Miles, *Authentic Correspondence with M. Le Brun, the French Minister* (3rd. ed.; London, 1796), 67, and Appendix, 66–69, 81–85; Charles P. Miles (ed.), *The Correspondence of William Augustus Miles on the French Revolution* (London, 1890), II, 25, 26, 61. Maret was an able man, and later, as the duc de Bassano, a trusted servant of Napoleon.

24. This extraordinary affair is described in Alger, *Paris in 1789–1794*, 324–29; Thomas Moore, *The Life and Death of Lord Edward Fitzgerald* (London, 1831), I, 172–73.

action in Belgium. In February Britain and France fell to blows. As war approached, Colonel George Monro, a British spy who had lived at White's Hotel and was familiar with the activities of its denizens, reported that the many British members of the society were turning against the relatively few Americans in it, feeling that the Americans had too much influence in the club. The Englishmen even considered a motion to expel the Americans. Some members regretted that they had signed the address to the Convention. The club languished, and Monro assured his masters in London that there was no need to be concerned about it. It did indeed die away, although Paris continued to supply inspiration to both English and American reformers.[25]

It is reported that at least thirteen of the diners of November 18 were later imprisoned in Paris, and at least six were killed for political cause. Lord Edward Fitzgerald afterward died in a stillborn Irish rebellion. Sayre's former partner, Jacob Pereyra, an extreme radical, was guillotined. Continuing as a tobacco manufacturer in the rue St. Denis after the dissolution of the partnership, Pereyra served as one of three commissioners who investigated the conduct of General Dumouriez. Since the general had not been victorious, the three men denounced him as a traitor. Dumouriez made his escape, but Pereyra himself was attacked in 1794 as a traitor and agent of Pitt and was found guilty— accused persons were seldom found innocent in France at that time. He was guillotined with other plotters about five o'clock in the afternoon of March 24 in the Place de la Révolution, to the general satisfaction of the crowd. Count Gorani fled to Switzerland in 1793 to escape the knife, and Tom Paine, who made an appearance at White's, sojourned for a time in a French prison. Sayre himself left France with his wife, with due formality, and without pursuit by terrorists.[26]

There can be no doubt that Sayre was devoted to the French republic—so much so, indeed, that he may have failed to see reasons for a clash between the revolutionary regime and the United States. In the draft of a treaty between the two nations, which he prepared late in 1792

25. Oscar Browning (ed.), *The Despatches of Earl Gower* (Cambridge, 1885), 260, 268–69; Alger, *Paris in 1789–1794*, 330–32.

26. *Réimpression de L'ancien Moniteur*, XVI, 15–16, 18–21, XVIII, 507–509, XX, 17–20, 40.

or in 1793, he proposed the establishment of a remarkable relationship between the two republics. "The citizens of France & of the United States of America," the paper began, "having duly consider'd the singular situation in which they now stand, with respect to other nations—reflecting that the world is yet wrap'd in slavery, or held in a condition of indignity & degradation—having emancipated our persons from the fangs of assumed power, and our minds from ignorance, we now resolve to unite as firmly in the bonds of mutual friendship & mutual interest, as we are united in the principles & the love of liberty." The paper continued, "We therefore hereby declare, & proclaim, to all the universe, that our great & leading object for union is, to procure & obtain for all the inhabitants of the earth the rights, & the lost dignity of *man*. Henceforth therefore, as long as other nations are held in chains—as long as other men are injur'd & oppress'd, the citizens of France & those of the United States of America will & shall be united in one common effort, & one common cause—mutual safety, & the safety & happiness of the oppress'd." What was more, "henceforth every citizen of France is, or may become a citizen of the United States of America—every citizen of America is, or may become a citizen of France." Moreover, although it is specifically stated that no military obligation would exist between the two nations, each would permit vessels of war of the other to use its ports and would not discriminate by taxation against the merchant ships of the other. Besides, explained Sayre, this peculiar union would supply "two abutments of the political arch, to secure the safe, & easy passage of the Atlantic against all the storms of contending nations, or the utmost efforts of disappointed ambition."[27] Did he truly believe that most American republicans thought of French republicans as ideological brothers, or that American leaders would sign such a treaty, almost certain to lead to a revival of hostilities with Britain?

Apparently so. War between France and Spain came. On March 4, 1793, with Pereyra, who was not yet consigned to the guillotine, and Beaupoils, who had served in Poland, Sayre presented a revised plan for an attack upon the Spanish. Since France did not have a fleet and army to

27. The draft of the treaty is preserved, with "Observations," in Sayre's handwriting in the Duane Papers. The political philosophy and the originality of the provisions regarding citizenship also point to Sayre as the author. It is not surprising that Sayre was accused of Gallomania.

make a direct attack south of the Caribbean, the plan called for a Franco-American expedition to move down the Mississippi River against New Orleans. American veterans of the War of Independence would be enlisted and would gather at Louisville for the attack. Supplies for three thousand men for two months would be needed. The troops would move down the river in batteaux and would be joined in Louisiana by French Creoles. Alternatively, the expedition would move to the westward of New Orleans, enlist the help of Indians in Mexico restless under Spanish rule, and move into that Spanish viceroyalty. Then, if Mexico fell, the rest of Spanish America would strike for freedom. The planners estimated that the expedition would cost only 280,000 francs, plus artillery and ammunition. Most important for France, the expedition, embroiling the United States in the contest for Louisiana or Mexico, would force American entrance into the war.

Other men were scheming for such an advance down the Mississippi. George Rogers Clark, the doughty frontier fighter who had defended Kentucky in the War of Independence and who believed that he had not been rewarded sufficiently, was ready to lead the expedition. In Paris, Joel Barlow, like Sayre, desired to lay the groundwork for a campaign in the American backwoods. French officials also listened to one Lyonnet, formerly a resident of New Orleans, who was willing to accept American ownership of Louisiana. They conceived that neither Sayre nor Barlow, for lack of familiarity with the valley of the lower Mississippi, would be useful in the North American interior. The French reached a decision to employ Clark and placed general direction of the expedition under Edmond Charles Genêt, a veteran diplomat who was about to sail across the Atlantic as minister to the United States, with the help of a committee consisting of Sayre, Beaupoils, and Lyonnet. At Philadelphia, which had become the American capital, Genêt and his associates were to get money to support Clark by collecting part of the debt owed to France in consequence of French assistance to the Americans in the War of Independence. Sayre was to be watched to make sure that he toiled for France.[28]

Such an appointment would have been in itself of little value to

28. Turner, "Genét's Attack on Louisiana and the Floridas," 650–71. For Sayre's role, see particularly pp. 656, 661–62.

Sayre. Conceivably he accepted it in part in order to secure a comfortable departure from a France torn by war, internal strife, and shortages of food. It may be that his wife, sickened and deeply frightened by the mobs and fanatics in Paris that killed for little or no reason, urged him to take her out of France. Perhaps his tobacco business was not flourishing; perhaps he was willing to abandon a profitable but small business to seek once more rewards from the United States for his former services or for his naval invention. He secured a passport from the ruling Committee of Public Safety and returned to America for the last time, with Elizabeth. They arrived in Philadelphia in the late spring or early summer of 1793. Sayre remained a passionate defender of the French republican revolutionaries, who he believed were leading the way to a better world—and were enemies of George III. That royal wretch, wrote Sayre ten years later, was determined to fight rather than to bargain with the French republicans in the autumn of 1792, and his Queen Charlotte "wanted to make more money out of the loans as she had done in our revolutionary war." The charge against the king was ill founded; the condemnation of the queen is ridiculous. Only a violent partisan remembering his sufferings could have written in such vein.[29]

29. Sayre to William Duane, August 4, 1803, in Duane Papers.

11
The American
Gentleman Farmer

E DMOND CHARLES GENÊT was learned and experienced in the ways of European diplomacy, but he was hopelessly ignorant of things American. He looked upon the nation that had been created with Bourbon help as a client state of France and assumed that the new republic on the western side of the ocean should and would gladly assist the still newer but more powerful one in Europe assailed on land and sea by wicked tyrants. Stephen Sayre might agree that America owed and should repay a heavy debt to France, even as an ally seduced into the great war, but not as a nation that must accept direction from Paris or from a French minister. Landing at Charleston, South Carolina, on April 8, Genêt was enthusiastically welcomed, and he slowly moved northward by land to Philadelphia amidst vast applause. He immediately began to commission privateers to use American ports as bases for attacks upon British shipping and as markets for their captures, and also to appoint officers for an assault upon Spanish Florida as well as the long-projected assault upon Louisiana. Friends of France formed Democratic Societies, similar to the clubs of revolutionists in Paris.

Sayre became a member of such a club in Philadelphia and earned a reputation as an extreme partisan of France—to his sorrow, so far as preferment and payment of his claim against the United States were concerned. Perhaps a third of the Americans acclaimed the rise of the French republic, and of that fraction many rejoiced over the execution of Louis XVI and other exploiters of a long-oppressed people. Another third saw the French revolutionaries as mad, bloodthirsty enemies of order and religion, as thieves who seized the property of their betters, the ancient and legitimate leaders of state and church. Such Americans were disposed to look with sympathy upon the efforts of Britain—if not those of Austria, Prussia, and Spain—to deal with the revolutionaries. Cooler Americans, perceiving that virtue did not dwell exclusively upon one side of the Channel or that wickedness was not confined to the other, sought to avoid involvement in the struggle. There was a division in the cabinet of President Washington—Secretary of State Jefferson favored the revolutionaries, Secretary of the Treasury Alexander Hamilton gave his blessing to England—but both men believed that America should refrain from taking part in the war. At first pleased by the overthrow in France of absolute monarchy and vicious privilege, Washington learned that French officers who had served with him in his hours of direst need in the War of Independence were despoiled and driven into exile or guillotined. With the approval of Jefferson and Hamilton, he issued a proclamation on April 22 urging all Americans to abstain from committing a hostile act against any of the nations at war.

When Genêt reached Philadelphia on May 18, he received a very cool reception from Washington. He threatened to appeal for his cause over the head of the president, and thus he offended Jefferson. Genêt's behavior threatened, said Washington, "war abroad, and discord and anarchy at home." Consequently, Genêt was prevented from launching the expedition down the Mississippi. When Genêt was recalled—and became a candidate for the guillotine—Washington gave him asylum in the United States in 1794. Washington did nothing for Stephen Sayre.

If Sayre did not approve of Genêt's tactics, if he was not trusted by the French, he remained for at least a time their devoted, passionate ally. He settled in Philadelphia and lived there for many months, except for a flight into the country to escape the great epidemic of yellow fever that struck the city in August, 1793. In December of that year he bought a handsome three-story house together with a farm of 150 acres on Point Breeze at Bordentown, New Jersey. Point Breeze jutted out into the Delaware River, and the house, with its fine view of the river and the opposite shore, occupied an almost idyllic spot.[1]

Whether at Philadelphia or Bordentown, Sayre did what he could to

---

1. Sayre to William Duer, September 15, 1793, in Duer Papers; E. M. Woodward, *Bonaparte's Park, and the Murats* (Trenton, 1879), 23–24. Tom Paine had lived in Bordentown some years earlier and could have recommended the location to Sayre. More likely, Sayre heard about the house through independent inquiry.

support the French republic. Before leaving Paris, he undertook to secure dismissal of Gouverneur Morris as minister, Morris being an able and determined enemy of the French republicans. Soon after his arrival in America, Sayre not only joined the Democratic Society in Philadelphia but went to see Washington to urge that Morris be brought home. In letters to the president and Jefferson, he also asked for a diplomatic appointment for himself. Washington coldly rejected his advice with respect to Morris, and Jefferson coolly notified the office seeker that the secretary of state had read the letters and that "I have the honor to inform you that the circumstances of the case not leaving room for the appointment therein proposed, the offer of service you are pleased to make cannot be made use of." Had Sayre asked to be appointed in place of Morris, or to represent the United States in the expedition, which aborted, down the Mississippi? Did he consort with Genêt? Evidence that he supported the French envoy has not been found.[2]

But Sayre wrote vehemently as a revolutionary under the pseudonym of "A New-Jersey Farmer" in a Philadelphia newspaper early in 1794. Seventeen years earlier, John Dickinson as a "Pennsylvania Farmer" had successfully stimulated American resistance to the Townshend duties. Emulating Dickinson, Sayre sought to arouse his readers against foreign and domestic exploiters and savagely condemned kings and aristocrats. "The great omniscient author of our being never designed that the few and those few too the scum and offscouring of humanity should lord it and tyrannize over the many." Kings were "bloodthirsty monsters," and it was preposterous to contend that England or the English monarch deserved American respect, much less liking. The American Patriots, by rising in behalf of freedom and achieving it, had laid a foundation for the happiness of the entire human race. France was destroying not only royalty but aristocratic oppressors; England, on the other hand, was exploiting the people of India. The killing in France was unavoidable: "France is wisely ridding herself of such vermin by the aid of the guillotine as we ought to have done, or forever banished them." He

2. Dávila (ed.), *Archivo del General Miranda*, VI, 203; Sayre to James Madison, January 20, 1809, in Madison Papers. "I offended Genl. W. very innocently," wrote Sayre to Madison, "by giving my opinion (tho' grounded on facts, for I was at Paris, & had them from all the ministers) that Mr. Gr. Morris ought not to be continued in France." See also Jefferson to Sayre, July 17, 1793, Jefferson Papers.

assailed a "tory junto" in America that favored Britain against France. Those Tories who had supported George III in the War of Independence were reaping the profits of American freedom, while the Patriots who struggled for it were denied reward for their sacrifices. There was a hint that the time to act against the wicked Tories had not yet passed. Ultimately, all exploiters of humanity ought to disappear, and all the peoples of the world should be united in one republic.[3]

By implication Sayre also attacked the developing Federalist party, led by Alexander Hamilton and John Adams, which was hostile to French revolutionaries and contained many men of aristocratic bent, including former Tories. It was known that Sayre held such opinions, and his authorship of the essay was suspected by Hamilton's friends. Accordingly, in 1795 they mistakenly believed that Sayre might be the author of "Features of the Treaty," a series of essays that appeared in the Philadelphia newspaper that published "A New-Jersey Farmer" and denounced the Jay Treaty on the ground that it conceded too much to Britain. Actually, the author of "Features of the Treaty," a very dry disquisition utterly unlike the writings of Sayre, was Alexander Dallas, a rising young Philadelphia lawyer and a fellow member with Sayre of the Democratic Society of that city.[4]

Personal disappointments continued to push Sayre toward extreme positions in politics. He was held at arm's length by Jefferson, despite the fact that he gave allegiance to the Democratic-Republican party that was emerging under the leadership of Jefferson, Aaron Burr, and George Clinton. He was kept at a greater distance by Washington. Late in 1793, he was accorded a hearing by Henry Knox regarding the "mistery" of his naval invention, during which Sayre again urged the merits of the vessel he had devised fourteen years earlier. The United States now had money

3. The essay appeared in Dunlap & Claypoole's *American Daily Advertiser* on February 17, 1794. Internal evidence demonstrates that the New Jersey tiller of political ground was Sayre: the arguments and conclusions fit him, and the writer was familiar with military service. The essay contained a reference to Lord Chatham characteristic of Sayre. It quickly reached France, where it stimulated General John Skey Eustace, an American whose views at that time were very much like those of Sayre. J. S. Eustace, *Letters on the Crimes of George III* (Paris, [1794]), Part I, 19.

4. Pointing toward Sayre as a possible author, Oliver Wolcott, Jr., said, "S. Sayre of New Jersey is I understand very violent" against the Washington regime. Harold C. Syrett *et al.* (eds.), *The Papers of Alexander Hamilton* (New York, 1961–), XIX, 294–96.

to spend, and superior warships would be useful. Knox cautiously expressed interest in Sayre's naval architecture but expressed doubt that it would be approved by others. He declined to bring it to the attention of the president. Thereupon Sayre asked the secretary for a letter to Washington that would enable him to make his case before the president. Knox invited Sayre to a second interview, but the records do not say that the inventor was granted a hearing by the president. Sayre did make a plea in a letter to Washington, claiming that the two ships he had built in St. Petersburg were superior and that he had acquired additional expertise by visiting English dockyards in the later 1780s. He insisted that he could build frigates "costing no more than those of 36 guns, now in use in England, that shall defend themselves against those of 74 guns." What was more, he could "make us the only naval power on the seas—*I can build ships which cannot be taken by ships now in use.*" He asked to be allowed to demonstrate the validity of his claims, which could be established in an inspection requiring only one day. No evidence of such a demonstration has been found; most of the secrets of Sayre's naval architecture remained secret.[5]

A last plea to Washington for a job in 1795 also failed, nor did Sayre encounter better fortune when he renewed his plea for pay as an American diplomat in the War of Independence. He presented a new petition for it to the House of Representatives immediately after Christmas in 1793. Jefferson had resigned from the Department of State, and his successor, Edmund Randolph, was asked to examine the claim and documents supporting it, since the business concerned his department. With time and distance, Sayre's achievements had grown in his own mind. He now specifically asserted that he should have received the salary of a secretary of legation—£1,000 per annum—for his services during the years 1777–1779. With interest, that claim amounted to

5. Sayre to Knox, December 16, 1793, Knox to Sayre, December 18, 1793 (Private), both in Knox Papers; Sayre to Washington, December 10, 1793, in Department of State, Miscellaneous Letters. Sayre explained that he used pine instead of oak in parts of the ships he built in Russia, thus lightening them and increasing their speed, and that had had done so independently of Captain John Peck of Massachusetts, who had built a schooner on the same plan for Congress during the War of Independence. Peck's *Mercury* was also a swift sailor, but it proved unsatisfactory in combat. William M. Fowler, Jr., *Rebels Under Sail* (New York, 1976), 212–13.

£4,375. Moreover, he asked to be rewarded because he had served America by initiating the League of Armed Neutrality, claiming that he had stirred Frederick the Great to work quietly for that combination, also Gustavus III. Britain had suffered in consequence of his work. However, except for a statement by Matthew Lewis that he had known Sayre since 1762 and that he was a person of good character, Sayre offered no new evidence of importance.[6]

Randolph urged that Sayre did indeed deserve some recompense, and the committee responded generously. It proposed that Sayre be allowed seven months pay as a secretary of legation, with interest, three months pay in lieu of passage money from Europe to America, and also that his services with respect to the League be recognized. But the House was less impressed than Randolph and the committee; after all, Sayre had not secured documents from Franklin or Arthur Lee to support his claims after their rejection in 1785. Publication of a pamphlet by Sayre defining his services and handsomely estimating that he had suffered direct and indirect losses of £93,700 because of his patriotic endeavors probably did not strengthen his case. He explained that he could not produce papers to prove that he had effectively worked for the League because the Prussians, remembering the Elliot theft in Berlin, would not let him carry away the documents. Moreover, his political views were undoubtedly anathema to many of the legislators. His claims were rejected in December, 1794. Presented again in 1796, they were rejected again, after much delay, on March 4, 1800. They were not sympathetically considered by Congress until after the Democratic-Republicans gained control of the national government.[7]

WEALTH continued to elude Sayre. The money of his second wife enabled him to live as a gentleman farmer at Point Breeze, but it did not relieve him from financial worries. The title to his home for at least a decade was vested in her name or that of his son, doubtless to protect it against his creditors. Perhaps those arrangements were in part dictated by his wife to prevent his mortgaging the property to secure money for speculative enterprises. Sayre was involved in some transaction in Sep-

6. Sayre to Washington, January 3, 1795, in Department of State, Miscellaneous Letters.

7. Sayre, *A Short Narrative*; *American State Papers*, IX, 81–83, 123–24, 223–26.

tember, 1793, that kept him in "a state of doubt and anxiety." His old friend William Duer was acting as his agent. "I was the other day at Trenton," Sayre wrote to Duer, "& would have come to New York, but had my apprehensions." Presumably Sayre feared he would be arrested for debt. This affair or another led to a financial and domestic crisis for him in the late spring of 1794.[8]

Duer was in much worse trouble. Serving under Alexander Hamilton in the Treasury, Duer had used public money for his own purposes. He was forced from office and was imprisoned for debt in New York. Sayre wrote to him from Trenton on June 19: "I found your favr. of the 14th inst. Don't imagine me capable of refusing to settle any former accots we have had together; but for God's sake do not withhold the 1500 dollars—not my own property, but my wife's son's, she holds in trust." The appeal went on. "I have been compel'd to let her know how I was necessitously obliged to leave it in your hands—assuring her you had too much honor, tho' confined, to abuse my confidence a single moment. She begins now to express some fears— my dear friend, you say it is not your intention to retain the money—why then give me so much as an unpleasant thought—by delaying it longer you may make me unhappy thro' life." "What purpose would it answer," pleaded Sayre, "to set your creditors upon me to tear me to pieces after all my sufferings." He begged Duer "*by all our former friendships*" to return the $1,500 document. For the sake of his domestic tranquillity one hopes he received it. Sayre apparently visited Duer in prison and remained on good terms with him. "Let me know what are your prospects as to getting out of that damnible place," he wrote to Duer in 1796. Poor Duer died in prison, leaving behind him a family in distress. Sayre's days in jail had ended. He was doubtless forced to listen at night to reproaches from his wife because of his risky ventures, but he could console himself with the thought that he had at least escaped the sad fate of Jacob Pereyra and other friends and acquaintances who perished in the Great Terror in France in 1794.[9]

8. Woodward, *Bonaparte's Park*, 25–26; Sayre to Duer, September 15, 1793, in Duer Papers.

9. Sayre to William Duer, June 19, 1794, July 10, 1796, both in Duer Papers. In 1805 John Duer, son of William, told Miranda that the money he had borrowed to go to Europe in 1784 came exclusively from William Duer and that Sayre had not been a lender

Despite the illnesses from which he had suffered, Sayre was remarkable, like so many leaders of the Revolutionary generation, for physical hardihood. In 1796, at the age of sixty, he arranged to journey to Pittsburgh and beyond, probably in connection with a speculation in land located beyond the Allegheny divide. The decisive victory won by General Anthony Wayne over the Indian warriors of the Old Northwest two years earlier in the Battle of Fallen Timbers, and Jay's Treaty, had brought about the withdrawal of British troops from forts south of the Great Lakes, and an extensive territory thus became open to settlement.[10]

But that venture was too small to occupy his mind entirely or lengthily. In February, 1797, from headquarters in Philadelphia, Sayre proposed a scheme that contained an excellent suggestion to John Adams, who was soon to succeed Washington as president. Relations between America and France, then ruled by the Directory, were tense. It was generally believed in France that America was ungrateful for the assistance rendered by France in the War of Independence. At war with Britain, the French held that America ought not to have composed its differences with Britain in Jay's Treaty, ought indeed to assist a sister republic in its struggle with a common enemy. War between France and America was threatened, and Sayre urged Adams to send a minister extraordinary to Paris to put an end to Franco-American quarrels. He also proposed that the two nations agree to take a strong stand in behalf of the rights of neutrals on the seas, such rights being limited once more by a Britain seeking to distress the French republicans and also injured in a minor way by the French in their efforts to hurt the British. Also, suggested Sayre, his familiar device of a free port in the Caribbean could be used to prevent British searches and seizures of American merchant

---

to Miranda. If so, Sayre must have forged at least one signature of William Duer in order to get $500 from Miranda in 1788—Sayre was desperate at that time. But the evidence indicates that the older Duer harbored no resentment against Sayre, that he was in economic straits as early as 1784, and that Sayre may indeed have become a participant in the loan to Miranda. Joseph S. Davis, *Essays in the Earlier History of American Corporations* (Cambridge, Mass., 1917), 121–22; Dávila (ed.), *Archivo del General Miranda*, VII, 95, 107, 115–17, XVI, 335–37. In 1806 Sayre asserted that he had lent money to Miranda in "1783." Sayre to Jefferson, November 15, 1806, in Thomas Jefferson Papers, Library of Congress, Washington, D.C.

10. Sayre to William Duer, July 10, 1796, in Duer Papers.

vessels on the ocean. France and America could work together with other nations to establish Puerto Rico as such a free area.

It was obvious to Adams that Sayre desired appointment as the special emissary. The proposal had peculiar merit in that Sayre was known to be an ally of Jefferson, who was about to take office as vice-president, rather than of Adams. He could thus appear in Paris as a person who spoke for all Americans. The president cautiously referred Sayre to Jefferson for his opinion, and the Virginian agreed that an envoy ought to go to Paris to settle matters with the French, although Jefferson was not much interested in establishing a free port in the Caribbean. Jefferson told Sayre that he would confer with Adams regarding the proposal. Sayre then urged Adams to make it clear to the French that the emissary, whoever was appointed, was acting for the United States, not as a party man. Secretary of State Timothy Pickering, a passionate enemy of the French, ought not to deal with them. Instead, Adams ought to make use of Sayre, not a political ally of the president. With Adams and Jefferson acting together, America could insist upon true neutrality, favoring neither of the European combatants. Sayre agreed that the matter of a free port was secondary and vowed that he would return to private life as soon as the special mission was completed. Adams let a splendid opportunity pass: the proposal was statesmanlike, even if its proposer was less than ideal for the mission.[11] After much travail and even armed conflict on the sea with France, Adams did send emissaries to Paris who could and did secure peace and improvement in relations between the two countries.

Sayre did secure a federal appointment while Adams occupied the presidency. French leaders were openly contemptuous of the western republic and insisted upon American help against Britain. In May, 1798, Benjamin Stoddert became secretary of the navy, with the task of building shipyards and frigates to defend American merchant vessels. Sayre went to Washington in search of an appointment, and Stoddert employed him in 1799 as an inspector to examine shipyard transactions. It would seem that Sayre was well qualified for the post, since he had visited every such naval establishment in Europe, except for the one at Constantinople. He examined yards at Boston and Portsmouth, and he

11. Sayre to John Adams, February 23, 1797, March 20, 1797, both in Adams Family Papers.

submitted an opinion on a plan to build the Navy Yard in Brooklyn in a report to Stoddert in November. He denounced agents at Boston and Portsmouth as grafters. "I did not recommend Long Island," he wrote afterward. "*I did not propose giving 40000 dollars for the worst* situation— or 4000 dollars per acre—worth only 100." However valuable his work, he could hardly have pleased Adams, who was not impressed by Sayre's abilities, found him vain, and knew him to be a Democratic-Republican. Adams instructed Stoddert, so Sayre believed, to discharge him.

The secretary did remove Sayre from his post, presumably because of misconduct. Sayre sought an interview with Adams in order to protest but was unable to see him. Sayre then wrote to the president to defend his character. Relating his history, he now asserted that he could prove that he had laid the foundations of the League of Armed Neutrality at the behest of Frederick the Great "by letters from his ministers" (he had earlier asserted that he had not been allowed to carry such documents from Berlin).[12] Evidence of misbehavior on Stoddert's part is lacking, and the frigates built under his direction performed splendidly against French warships, Barbary pirates, and British frigates in the War of 1812. It is worth mention that Stoddert was a poor man when he died in the midst of that conflict.

If Sayre tried to soften his political bent when he was in government under John Adams, he was a vigorous, even violent Democratic-Republican in the election of 1800. He actively participated in selecting members of the party as candidates for Congress, and he campaigned for several months for Jefferson as president. As "Secretary of the Republican Citizens of Burlington County," he delivered a vehement speech in which he condemned the Federalists as speculators and spendthrifts and demanded the election of Jefferson. "Is it not time for a change?" he inquired rhetorically. As a fiery partisan, he became very unpopular in his county, where the Federalists were in the majority, and he relates that he was in consequence compelled to move to Philadelphia for safety. There he established himself in a house at the corner of Eighth and Walnut Streets that he had secured the preceding year. He maintained a home there for many months.[13]

12. Sayre to Albert Gallatin, April 24, 1801, in Gallatin Papers; Sayre to John Adams, February 21, 1799, in Adams Family Papers.

13. Carl E. Prince, *New Jersey's Jeffersonian Republicans* (Chapel Hill, 1964), 58, 62; Ronald L. Becker (ed.), "From the Collections: A Republican Meeting in Burlington

From Philadelphia and Point Breeze Sayre carried on a long campaign to get a federal post after the victory of the Democratic-Republicans in the election. Indeed, he began it even before the contest between Jefferson and Aaron Burr for the presidency had been settled in favor of Jefferson. Sayre believed that his services in behalf of Jefferson deserved reward. He had lost his enthusiasm for a France that had come under the sway of Napoleon and urged Jefferson to avoid entanglement in the continuing European war. Jefferson replied on February 14, 1801, that he would steer away from the "convulsions of Europe" if he actually became president. After he was chosen, he received both direct and indirect pleas for office from Sayre, coupled with more advice. Eventually, Jefferson ordered a dockyard investigation in response to information from Sayre. He also considered remarkable counsel from Sayre in regard to the acquisition of territory in the Caribbean. Sayre suggested that America acquire one of the islands in that sea, then proposed that at the end of the wars in Europe America should secure the western half of Puerto Rico, with Russia and other European nations taking the other half. Blacks from the United States could settle on the island, which could serve, of course, as a base for opening trade with Spanish America. The president decided not to answer petitions for office. He was not at all eager to find a place for the imaginative—and possibly unreliable—Mr. Sayre.[14]

The office seeker went to Washington to push for preferment in person. The president granted him an interview but indicated that he did not enjoy the conversation. It was, reported Sayre, "necessary to retire, that I might release him from pain, & prevent myself being disliked by the man, by whom I wished to be beloved." Jefferson referred him to Secretary of State James Madison for possible employment in the diplomatic service. Madison did not respond to pleas from Sayre, who then began a long-continued bombardment of letters to Jefferson, to the secretary of state, and to Secretary of the Treasury Albert Gallatin that

---

County, 1800," *New Jersey History*, XCII (1974), 110–11; Walter R. Fee, *The Transition from Aristocracy to Democracy in New Jersey, 1789–1829* (Somerville, N.J., 1933), 94; Sayre to Albert Gallatin, April 24, 1801, in Gallatin Papers. Sayre was listed in the Philadelphia city directory as "Stephen Sayre, Esq."

14. Thomas Jefferson to Sayre, February 14, 1801, Sayre to Thomas Jefferson, April 10, 1801, both in Jefferson Papers, L.C.; Thomas Jefferson to [Samuel Smith], April 17, 1801, in Jefferson Papers, U.V.

recounted again and again his services, his qualifying experiences, and his financial troubles, and asked for various offices. He claimed the support of Governor Thomas McKean of Pennsylvania. He asked to be sent to Europe as a minister, to London, to The Hague, to one of the countries bordering upon the Baltic Sea. "I am more esteem'd, respect'd, & beloved in those countries than in my own," he boasted. He offered to serve as consul in London, that post being a profitable one with diplomatic status, and indicated that he was willing to be secretary of the navy, to be collector of customs at the port of Philadelphia, to be postmaster of that city. [15]

Had a tale of woe been the primary requirement for office, Sayre should have been successful. If he was vain, if he was arrogant in youth, he abased himself in his sixties in fruitless efforts to win sympathy. He enlarged upon his early prospects, his successes in middle life, and his recent sufferings caused by the ingratitude of the Republic and the importunities of his creditors. To Madison he asserted that "had I served England as I have America, I would not have suffered the injustice I have met." Moreover, "as to any immoral action tending to dishonor—I never have committed one." He claimed that he was respected in England for character as well as talent and that he did not acquire "this estimation by family influence, or the weight of property, or by flattery. No, I became respected by my honest principles, my steady conduct, my ardent zeal & the manners of a gentleman." Even if he deserved no credit for his activities in Berlin or for the Armed Neutrality, he asked Gallatin in a final appeal whether he did not have "some claim on the justice of my country for the loss of my fortune & high situation in England, where I was more caress'd & respected than any man who was born in America . . . does it do honor to my country to benefit by my personal connections, & when no longer useful, leave me to suffer for my credulity, & lament my misplaced confidence?" As it became evident that his begging was in vain, he wrote bitterly to Gallatin, "I trust the apathy, which shields you so happily against the solicitations of needy friends, will also protect me against your anger & resentment." He wrote to Governor John Page of Virginia in pathetic language, saying that he had

15. Sayre to James Madison, May 16, 1801, March 10, 1802, both in Madison Papers; Sayre to [Governor John Page], June 5, 1803, in the Emmett Collection, New York Public Library.

"a broken heart," and that Jefferson and his cabinet "treat me like cruel inquisitors." He told Page that he was living in Philadelphia in part in order to avoid legal action against him as a debtor, since he had not been able to repay some Bordeaux men who had lent him money to meet his obligation to Isaac Panchaud. Nor did the Jeffersonians quickly respond to Sayre's renewed petition for pay as a diplomat during the War of Independence—he was turned away again by the House of Representatives in March, 1802.[16]

But there was also cause for joy in the Sayre establishment after Sayre and Elizabeth settled in Bordentown, in the progress of their son, Samuel William. In October, 1801, probably after spending his early years with relatives, he was engaged to marry in England. If the marriage took place, it did not long continue. Samuel became an ensign in the second regiment of infantry of the United States Army on April 14, 1803, and went to duty in Tennessee in June. He left the army after serving less than a year. Like his father, he became allied with families of good standing. In September, 1804, he married Mary Grymes, who brought him Brandon plantation in Middlesex County, Virginia, and a daughter. Mary Grymes Sayre died young, and Samuel then took a second wife, Virginia Bassett. He eventually had many descendants.[17]

IN NOVEMBER, 1805, Francisco de Miranda returned to New York. There, having been promised English support, he laid plans for an expedition to free Venezuela, and even Spanish America, with his old friend Colonel William Smith, who had become collector of the port of New York, and with Samuel Ogden, who undertook to supply

16. Sayre to James Madison, May 16, 1801, June 9, 1801, October 30, 1801, March 10, 1802, all in Madison Papers; Sayre to Albert Gallatin, April 24, 1801, June 30, 1801, August 3, 1801, October 15, 1801, April 28, 1802, all in Gallatin Papers; Sayre to [John Page], June 5, 1803, in Emmett Collection; *Annals of the Congress of the United States*, 7th Cong., 1st Sess., 854–76.

17. Sayre to Albert Gallatin, October 15, 1801, in Gallatin Papers; Francis B. Heitman, *Historical Register and Dictionary of the United States Army* (Washington, 1903), I, 863; Sayre to [John Page], June 5, 1803, in Emmett Collection. A 1978 letter from Stuart L. Butler of the National Archives to the author states that young Sayre was recommended for a commission by General John Peter Muhlenberg and a Colonel Shea. It would appear that Samuel William Sayre was the son of Elizabeth II by a first marriage, mentioned above, and that he took the surname of his stepfather. It is unlikely that he

the necessary vessels to transport Miranda with men and weapons to the Caribbean. Proceeding to Washington, in December Miranda consulted Jefferson and Secretary of State Madison, who warned him that American law forbade a military attack upon a friendly nation from an American base.[18]

Sayre was in Washington at the time. If Miranda had severed relations with Sayre in France thirteen years earlier, he revived their friendship in astonishing fashion and informed Sayre of his plans. Two months later Sayre was in the capital of Virginia. The Richmond *Enquirer* published on February 25, 1806, a "communication" which said that "Stephen Sayre, Esq. is now in our city and lodges at the Bell; he has been on a visit to his son, Capt. Sayre. We hope he may be induced to reside here, as his only son has now a considerable property in the state." It was well known, asserted the letter, that Sayre was once sheriff of London; that he was a remarkably zealous champion of American rights at the beginning of the War of Independence; "that he first prevailed on the King of Prussia to enter into the armed neutrality, he then proceeded to Denmark and Sweden, united those two powers in the object, which was finally carried into effect in 1780 by the empress of Russia, who fitted out 20 ships of the line to support it." "We have made the above remarks," declared the newspaper, "because since his arrival, Mr. Sayre has made some communications to a friend here, that must, when publicly known, not merely excite curiosity, but the wonder of every citizen of America." By that time it was known that Miranda had sailed from New York in the *Leander*. Sayre had said, according to the newspaper, that Miranda was executing a "most extensive" plan, one "above all things, most likely to change the face of affairs through the universe." Three

---

was the product of the union of Sayre and Elizabeth I, in view of her age at the time of the marriage. It is just possible, though improbable, because of the references of London newspapers to Sayre "and family" in 1786, that he was the child, renamed, of Sophia Baddeley. The prenuptial agreement between Sayre and Elizabeth II, cited above, indicates that she was connected with the great Courtauld family. The name Samuel appears in that family generation after generation, but not among the Noels or Sayre's ancestors. *The Parish Register of Christ Church, Middlesex County, Va. from 1653 to 1812* (Richmond, 1897), 161, 198, 281; Banta, *Sayre Family*, 89–91, 94, 445–47.

18. Robertson, *Life of Miranda*, I, 293–97.

days later, challenged to tell more, Sayre published a statement in the *Enquirer* that praised the Latin American for natural abilities enhanced by travel and experience and declared that Miranda intended to free South America.[19]

Amidst excitement in Richmond, Thomas Ritchie, editor of the *Enquirer*, expressed doubt that a rebellion in Spanish America could succeed and questioned the accuracy of Sayre's prediction.[20] Sayre then came forth with a second statement, published in the *Enquirer* on March 4: "I am not in the habit of making communications, either to the public or in private company, which are not supported by facts." He insisted that Miranda was not a mere adventurer. "I have been a witness," he said, to important events in France and England in which Miranda displayed "talents integrity and perseverance." As proof of his own intimate knowledge, Sayre declared that he had placed a sealed letter describing the plan of the expedition in the hands of federal court clerk Daniel Hylton, which would not be opened until the information contained in it could not injure Miranda's chances for success.

Thomas Ritchie prudently refrained from questioning Sayre's veracity, but he challenged Sayre in that respect upon a related and rather remarkable matter. Sayre was attempting to form a company for a "legal" trading voyage to South America that would take advantage of the Miranda expedition. The company was to have thirty members, each one investing a thousand dollars. Profits of at least 400 percent were envisaged. Ritchie observed that the capital of the company, "the entire management of it, the port of destination, and every arrangement connected with the voyage, is to be under the direction of a certain gentleman." It had been urged, said the editor, that Richmond men must hasten to act so as to compete with rival companies already under way in the northern states. Ritchie, expressing best wishes for the freedom of Spanish Americans, warned his readers that Richmond, "an inland city," was not a suitable place for such an enterprise, that they must not be enticed into another South Sea Bubble. Three days later, Ritchie gave a

19. Sayre to Thomas Jefferson, November 15, 1806, in Jefferson Papers, L.C. Sayre also asserted that Chatham had encouraged revolution in Spanish America as early as 1767.

20. Richmond *Enquirer*, February 28, 1806.

name to "The Miranda South American Company," argued that its political background was dubious, and denounced gossip that it had the blessing of President Jefferson.

Sayre arranged for the publication of the statement he had entrusted to Hylton in the *Enquirer* on April 4, after it had become clear that it could not injure Miranda's chances. It said, "Miranda has permission from the British government to make Trinidad the place of rendezvous; he is gone there. The delegates of Caracas, Sta. Fee [Colombia] and Mexico, are now there, or expected to meet him. Some delay may take place; therefore it would be imprudent to name the place of attack, *rather the place to be surrendered,*—to be made the seat of confederation." Sayre went on, "If Miranda is not gone to this island, you may laugh at my credulity—if you hear of his being there, you may put more confidence, than heretofore, in any communications I shall make as to this subject." Ritchie commented that he would welcome "a United States of South America," which might at last emerge after much tumult. In the end, Sayre proved that he had had prior knowledge of Miranda's intentions, demonstrated in the form of a letter to Ritchie of March 1, but his projected company collapsed under the weight of the common sense and arguments of the cautious Ritchie.

Established once more at Point Breeze in 1803, Sayre informed Chancellor Livingston in the spring of 1806 that he lived there in a "domestic & tranquil manner." He claimed that he had made his house into the finest one in New Jersey. In rural peace he read the works of Tom Paine and immaturely declared, "I can declare solemnly that there is more wisdom in the two volumes than in twenty volumes of any other work on earth. He will be admired & reverenced when he is long gone to the tomb of his fathers." He thought at one time of raising thoroughbred sheep; he acquired a stock of cows, sheep, oxen, and pigs; and he built a race track on his farm. Was he subsiding into the role of a country gentleman at the end of his seventh decade of life? He could not even then accept a modest mode of life, and his finances remained dubious.[21]

The Miranda expedition failed miserably. John Steuben Smith, a son of Colonel Smith, was a volunteer under Miranda and spent months in a

21. At least Sayre wrote a letter from Point Breeze as early as August, 1803, and his name was dropped from the Philadelphia city directory in 1804. Sayre to Robert R.

Spanish colonial jail after the rebels were driven away by Spanish forces. Jefferson discharged Colonel Smith from his post in New York City. A jury found the colonel innocent of violating federal law; he was obviously guilty, but it was generally believed that the Miranda venture had been secretly endorsed by Jefferson and Madison. Colonel Smith sank into temporary obscurity.

Miranda was available for another effort. In November Sayre urged Jefferson to restore Smith to his office and to assist Miranda. The European powers seemed to be stalemated in war, and Spain was weak. With American help, Miranda could defeat the Spanish armies in the New World and arrange for the establishment of free Latin American republics that could then form a federation with their North American benefactor. Sayre praised Miranda enthusiastically for idealism, intelligence, imagination, and virtue, and he warned Jefferson that Britain would eventually act to help Miranda if America did not, that sons of George III—Heaven forbid—might appear upon thrones south of the Rio Grande. His advice was obviously worth consideration, but it was not taken.[22]

Nor did Jefferson adopt most remarkable counsel offered by Sayre in the following February. Napoleon then seemed to be triumphant in Europe. He would, predicted Sayre, foster French economic penetration of Spanish America and should be checked for the sake of the freedom of that area. How? By sending Sayre as a special emissary to Europe, where "I hold a high character in every nation." With James Monroe, who had been serving as American minister in London, Sayre would undertake to persuade the heads of the European states—including France?—to seek freedom of international trade. He assured Jefferson that "men who know the influence of women" might be able to exert it to achieve that goal. Presumably Sayre was to fascinate the ladies, since Monroe was not specially distinguished for charm among queens, duch-

Livingston, April 30, 1806, August 14, 1805 (?), both in Livingston Papers, New-York Historical Society, New York; Sayre to William Duane, August 4, 1803, in Duane Papers; "An Account of Sales of property conveyed by Stephen Sayre to John Chowning . . . by Deed Executed 12th March 1818," in Middlesex County Records, Virginia State Library, Richmond, Virginia; Woodward, *Bonaparte's Park*, 26.

22. Sayre to Thomas Jefferson, November 15, 1806, in Jefferson Papers, L.C.

esses, or mistresses. Although old George III hated America, England would welcome intervention, for it would rescue that country "from disgrace—perhaps total ruin." The promoter was at his worst if he believed that the president would consider the scheme. It would seem that Sayre was displaying his knowledge of the world and prescribing a remedy for its ills in the assurance that he would not be compelled to offer proof of his genius. Or was he, just possibly, near the border of megalomania?[23]

That curious proposal was sent to Jefferson from a hotel in Washington where Sayre was staying while he tried once more to secure pay for his diplomatic services three decades earlier. The finances of the nation were now in good order, and no one could doubt that Sayre had suffered, even if he had not achieved much, for the American cause. Perhaps politicians were moved by pity for an aging man. In any case, he was at last granted, in March, 1807, the generous award so long ago proposed for his labors in Prussia. If Washington politicians hoped they would hear no more from Mr. Sayre, they were wrong. He was not satisfied with that award, and in 1808 he sought compensation for his achievements "in the north of Europe." His petition was peremptorily rejected by the House of Representatives.[24]

Sayre then sought an office. Thomas Newbold, a member of the House from New Jersey, urged James Madison to give him one, in January, 1810. Madison, who was to succeed Jefferson on March 4, incautiously asked what sort of appointment Sayre sought. Responding to that inquiry, Sayre did not modestly confine himself to a brief answer. In a letter to Madison he said that he wished to be employed in the supply division of the navy. But the letter began haughtily, and it became worse. "Mr. Newbold," wrote Sayre, "informs me that you had so far condescended to take notice of our application as to ask what I might particularly think of, or expect." There followed a substantial chronicle of explanations why Washington, Adams, and Jefferson had not desired his services. Sayre wished only to have a post where he could honorably serve Madison. But then came gratuitous advice and, once

23. Sayre to Jefferson, February 2, 1807, in *ibid*.
24. *Annals of the Congress of the United States*, 9th Cong., 2nd Sess., 69, 70, 78, 91, 94, 95, 428–29, 485, 657, 681, 10th Cong., 473–74.

more, mysterious reference to his naval invention. He contended that America ought to respond to injuries inflicted by Britain by waging war against that nation, which would secure for America "the friendship of the rest of the world—*and what honors will you bestow on the man, who shall point out the means by which their navy may be rendered useless & contemptible?*" Would Madison wish to confer with him *"alone?"* It is to be suspected that Madison did not desire to talk with Sayre, in private or in company. Four months later Sayre reminded the president of his application in a letter with a very different tone. The award he had received from the Congress had not been enough to cover all his debts, and he asked Madison to act to save him from the disgrace of bankruptcy. Nothing happened.[25]

Was there ever a more persistent seeker of office than Stephen Sayre? In 1813 he asked Secretary of State James Monroe to send him to London with money to bribe the right people in order to bring peace to Europe and America. By that time he had almost lost touch with reality. "All Europe knows that I originated and carried the Arm'd Neutrality into effect," he asserted. Lord Stanhope and Lebrun were still his friends beyond the Atlantic, and Sayre presumed that "no man would be received with equal expectation" in Europe. "The people of England would hear the news" of his coming "with cordiality and hope." Washington could only be silent. Sayre asked in the same year for an appointment as an army paymaster, as consul in Guadeloupe. His pleas went unheeded. In October, 1817, at the age of eighty-one, he offered advice to Secretary of State John Quincy Adams and nominated himself as a person fitted to begin American penetration into Mexico. Since America lacked great naval power, it would be imprudent to try to take Cuba, valuable as that island might be, because the Holy Alliance might interrupt such a venture. But America could expand southward by land. Sayre desired to lead an expedition into Mexico, either as an American official or as a member of a company supported from Washington. He continued in vain to seek appointments almost to the very end of his life.[26]

25. Sayre to Madison, January 20, 1810 (dated 1809 by mistake), May 12, 1810, both in Madison Papers.

26. Sayre to Monroe, January 10, 1813, July 15, 1813, September 4, 1813, Sayre to

Sayre was still able to travel in 1817. He visited New York City and conferred with President Monroe in Washington. By that time, however, he had abandoned residence at Point Breeze, probably compelled to sell his home in order to pay his debts. In the spring of 1816, Joseph Bonaparte, the oldest brother of Napoleon and formerly king of Spain, came to the house. He had not only escaped from France after the Battle of Waterloo but had managed to save much money, jewelry, and art treasures. He bought Point Breeze for $17,500, in July, 1816 (the house afterward burned down). Ironically, Sayre was later remembered in the neighborhood of Bordentown and Philadelphia as "the handsome Englishman."[27]

The Sayres went, perhaps in part for financial reasons, to Virginia to live with Samuel William Sayre. Stephen died there on September 27, 1818, and his wife on the following day. He left no will, for he owned neither land nor property to bequeath. He had not exhausted his second wife's fortune. She tried to give him by will the income from five thousand dollars in United States bonds that he did not live long enough to inherit. In a remarkable codicil to her will, she also desired that he should receive the annuity of one hundred pounds per annum that she had bought from Lady Anne Stuart Percy Poellnitz. Her principal heir was "my son," Samuel William.[28]

Stephen Sayre was not legally insolvent in Virginia when he died. To be sure, his long-continued effort to move from Presbyterian respectability in a Long Island village to riches and rank had largely failed, but not quite. Before his death, descendants of the first cousin of his first wife had achieved fame that would grow. Lady Annabella Milbanke, wife of

John Quincy Adams, October 7, 1817, all in Department of State, Miscellaneous Letters.

27. According to the letter to John Quincy Adams cited above. Charlemagne Tower, "Joseph Bonaparte in Philadelphia and Bordentown," *Pennsylvania Magazine of History and Biography*, XLII (1918), 301–309; Woodward, *Bonaparte's Park*, 26; "Reminiscences of Admiral Edward Shippen: Bordentown in the 1830's," *Pennsylvania Magazine of History and Biography*, LXXVIII (1954), 214.

28. Richmond *Enquirer*, December 10, 1818; statement by Robert Healy, administrator of the estate of Stephen Sayre, June 27, 1826, in Middlesex County Records; Banta, *Sayre Family*, 89–91.

Lord Byron the poet, would eventually inherit and inhabit Kirkby Mallory, and Byron himself took the name of Noel in consequence of his marriage to her.[29] The family tree of Elizabeth Sayre I, as has been mentioned, also included the novelist Anthony Trollope. It was no small achievement for a tanner's son from the colonies to climb as high as did Stephen Sayre, to associate with the earl of Chatham and the marquis of Rockingham, to be the object of the solicitude of Edmund Burke and John Wilkes, to be the consort of the lovely Sophia Baddeley, to be the trusted agent of the first French republic. The time came when remarkable personal attractions, graciousness, and fine manners failed to prevent his confinement in jail—but he was locked up in the most famous of all prisons. The time came when all his efforts to secure great and quick wealth proved to be in vain. His imagination was undisciplined; his thought was not profound; and he lacked good judgment. Sayre was a promoter, fertile in device but deficient in execution. His attacks upon monarchs and aristocrats, so long as they were directed toward obtaining recognition of himself as a gentleman, were not entirely altruistic. It may be that his periods of confinement, of poverty, at last destroyed much of the conceit he displayed in youth, that his later vision of free world republics was founded at least in part upon sympathy with fellow sufferers in a European world of brutal elegance. His disappointments seem to have driven him almost to madness in middle life.

As a hero of the American Revolution who ended his days in less than stateliness, Sayre was not singular. His friend Colonel William Smith, abandoning revolutionary enthusiasm, turned Federalist and became a member of Congress. But William Duer died in prison as a debtor; Miranda, failing to establish a South American republic, finished his life in a Spanish prison; and General Henry Knox died in near poverty.

It has often been remarked that revolutions consume their originators. The convulsion in America in the last half of the eighteenth century, less destructive than others of its leaders, impoverished many of them. Stephen Sayre left behind him no great monument, and he has

29. There was another association between Sayre and Byron. Lady Caroline Lamb, the poet's mistress, was the daughter-in-law of Peniston Lamb, Lord Melbourne, who shared the favors of Sophia Baddeley with Sayre.

been virtually forgotten. But he rose far, and he enjoyed himself thoroughly before politics, prisons, and rash speculations reduced him to the substantial status of an American country gentleman living in his own mansion on the banks of the Delaware and thence to the hospitality of a Virginia plantation.

Bibliography

Manuscripts

BOSTON, MASSACHUSETTS

Massachusetts Historical Society
Adams Family Papers
Knox, Henry, Papers

CAMBRIDGE, MASSACHUSETTS

Houghton Library, Harvard University
Lee, Arthur, Papers

CHARLOTTESVILLE, VIRGINIA

University of Virginia Library
Jefferson, Thomas, Papers

EAST HAMPTON, NEW YORK

East Hampton Free Public Library
Will of John Sayre, Sr.
Will of Matthew Sayre

LONDON, ENGLAND

British Museum
Additional MSS. 5823
Additional MSS. 30,870
Additional MSS. 35,427
Egerton MSS. 2697
House of Lords Record Office
Main Papers
Public Record Office

Bankruptcy, Series 1
Colonial Office, Series 5
Prisons, Series 4
State Papers, Domestic, Series 44
Treasury Solicitor, Series 11
Wills (William Noel)

NEW HAVEN, CONNECTICUT

Yale University Library
Duane, William, Papers

NEW YORK CITY

New-York Historical Society
Duer, William, Papers
Gallatin, Albert, Papers
Livingston, Robert, Papers
Reed, Joseph, Papers
New York Public Library
Emmett Collection

NORTHAMPTON, ENGLAND

Northamptonshire Record Office
Burke, Edmund, Papers

PHILADELPHIA, PENNSYLVANIA

American Philosophical Society
Franklin, Benjamin, Papers

RICHMOND, VIRGINIA

Virginia State Library
Middlesex County Records

RIVERHEAD, NEW YORK

Suffolk County Historical Society
Ackerley Record Books

SALT LAKE CITY, UTAH

Archives of the Church of Jesus Christ of Latter-Day Saints
Stamford, England, Parish Register

SOUTHAMPTON, NEW YORK

   Southampton Historical Museum
     Sayre, John, Account Book

WASHINGTON, D.C.

   National Archives
     Department of State, Miscellaneous Letters, 1789–1906.
      Record Group 59.
     United States Army Records
   Library of Congress
     Franklin, Benjamin, Papers
     Jefferson, Thomas, Papers
     Madison, James, Papers
     Washington, George, Papers

Printed Materials

Adams, Charles Francis, ed. "Correspondence Between John Adams and Mercy Warren, Relating to Her 'History of the American Revolution,' July–August, 1807." *Collections of the Massachusetts Historical Society*, 5th Ser., IV (1885).

———, ed. *The Works of John Adams*. 10 vols. Boston, 1850–56.

Alger, John Goldsworth. *Paris in 1789–94: Farewell Letters of Victims of the Guillotine*. New York, 1902.

Almon, John. *The Correspondence of the Late John Wilkes with His Friends*. 5 vols. London, 1805.

Alvord, Clarence W., and Clarence E. Carter, eds. *The Critical Period, 1763–1765*. Springfield, Ill., 1915. Vol. X of *Collections of the Illinois State Historical Library*.

American State Papers. Documents, Legislative and Executive, of the Congress of the United States . . . Commencing March 4, 1789, and Ending March 3, 1823. Washington, 1834. Vol. IX.

Annals of the Congress of the United States. Seventh, Ninth, and Tenth Congresses.

Annual Register. Vol. XVIII (1775).

Anson, William R., ed. *Autobiography and Political Correspondence of Augustus Henry Third Duke of Grafton*. London, 1898.

Aulard, François V. A., ed. *La Société des Jacobins*. 6 vols. Paris, 1889–97.

Banta, Theodore Melvin. *Sayre Family: Lineage of Thomas Sayre, A Founder of Southampton*. New York, 1901.

Beaufort, W. H. De, ed. *Brieven von en aan Joan Derck Van Der Capellen Van De Poll*. Utrecht, 1879.

Beaven, Alfred B. *The Aldermen of London*. 2 vols. London, 1908.

Becker, Ronald L., ed. "From the Collections: A Republican Meeting in Burlington County, 1800." *New Jersey History*, XCII (1974), 110–11.

Belsterling, Charles S. "Baron Poellnitz of New York City and South Carolina." *New York Genealogical and Biographical Record*, LXXX (1949), 130–41.

Bénétruy, J. *L'Atelier de Mirabeau*. Paris, 1962.

Benson, Adolph. *Sweden and the American Revolution*. New Haven, 1926.

Bickley, Frances, ed. *The Diaries of Sylvester Douglas (Lord Glenbervie)*. 2 vols. London, 1928.

Bigo, Robert. *La Caisse d'Escompte (1776–1793) et les Origines de la Banque de France*. Paris, n.d.

Bleackley, Horace. *Life of John Wilkes*. London, 1917.

Boyd, Julian, ed. *The Papers of Thomas Jefferson*. Princeton, 1950–.

———, ed. *The Susquehannah Company Papers*. 11 vols. Wilkes-Barre, 1930–71.

Brown, Mrs. Charles, and Harold Simpson. *A Century of Famous Actresses, 1750–1850*. London, n.d.

Brown, John. *Secret Memoirs of the Courts of Europe: The Courts of Sweden and Denmark*. 2 vols. Philadelphia, 1897.

Browning, John, and Richard Morton, eds. *1776*. Toronto, 1976.

Browning, Oscar, ed. *The Despatches of Earl Gower*. Cambridge, 1885.

Buell, Augustus C. *Paul Jones*. 2 vols. New York, 1906.

Burnett, Edmund C., ed. *Letters of Members of the Continental Congress*. 8 vols. Washington, 1921–36.

Burr, Leon, ed. *An Indian Preacher in England*. Hanover, N.H., 1933.

Butterfield, Lyman H. *John Witherspoon Comes to America*. Princeton, 1953.

Carter, Clarence E., ed. *The Correspondence of General Thomas Gage*. 2 vols. New Haven, 1931–33.

Chapman, John H., ed. *The Register Book of Marriages Belonging to the Parish of St. George, Hanover Square*. London, 1886. Vol. I.

Christelow, Allan. "Contraband Trade Between Jamaica and the Spanish, and the Free Port Act of 1766." *Hispanic American Historical Review*, XXII (1942), 309–343.

Christie, Ian R. *Myth and Reality in Late Eighteenth-Century British Politics and Other Papers*. Berkeley, 1970.

Clark, William Bell, ed. *Naval Documents of the American Revolution*. Washington, D.C., 1964–.

Cobbett, William, ed. *Parliamentary History of England*. London, 1813. Vol. XVIII.

Cokayne, George Edward. *The Complete Baronetage*. 8 vols. Exeter, 1887–88.

Copeland, Thomas W., *et al.*, eds. *The Correspondence of Edmund Burke*. 10 vols. Chicago, 1958–78.

Croft, Herbert. *Abbey of Kilkhampton*. London, 1780.

Cushing, Harry A., ed. *The Writings of Samuel Adams*. 4 vols. New York, 1904–1908.

Dangerfield, George. *Chancellor Robert R. Livingston of New York, 1746–1813*. New York, 1960.

Dávila, Vicente, ed. *Archivo del General Miranda*. 24 vols. Caracas, 1924–50.

Davis, Joseph S. *Essays in the Earlier History of American Corporations*. Cambridge, Mass., 1917.

Deas, Anne Izard, ed. *Correspondence of Mr. Ralph Izard, of South Carolina, from the Year 1774 to 1804*. New York, 1844.

Dexter, Franklin B., ed. *The Literary Diary of Ezra Stiles*. 3 vols. New York, 1901.

Domett, Henry W. *A History of the Bank of New York*. 3rd ed. [Cambridge, Mass.], 1884.

Donne, William B., ed. *Correspondence of King George the Third with Lord North from 1768 to 1783*. 2 vols. London, 1867.

Durnford, Charles, and Edward Hyde East. *Term Reports, in the Court of King's Bench*. 8 vols. in 4. New York, 1834.

Edler, Friedrich. *The Dutch Republic and the American Revolution*. Johns Hopkins Studies in Historical and Political Science, Ser. XXIX, No. 2. Baltimore, 1911.

Einstein, Lewis. *Divided Loyalties*. Boston, 1933.

Eustace, J[ohn] S. *Letters on the Crimes of George III*. Paris, [1794].

Everard, Edward C. *Memoirs of an Unfortunate Son of Thespis*. Edinburgh, 1818.

Faucille, Paul. *La Diplomatie française et la Ligue des Neutres de 1780*. Paris, 1893.

Fee, Walter R. *The Transition from Aristocracy to Democracy in New Jersey, 1789–1829*. Somerville, N.J., 1933.

Fitzpatrick, John C., ed. *The Writings of George Washington*. 39 vols. Washington, 1931–44.

Ford, Worthington C. "Franklin's Accounts Against Massachusetts." *Proceedings of the Massachusetts Historical Society*, LVI (1922).

———, ed. *Letters of William Lee*. 3 vols. in one. Brooklyn, 1897.

Ford, Worthington C., *et al.*, eds. *The Journals of the Continental Congress, 1774–1789*. 34 vols. Washington, D.C., 1904–1937.

Fortescue, John W., ed. *The Correspondence of King George the Third*. 6 vols. London, 1928.

Foss, Edward. *The Judges of England*. London, 1864. Vol. VIII.

Fowler, William M., Jr. *Rebels Under Sail*. New York, 1976.

Frothingham, Richard. *The Life and Times of Joseph Warren*. Boston, 1865.

Fyvie, John. *Comedy Queens of the Georgian Era*. London, 1906.

Galt, John. *The Lives of the Players*. 2 vols. Boston, 1831.

Gayet, Robert Lacour. *Calonne*. Paris, 1963.

Gipson, Lawrence H. *The Triumphant Empire, 1763–1766*. New York, 1956. Vol. IX of *The British Empire Before the American Revolution*.

Griffiths, David M. "American Commercial Diplomacy in Russia, 1780–1783." *William and Mary Quarterly*, 3rd Ser., XXVII (1970).

Hawke, David F. *Paine*. New York, 1974.

Hays, A. Minis. *Calendar of the Papers of Benjamin Franklin in the Library of the American Philosophical Society*. 5 vols. Philadelphia, 1908.

Heitman, Francis B. *Historical Register and Dictionary of the United States Army*. Washington, 1903. Vol. I.

Higginbotham, R. Don, ed. *The Papers of James Iredell*. 2 vols. Raleigh, 1976.

Highfill, Philip H., Jr., Kalman A. Burnim, and Edward A. Langhans, eds. *A Biographical Dictionary of Actors, Actresses, Musicians, Dancers, Managers & Other Stage Personnel in London, 1660–1800*. Carbondale, Ill. 1973–. Vol. I.

Hoffman, Ross J. S. *The Marquis: A Study of Lord Rockingham, 1730–1782*. New York, 1973.

Howell, George Rogers. *The Early History of Southampton, L.I., New York, with Genealogies*. 2nd ed. Albany, 1887.

Howell, T. B., comp. *A Complete Collection of State Trials*. London, 1814. Vol. XX.

Hutchinson, Peter O., ed. *The Diary and Letters of His Excellency Thomas Hutchinson*. 2 vols. Boston, 1884–86.

Hutton, James, ed. *Selections from the Letters and Correspondence of Sir James Bland Burges*. London, 1885.

Index of Ancestors and Roll of Members of the Society of Colonial Wars. New York, 1922.

Isham, Charles, ed. *Deane Papers*. 5 vols. New York, 1887–1891. Vols. XIX–XXIII of *Collections of the New-York Historical Society*.

Johnson, Amandus. *Swedish Contributions to American Freedom*. Philadelphia, 1953. Vol. I.

Johnston, Henry P., ed. *The Correspondence and Public Papers of John Jay*. 4 vols. New York, 1891.

Journals of the House of Commons from 1774 . . . to . . . 1777. London, 1803.

Kammen, Michael G. *A Rope of Sand: The Colonial Agents, British Politics, and the American Revolution.* Ithaca, 1968.

Kapp, Friedrich. *Friedrich der Grosse und die Vereinigten Staaten von Amerika.* Leipzig, 1871.

Knollenberg, Bernhard. *Growth of the American Revolution, 1766–1775.* New York, 1975.

Labande, L. H. *Un Diplomate Français à la Cour de Cathérine II, 1775–1780.* 2 vols. Paris, 1901.

Lee, Richard Henry. *The Life of Arthur Lee.* 2 vols. Boston, 1829.

Letters from Mrs. Elizabeth Carter, to Mrs. Montagu. 3 vols. London, 1817.

"Letters from Mrs. Ralph Izard to Mrs. William Lee." *Virginia Magazine of History and Biography*, VIII (1900–1901).

Lewis, W. S., *et al.*, eds. *Horace Walpole's Correspondence with Sir Horace Mann.* New Haven, 1960–1967. Vols. VI and VIII.

Lhomet, J. *Le Banquier et Sa Fille, la Duchesse de Raguse.* Paris, 1926.

Lilly, Edward P. *The Colonial Agents of New York and New Jersey.* Washington, D.C., 1936.

Lodge, John. *The Peerage of Ireland.* Edited by Mervyn Archdall. 7 vols. London, 1789.

McLachlan, James. *Princetonians, 1748–1768.* Princeton, 1976.

Maclean, John. *History of the College of New Jersey.* 2 vols. Philadelphia, 1877.

Madariaga, Isabel de. *Britain, Russia, and the Armed Neutrality of 1780.* New Haven, 1962.

Maddison, A. R. *Lincolnshire Pedigrees.* 3 vols. London, 1902–1904.

Magazine of American History, X (1883), 508–509.

Malmesbury, Earl of, ed. *Diaries and Correspondence of James Harris, First Earl of Malmesbury.* 4 vols. London, 1844.

Malvezin, Théophile. *Histoire du Commerce de Bordeaux.* 4 vols. Bordeaux, 1892.

Mather, Frederic Gregory. *The Refugees of 1776 from Long Island to Connecticut.* Albany, 1913.

Mathews, Albert, ed. "Letters of Dennys De Berdt, 1757–1770." *Publications of the Colonial Society of Massachusetts*, XIII (1911).

Miles, Charles P., ed. *The Correspondence of William Augustus Miles on the French Revolution.* 2 vols. London, 1890.

Miles, W. *Authentic Correspondence with M. Le Brun, the French Minister.* 3rd ed. London, 1796.

Minto, Lady. *Memoir of the Right Honourable Hugh Elliot.* Edinburgh, 1868.

Monnier, Marc. *Un Aventurier Italien du Siècle Dernier: Le Comte Joseph Gorani.* Paris, 1884.

Moore, Frank, ed. *Materials for History.* New York, 1861.

Moore, Thomas. *The Life and Death of Lord Edward Fitzgerald*. 2 vols. London, 1831.

―――. *Memoirs of the Rt. Hon. Richard Brinsley Sheridan*. 2 vols. New York, 1853.

Morison, Samuel E. *John Paul Jones: A Sailor's Biography*. Boston, 1959.

Morris, Gouverneur. *A Diary of the French Revolution*. Edited by Beatrix C. Davenport. 2 vols. Boston, 1939.

Nelson, William, and A. Van Doren Honeyman, eds. *Documents Relating to the Colonial History of the State of New Jersey*. 1st Ser., XXIX. Paterson, 1917.

New York. *Second Annual Report of the State Historian of the State of New York*. Albany, 1897.

―――. *Third Annual Report of the State Historian of the State of New York*. New York, 1898.

Nichols, John. *The History and Antiquities of Leicestershire*. 4 vols. London, 1795–1811.

―――. *Illustrations of the Literary History of the Eighteenth Century*. 8 vols. London, 1817–18.

―――. *Literary Anecdotes of the Eighteenth Century*. 8 vols. London, 1812–15.

Norton, J. E., ed. *The Letters of Edward Gibbon*. 3 vols. London, 1856.

Nugent, Nicholas. *The Case of Nicholas Nugent, Esq.: Late Lieutenant in the First Regiment of Foot Guards*. London, 1776.

Parish Register of Christ Church, Middlesex County, Va. from 1653 to 1812. Richmond, 1897.

Porter, Kenneth W. *The Jacksons and the Lees: Two Generations of Massachusetts Merchants, 1765–1844*. 2 vols. Cambridge, Mass., 1937.

Price, Cecil, ed. *The Letters of Richard Brinsley Sheridan*. 3 vols. Oxford, 1966.

Prince, Carl E. *New Jersey's Jeffersonian Republicans*. Chapel Hill, 1964.

Quincy, Josiah. *Memoir of the Life of Josiah Quincy, Junior, 1774–1775*. Boston, 1874.

Rae, W. Fraser. *Sheridan*. 2 vols. London, 1896.

Reed, William B. *Life and Correspondence of Joseph Reed*. 2 vols. Philadelphia, 1847.

―――. *The Life of Esther De Berdt, Afterwards Esther Reed of Pennsylvania*. Philadelphia, 1853.

Réimpression de l'ancien Moniteur. Paris, 1854. Vols. XVI and XX.

"Reminiscences of Admiral Edward Shippen: Bordentown in the 1830's." *Pennsylvania Magazine of History and Biography*, LXXVIII (1954).

Represa Fernandez, María Francisca, *et al.*, eds. *Documentos Relativos a la Independencia de Norte América Existentes en Archivos Españoles*. 3 vols. Madrid, 1976.

Reynolds, Frederic. *The Life and Times of Frederic Reynolds, Written by Himself.* 2 vols. London, 1826.

Richardson, Francis. *An Appeal to the Officers of the Guards.* London, 1776.

Roberts, W[illiam]. *Memorials of Christie's.* 2 vols. London, 1897.

Robertson, William S. *The Life of Miranda.* 2 vols. Chapel Hill, 1929.

Robinson, Mary. *Memoirs of the Late Mrs. Robinson, Written by Herself.* 2 vols. London, 1801.

Robinson, Stewart M. "Campus Evangelism Two Centuries Ago." *Proceedings of the New Jersey Historical Society,* LXXVIII (1960), 118–24.

Roche, John R. *Joseph Reed: A Moderate in the American Revolution.* New York, 1957.

Royal Historical Manuscripts Commission, Fourteenth Report. Appendix, Part X. London, 1895.

Rudé, George. *Wilkes and Liberty: A Society Study of 1763 to 1774.* Oxford, 1962.

Sabine, William H., ed. *Historical Memoirs from 16 March 1763 to 9 July 1776 of William Smith.* New York, 1956.

Sayre, Stephen. *A Short Narrative.* N.p., n.d.

Sellers, John R., *et al.,* eds. *Manuscript Sources in the Library of Congress for Research on the American Revolution.* Washington, D.C., 1975.

Shipton, Clifford K. *Sibley's Harvard Graduates.* Boston, 1968. Vol. XIV.

Sitwell, Edith. *English Eccentrics.* New York, 1957.

Smyth, Albert H., ed. *The Life and Writings of Benjamin Franklin.* 10 vols. New York, 1905–1907.

Sosin, Jack M. *Agents and Merchants: British Colonial Policy and the Origins of the American Revolution, 1763–1775.* Lincoln, Neb., 1965.

Stanhope, Ghita, and G. P. Gooch, *The Life of Charles Third Earl Stanhope.* London, 1914.

Steele, Elizabeth. *The Memoirs of Mrs. Sophia Baddeley, Late of Drury Lane Theatre.* 3 vols. Dublin, 1787.

Steuart, A. Francis, ed. *Last Journals of Horace Walpole.* 2 vols. London, 1910.

Stevens, Benjamin Franklin, ed. *Facsimiles of Manuscripts in European Archives Relating to America, 1773–1783.* 26 vols. London, 1889–95.

Sullivan, James, *et al.,* eds. *The Papers of Sir William Johnson.* 14 vols. Albany, 1921–45.

Sumner, William Graham. *The Financier and the Finances of the American Revolution.* 2 vols. New York, 1891.

Syrett, Harold C., *et al.,* eds. *The Papers of Alexander Hamilton.* New York, 1961–.

Taylor, William S., and John H. Pringle, eds. *Correspondence of William Pitt, Earl of Chatham.* 4 vols. London, 1840.

Thomas, George, Earl of Albemarle, ed. *Memoirs of the Marquis of Rockingham and His Contemporaries.* 2 vols. London, 1852.

Tower, Charlemagne. "Joseph Bonaparte in Philadelphia and Bordentown." *Pennsylvania Magazine of History and Biography,* XLII (1918).

Trefman, Simon. *Sam. Foote, Comedian, 1710–1777.* New York, 1971.

Treloar, William Purdie. *Wilkes and the City.* London, 1917.

Trench, Charles C. *Portrait of a Patriot: A Biography of John Wilkes.* Edinburgh, 1962.

Turner, Frederick Jackson. "Genêt's Attack on Louisiana and the Floridas." *American Historical Review,* III (1898).

Van Schaack, Henry C. *The Life of Peter Van Schaack.* New York, 1842.

Vlieger, A. de. *Historical and Genealogical Record of the Coote Family.* Lausanne, 1900.

Warren, Mercy. *History of the Rise, Progress and Termination of the American Revolution.* 3 vols. Boston, 1805.

Waterhouse, Ellis K. *Reynolds.* London, 1941.

Watson, Elkanah. *Men and Times of the Revolution: Or, Memoirs of. . .* 2nd ed. New York, 1856.

Watson, John F. *Annals of Philadelphia and Pennsylvania.* 2 vols. Philadelphia, 1850.

Werkmeister, Lucyle. *The London Daily Press, 1772–1792.* Lincoln, Neb., 1963.

————. "Notes for a Revised Life of William Jackson." *Notes and Queries,* CCVI (1961).

Wharton, Francis, ed. *The Revolutionary Diplomatic Correspondence of the United States.* 6 vols. Washington, D.C., 1889.

Wilson, James G. *Memorial History of the City of New York.* 4 vols. New York, 1892–93.

Woodward, E. M. *Bonaparte's Park, and the Murats.* Trenton, 1879.

Newspapers and Magazines

American Daily Advertiser, 1794
Bath *Journal,* 1775
Bristol *Journal,* 1775–77
Cambridge *Chronicle*
Connecticut *Gazette,* 1776
Essex *Journal,* 1775–76

European Magazine, 1787, 1789, 1811
Gentleman's Magazine, 1731–1817
London *Chronicle*, 1759–1805
London Magazine, 1775–76
London *Times*, 1785–1817
Monthly Review, 1776
New York *Mercury*, 1759
Pennsylvania *Evening Post*, 1776
Pennsylvania *Mercury and Universal Advertiser*, 1785
Richmond *Enquirer*, 1806, 1818
Rivington's Royal Gazette
Scot's Magazine, 1776
Southern Literary Messenger, 1859
Town and Country Magazine, 1775–78
Virginia and Alexandria *Advertiser*, 1784
Virginia *Argus*, 1806
York *Courant*, 1775

Dissertation

Potts, Louis W. "Arthur Lee: American Revolutionary." Ph.D. dissertation, Duke University, 1970.

Index